THE COMPLETE BOOK OF
PATCHWORK, QUILTING & APPLIQUÉ

THE COMPLETE BOOK OF

PATCHWORK, QUILTING & APPLIQUÉ

LINDA SEWARD

FIREFLY BOOKS

BEFORE YOU BEGIN

This key explains the meaning of the colour, tone and texture used in the step-by-step drawings in *The Complete Book of Patchwork, Quilting and Appliqué*. It also defines the symbols that have been used throughout the book.

 Main fabric, right side (RS). The RS of the back of a quilt is illustrated in white.

 Main fabric, wrong side (WS); also used when necessary to indicate and additional fabric colour.

 Main Fabric (RS); used to indicate an additional fabric colour.

 Main fabric (RS); used to indicate printed fabrics.

 Sheer fabric such as organdy, organza or voile.

 Interfacing

 Template

 Press with a steam iron

 Machine sew

 Cut using scissors

 Dressmaker's ruler or rotary ruler

A FIREFLY BOOK

Published by Firefly Books Ltd. 2011

Copyright © Reed International Books Ltd 2011
Text copyright © Linda Seward 2011
Illustrations copyright © Linda Seward and Reed International Books Ltd 2011

First printing

Publisher Cataloging-in-Publication Data (U.S.)

Seward, Linda.
     The complete book of patchwork, quilting and appliqué / Linda Seward.
[184] p. : ill., photos. (some col.) ; cm.
Includes: Bibliographical references and index.
ISBN-13: 978-1-55407-804-2 (pbk.)
ISBN-10: 1-55407-804-0 (pbk.)
1. Patchwork. 2. Quilting. 3. Appliqué. I. Title.
746.46 dc22   TT835.S4937 2010

Library and Archives Canada Cataloguing in Publication

Seward, Linda
             The complete book of patchwork, quilting and appliqué / Linda
Seward.
Includes bibliographical references and index.
ISBN-13: 978-1-55407-804-2 (pbk.)
ISBN-10: 1-55407-804-0 (pbk.)
             1. Quilting. 2. Patchwork quilts. 3. Patchwork — Patterns.
4. Appliqué — Patterns. I. Title.
TT835.S457 2011   746.46   C2010-906425-9

Published in the United States by
Firefly Books (U.S.) Inc.
P.O. Box 1338, Ellicott Station
Buffalo, New York 14205

Published in Canada by
Firefly Books Ltd.
66 Leek Crescent
Richmond Hill, Ontario L4B 1H1

Printed in China

Edited and Designed by
Mitchell Beazley, an imprint of Reed Consumer Books Ltd,
Michelin House, 81 Fulham Road,
London SW3 6RB
and Auckland, Melbourne, Singapore and Toronto

Executive Editor: Judith More   Editor: Julia North
Art Editor: Glen Wilkins   Production: Juliette Butler
Illustration: Brian John Wilkins

Dedication

To my daughter, Alysson, who was born at the same time as this book, and to my husband, Robert, who played an important role in the creation of both.

CONTENTS

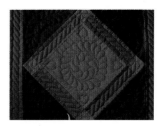

I've had a heap o' comfort all my life makin' quilts, and now in my old age I wouldn't take a fortune for 'em... You see, some folks has albums to put folks' pictures in to remember 'em by, and some folks has a book and writes down the things that happen every day so they won't forgit 'em; but honey, these quilts is my albums and my di'ries, and whenever the weather's bad and I can't git out to see folks, I jest spread out my quilts and look at 'em and study over 'em, and it's jest like goin' back fifty or sixty years and livin' my life over again. *From Aunt Jane of Kentucky written in 1898 by Eliza Calvert Hall.*

1
THE BASICS OF QUILTING

THE BASICS OF QUILTING

Quiltmaking has been a vital, living craft for hundreds of years. It originally evolved as an economical way of providing warmth, but quiltmaking has long since outgrown its prosaic beginnings. Today, it has become an outlet of artistic expression practised by people who would no more need to make a quilt solely for warmth than to sow their own wheat to make bread.

Why has quiltmaking survived through its long history, when other practical crafts have become obsolete—victims of the age of manufactured goods easily bought off the shelf? Those of us who are involved in quiltmaking will say that it is because it is so satisfying. Quiltmaking combines so many creative operations that it inspires the craftsperson to devise one project after another. Making a quilt can be as simple or demanding as one wishes, and a quilter can derive just as much satisfaction out of successfully completing an exact copy of a traditional example as from designing and making an original work of art. Also, there are so many variations of patchwork, quilting and appliqué that a quilter need never get bored with repeating the same technique.

The first chapter of this book will introduce you to the basics of quiltmaking, but there is nothing that this or any other book will teach you that hands-on experience won't bring home to you more solidly. If you are a skilled quilter, it might be a good idea to review the first chapter to find other ways of dealing with the same problem that you may have worked out on your own.

EQUIPMENT

Try to collect all the equipment you will need before starting a project. The equipment list I have compiled is complete; collect all your equipment in the beginning and store it in one place such as a pretty basket or bag so it will always be where you think it is. This may seem like simple advice, but you will appreciate it when you reach for a special needle or thread and it is there!

TEMPLATES AND MARKING FABRICS

Accuracy is the most important aspect of making templates and then using them to mark and cut out your fabrics. This point can't be stressed often enough. Precision at this stage of quiltmaking is more important than at any other stage in your work. If you make a patchwork template that is off by 3mm/⅛in, for example, by the time you have cut about 50 pieces, you have an error of 15cm/6in! Take your time at this stage and you can enjoy the rest of your quiltmaking, secure in the knowledge that everything will fit when you're done.

HAND VS. MACHINE SEWING

It's difficult to discuss this part of quiltmaking because those who only sew by hand wouldn't dream of doing it by machine, and those proficient with a machine wouldn't consider sewing by hand, except for finishing techniques. What is correct? The answer is that both methods are perfectly acceptable, and if you are comfortable with one, then stick with it.

Hand sewers discuss the joy of being able to pick up and put down a project at will, carrying it with them wherever they go. Matching seams, setting in corners and sewing curves are certainly easier when hand sewing. The main difficulty with hand sewing is that it is slow, and unless the stitches are absolutely tiny and perfectly even, the work will not be as strong as machine sewing.

Machine sewers revel in the fact that they can begin a project in the morning and finish it by the afternoon, leaving them free to spend their time more creatively, such as in the designing stage. There is no doubt that machine stitching is stronger and quicker than hand sewing, but because the work goes faster, it is easier to make mistakes which may be difficult to remove.

Since each group of sewers wouldn't trade their method for the other, it seemed sensible to give instructions that are flexible enough for both hand and machine sewing. When the technique makes a definite difference, both methods are covered.

Although it would take many years to make an individual quilt in each of the variations of patchwork, appliqué and quilting covered in this book, this trinity of crafts works so well together that you can combine several variations within one project, such as a sampler quilt. Allow yourself to be challenged while you learn. The step-by-step illustrations and directions in this book will guide you easily through every technique—even one you may never have tried before.

1 Block Style Quilt, late 19th century. This dramatic quilt is composed of patchwork blocks that were sewn together without sashing between them. This creates secondary designs and almost totally obscures the original pattern. The block design, called Young Man's Fancy, was often used to make a "coming of age" quilt for a young man. *Collection of the Ohio Historical Centre.*

2 Medallion Quilt, circa 1900. A pink eight-pointed star is surrounded by simple borders of pink and white strips quilted with twist and running feather designs. The quilt was probably "stamped" by Elizabeth Sanderson of Allenheads, Northumbria (1861-1934). Blue pencil markings are still visible on the quilt's surface. *Collection of Beamish, North of England Open Air Museum.*

3 Strippy Quilt, circa 1899. Made by Isabella Calvert of Thornley, County Durham, this typical North Country quilt of mustard and cream sateen is superbly quilted in running diamond, fan, rose and feather with a diamond filling. It was probably made as a wedding present for the donor's grandmother—Mrs Barbara Jane Clark. *Collection of Beamish, North of England Open Air Museum.*

4 Mosaic Quilt, mid 19th century. This Honeycomb coverlet in a Grandmother's Flower Garden arrangement was made by an elderly country woman from Allenheads, Northumbria. She constructed it using the English method of piecing over papers, most of which have not been removed; some are clearly dated 1841 and 1855. *Collection of Beamish, North of England Open Air Museum.*

TRADITIONAL QUILT STYLES

1

2

3

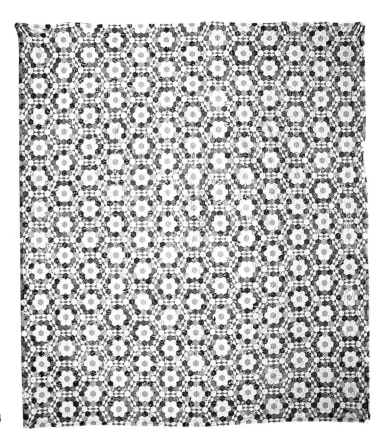

4

FABRIC AND COLOUR

Since quiltmaking is a textile art, the most important medium that you will be using is fabric. Although quiltmaking has always been fondly regarded as a thrifty way to use up scraps of fabric, there is a theory that very few surviving quilts were made totally from scraps.[1] So sort through your own fabric collection to see what you lack, and then make a visit to your local material store to purchase some fabric—for some quilters, this is one of the most enjoyable aspects of quiltmaking!

The first rule when buying fabric is: buy the best that you can afford. Do not skimp on this most essential element of a quilt. You will be putting so much of yourself into its creation that it would be a shame to sacrifice even a few years of your quilt's life by using inferior fabrics. The second rule is to begin working with 100% cotton fabrics; cotton fabrics will last longer, wear better and handle easier than any other material.

Experienced quilters will naturally turn to other fabrics in the course of their development. The only way to learn about special fabrics is to test them yourself to see how they handle, how easy they are to mark and cut, whether they will hold creases, etc.; *see page 90* for a discussion on special fabrics.

As your interest in quiltmaking grows, so will your fabric collection, and it is important to add judiciously and not haphazardly to your palette of colours in solids and prints. Study the different types of prints *(see pages 28-30)*, then sort through your own collection to determine which areas are deficient and which need supplementing. Try to include a complete rainbow of colours in pale tints and dark shades. Keep in mind that value (the lightness or darkness of a colour) is almost more important than colour in making a quilt. Use a range of values in your work for the best results.

The only way that you are going to know how successful you are at combining colours is to try it. This is why your first project should not be a gargantuan effort that will take years to finish; you may never complete it and the quilt world may be robbed of another great artist. Start small and work your way up; you'll then have the satisfaction of actually completing something.

Above Network by Inge Hueber, 1990, Köln, Germany. 165 x 218cm/ 65 x 86in. This leading German quilt artist hand-dyes all her own fabrics and is known for her expert handling of colour in her pieces. Using the Seminole piecing method of patchwork, Inge made Network to honour the friendship of quilters all over the world. *Collection of the artist.*

Left Movement by Lynne Edwards, 1989, Suffolk, England. 81 x 91cm/ 32 x 36in. Lustrous silks and glowing shades of yellow and gold drift across the surface of this wall hanging. By changing the size of the classic Cathedral Window blocks within the same piece, this well-known British quiltmaker has created a feeling of depth and movement. *Collection of Hazel Hurst.*

Left Cold-Warm with Perturbations by Ursula Stürzinger, 1986, Zürich, Switzerland. 106 x 106cm/42 x 42in. String patchwork has been refined to a high degree of sophistication with this simple yet striking quilt. The juxtaposition of several blocks has resulted in a dazzling yet playful effect. Ursula's subtle use of pink, orange and red contributes to the movement and excitement of the design. *Collection of the Zürich State Art Collection.*

Below left Arachnida by Linda Negandhi, 1993, Northumberland, England. 140 x 170cm/55 x 67in. Arachnida gleams with colour and swirls with movement. It was made completely by hand using the English method of piecing over papers. The 1993 winner of the Great American Quilt Contest, the quilt is constructed entirely of silk, and was hand-quilted with silk thread. Some of the fabrics were hand-dyed to achieve exactly the right shade. A detail, below right, shows the precision of the work and the delicate quilting stitches. *Collection of the artist.*

PATCHWORK

It is believed that patchwork evolved in America as a sensible method of teaching young girls the basics of sewing—cutting, stitching and successfully combining fabrics—so that they would be proficient at this important task when it came time to supply their own family's needs. A favourite and oft-repeated quilt legend is that a young girl would be expected to make a dozen quilts before she became engaged to be married. Each successive quilt was meant to be more skilfully sewn and better designed than the previous one. Then, when she actually became betrothed, the thirteenth quilt—the elaborate masterpiece—was designed and made. Quilt historians have been hard-pressed to prove many details of this narrative, but it has become a firm part of quilt lore.

Whether or not it is true, this story can actually teach today's quilters a lesson: learn the basics and work your way up to more complicated designs. There is no way that your first quilt is going to be as wonderful as your tenth or twentieth, so don't try to create an intricate masterpiece on your first attempt. Begin with a basic design that will teach you about your abilities to select fabrics, combine colours, cut and sew. Then, gradually challenge yourself with more difficult or intricate designs.

Left Sunburst or Pinwheel Quilt, by Lucy Tucker Catlett, circa 1860, Anderson County, South Carolina. 208 x 178cm/82 x 70in. One cannot help but smile upon viewing this delightful quilt. The brightly coloured triangle and diamond shapes illustrate the stitcher's sophisticated sense of design as well as her precision piecing and obvious mathematical ability. The contour quilting emphasizes the flower medallions in each corner. The quilt is signed "MACV from your mother." *Collection of the South Carolina State Museum.*

Right Spinning Stars, by an Unknown Maker, circa 1840, Texas. 183 x 213cm/72 x 84in. A rare pattern, this Spinning Stars quilt was made from fabric scraps, which is why each block is different. The difficulty of joining the sixteen seams in the middle of each block is apparent when you study the quilt closely. However, the eccentricity of the sewing adds to the charm of this piece of American folk art. *Collection of Laura Ann and Buddy Rau.*

PATCHWORK

Above Eating Disorder, by Sara Ann McLennand, 1992, Wellington, Florida. 221 x 163cm/87 x 64in. This is a close-up detail of Sara Ann's quilt which was inspired by the old patchwork pattern, Arabic Lattice. Sara Ann updated this design by setting the pieces into one another and adding teeth and eyes. The "creatures" appear to be eating each other in all different directions. *Collection of the artist.*

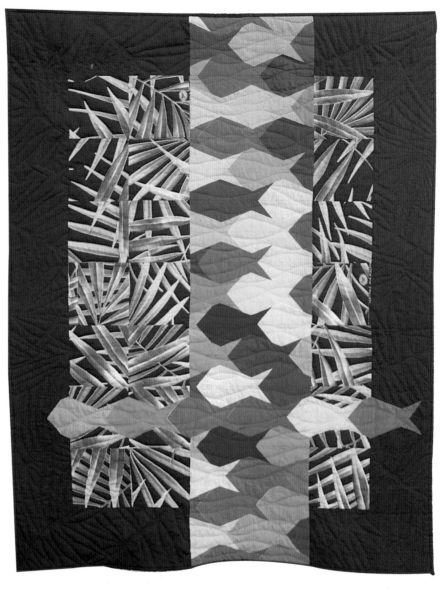

Left Keith's Quilt, by Linda Seward, 1994, London, England. 66 x 84cm/26 x 33in. This two-sided quilt was made to celebrate the birth of the author's son. Linda hoped that the child-like quality of the patchwork combined with the bright colours would appeal to him. The quilt wasn't pre-planned; patchwork and strips were added where necessary to make the blocks fit together. The work is embroidered with Keith's name and his birth date. *Collection of Robert George Keith Seward.*

Above Coral Reef by Irene MacWilliam, 1993, Belfast, Northern Ireland. 105 x 135cm/42 x 53in. Machine-pieced and hand-quilted, this colourful patchwork quilt sparkles and shimmers with shifting colours that draw the eye appreciatively over its surface. It is part of a series of quilts by this well-known Irish quilter featuring fish and the sea. The intricately pieced fish contrast with the large bold print of the background fabric. *Collection of the artist.*

Above Blue Glow by Nancy Herman, 1992, Merion, Pennsylvania, 122 x
122cm/48 x 48in. To create this remarkable work, Nancy first machine-pieced
two quilt tops. She set one aside for the background, and cut the other into
L-shaped strips. These strips were then machine-appliquéd onto the pieced
background. The silvery pieces are cut from satin, which adds a luminous
quality to the work. *Collection of Saul, Ewing, Remick & Saul.*

PATCHWORK

Above The Sun, the Moon...and the Stars by Paula Nadelstern, 1991, Bronx, New York. 223 x 152cm/88 x 60in. Paula achieves a dramatic impact through the complex detail of her work—her quilt is seamed from many thousands of pieces. The impression of circles and curves is an illusion created by piecing straight lines. *Collection of Ralph and Clara Lyman.*

Left By Moonlight by Diana Goulston Robinson, 1992, Brooklyn, New York. 155 x 145cm/61 x 57in. This is a close-up detail of Diana's quilt, which was inspired when she witnessed baby Loggerhead turtles, an endangered species, bursting forth from their nests and marching towards the moon-reflected sea. Her considered use of fabric and colour creates the impression of movement; it's hard to believe that the quilt is basically constructed from squares and triangles. *Collection of the artist.*

Below Emily's Quilt by Linda Seward, 1992, London, England. 203 x 203cm/80 x 80in. Finished the day before Emily was born, this quilt is used as a teacher's sample for rotary cutting workshops. It fulfilled a personal challenge to design a complex pattern using only three fabrics. *Collection of the author.*

Above Fissures by Ann Stamm Merrell, 1993, Cupertino, California. 180 x 183cm/71 x 72in. A strong and disturbing piece, this quilt was made as an abstract design, although many people have seen cataclysmic events like the Loma Prieta earthquake or the Oakland fire in it. *Collection of the artist.*

PATCHWORK

Left Emily's Animals by Linda Seward, 1995, London, England. 155 x 190cm/61 x 75in. This quilt was made for the author's daughter who took a keen interest in its progress over the two years it took to make it. It is the result of a challenge Linda imposed on herself to create a quilt using only plaid, striped and geometric fabrics. Emily chose the animals from Margaret Rolfe's book, *Go Wild With Quilts*, and she helped design the animals that have been featured in the quilting. The other blocks are favourite traditional ones. *Collection of Emily Ann Seward.*

Right Double Wedding Ring by a member of the Pearson family, circa 1940, Ohio. 132 x 132cm/52 x 52in. This quilt was made before World War II and serves as a catalogue of the different fabric prints that were popular during that period. You can create the same quilt using the full-size patterns on page 97 and following the instructions on pages 66-67. The extra square along the border is optional; attach by hand if desired. A quilting pattern for the flower in the middle of each ring can be found on page 136. *Collection of Edward and Rita Susse.*

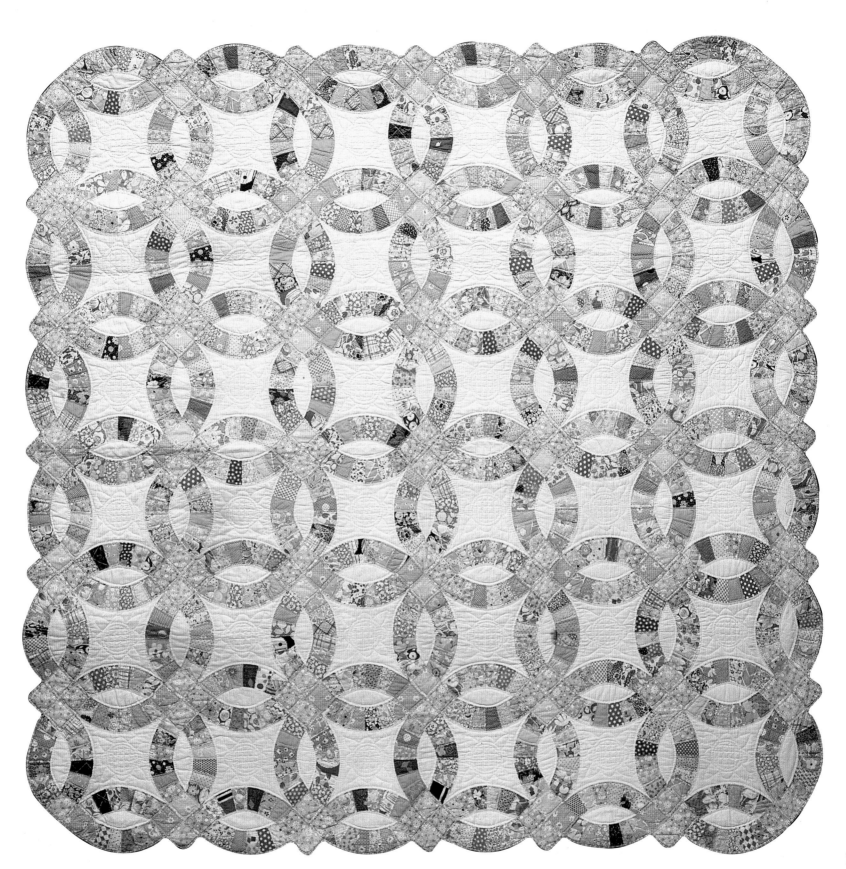

19

APPLIQUÉ

Joyful, carefree, unrestrained—these words can be used to describe the appliqué quilts on the following pages. Precise, well-executed, detailed: these words can also characterise the same quilts. Appliqué work has the ability to satisfy every quiltmaker, whether you prefer close detailed work, or a freer approach. Look at Chapter 3, The Art of Appliqué, which starts on *page 98*, to see the many diverse techniques that come under the heading of applied work.

If you have never tried appliqué, you might be put off attempting it when you study the magnificent masterpiece quilts that have been made using this technique, such as Susan McCord's Urn Quilt on the facing page. But if you have tried it, you will know that it is easier to camouflage a problem with appliqué. Often, depending, of course, on the pattern, measurements don't have to be as exact as in patchwork. You can be freer in your design and in your choice of fabrics. Moreover, decisions that you made when you started a piece can be changed without anyone being any the wiser.

Look at the spontaneity and jubilation that emanates from Martha by Jeanne Lyons Butler on this page. Jeanne designs her quilts very freely. Perhaps if you always pre-plan your quilts on paper and rigidly stick to your original design, you might try to make an adventurous appliqué quilt as an exercise—it just might reveal a talent that you didn't know you had! Look at the wonderful embellishments Jane Burch Cochran used on her quilt, Southern Devotion *(see page 22)*—search through your button box and look for other small treasures that you can sew onto your quilts to personalize them. If you don't feel comfortable about designing your own appliqués, try using the Broderie Perse technique, which has been done to create Memories of Days Under the Sea on *page 22*. Have fun collecting fabrics that feature your favourite subject, then cut them out and use them to design a small wall hanging or cushion.

Appliqué work done on the sewing machine can be just as successful as that done by hand—it will look different, of course, but it will have its own charm. Monica Millner machine-appliquéd the figures in her African Magic quilt on *page 22*, while Amelia Adams used only hand-sewing techniques on her Baltimore masterpiece on *page 23*.

Left Martha by Jeanne Lyons Butler, 1992, Huntington, New York. 105 x 152cm/41 x 60in. Jean designs her quilts in a collage-like manner employing diverse methods of appliqué and piecing in her work. She uses no drawings but works directly with the fabrics and embellishments. The life of the dancer Martha Graham and her dedication to her art and personal expression are the inspiration behind this quilt, which imparts an incredible feeling of music, energy, movement and beauty. The appliquéd figure is decorated with beads, buttons, hardware and paint. *Collection of the artist.*

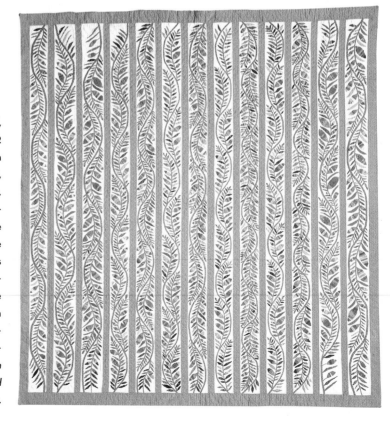

Right Vine by Susan Noakes McCord, 1880-1900, McCordsville, Indiana. 192 x 206cm/75 3/4 x 81in. Susan McCord, who lived from 1829-1909, was a talented and prolific quilt maker. This, her most famous quilt, is an example of American folk art at its best. The quilt displays such inventiveness, sense of colour and pure joy that it has received national renown. Close examination reveals that most of the appliquéd leaves and buds have been pieced with strips of fabric. The rose-coloured borders and sashes complement the harmonious design. *Collection of the Henry Ford Museum and Greenfield Village, Dearborn, Michigan.*

Above Urn Quilt by Susan Noakes McCord, circa 1860, McCordsville,
Indiana. 211 x 216cm/83 x 85in. Appliquéd urns have been filled with tulips,
fuschias, and flowers, and interspersed with bunches of grapes. The quilt's
colours are unfaded; it appears to have never been washed. Note how the
artist has solved the often difficult problem of turning corners. *Collection of the
Henry Ford Museum and Greenfield Village, Dearborn, Michigan.*

Appliqué

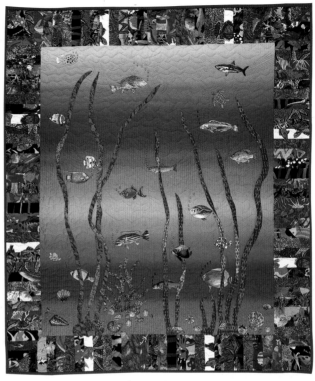

Left Memories of Days Under the Sea by Linda Seward, 1994, London, England, 119 x 137cm/47 x 54in. This quilt was made for the author's sister who is a scuba diver. Linda collected "fish fabrics" and dreamt about creating this quilt for 3 years while waiting for the right background fabric to come along — she finally found it in a shop (when she wasn't even looking for it) and started the quilt immediately after that. The wall hanging was quilted entirely by hand, with stipple quilting at the bottom to imitate sand. Beads and coral add texture.
Collection of Danae Tyler.

Above Southern Devotion by Jane Burch Cochran, 1992, Rabbit Hash, Kentucky, 173 x 216cm/68 x 85in. This quilt was made to honour Marie Sims of Clover, Virginia, who nourished her community with food, love and wisdom regardless of race. This detail of Jane's quilt shows the elaborate embellishments that she employs in her art quilts. Jane mostly decorates her pieces with buttons, beads, embroidery and paint. She likes to combine the loose, free feeling of abstract painting with the time-consuming and controlled techniques of beading and sewing.

Collection of the artist.

Right African Magic by Monica Millner,1993, London, England, 135 x 132cm/53 x 52in. Made of cotton and velvet, this powerful wall hanging was machine-appliquéd and machine pieced. The unusual fabrics were collected over many years and suddenly seemed to fit together. The figures were inspired by images seen at museum exhibitions and in books; the design was carefully pre-planned on paper. Monica used fabric crayons to draw the double circles, and embroidered some of the animals. Black bias binding was used to separate and define the blocks.

Collection of the artist.

Above Pride of Baltimore II by Amelia Adams, 1994, London England, 198 x 198cm/78 x 78in. This magnificent quilt was created entirely by hand over a two-year period. The background fabric is a fine Egyptian cotton—bought in the back streets of Luxor! The central design is a clipper ship that sails around the world as a goodwill ambassador for Maryland. *Collection of the artist.*

QUILTING

No matter how magnificent the patchwork or appliqué may be, a quilt is usually not deemed "finished" until it has been quilted. It is amazing how a simple running stitch, essentially meant to hold the three quilt layers together, can create so many different effects. Study the quilts in these photographs to discover the many ways that quilting can be used to enhance your work.

Wholecloth quilts such as the Welsh example shown below are, of course, the best way to display elaborate quilting. If you are confident of your stitches, try quilting a wholecloth quilt with a contrasting colour thread. Patchwork and appliqué quilts will benefit greatly from judicious quilting. To make appliqués appear to stand out from the background, first outline-quilt each appliqué and then cross-hatch the background with straight lines that form diamonds; this technique has been used to great effect by Amelia Adams on her quilt, Pride of Baltimore II *(see page 23)*. Quilt animal motifs, special messages, or your children's hands and feet on a whimsical piece such as Emily's Animals on *page 18*. Quilting can add details, such as the waves and sand on Memories of Days Under the Sea *(page 22)*, or the flowers on Linda Negandhi's quilt, Arachnida *(page 11)*.

Spectacular effects can be achieved when you quilt with a sewing machine. Traditional designs such as feathers and cross-hatching, intensive stipple quilting, or just plain outline quilting can now be accomplished quickly using a machine.

Right Amish Quilt by Emma Stoltzfus, 1994, Lancaster County, Pennsylvania, 89 x 89cm/35 x 35in. Antique Amish quilts are renowned for their elaborate and meticulous quilting. This small-scale quilt was made recently by an Amish woman; the sale of contemporary quilts to tourists has become a welcome source of income for the Amish. The wall hanging was pieced in a traditional pattern called Diamond in a Square using typical sober Amish colours. It has been beautifully quilted with hearts, a central wreath and an elaborate feathered border, skilfully turned at the corners. *Collection of Jan Jefferson.*

Right Welsh Wholecloth Quilt by an Unknown Maker, late 19th century, Wales, 173.5 x 207cm/68 x 81in. Made of cotton sateen, this magnificent design was probably created as a wedding quilt. Welsh wedding quilts were often made using fabrics in strong bright colours (the reverse side is a rust colour). Also, the use of hearts in the outer border would make it more than likely that a newly married couple were the first to sleep beneath it. The spiral "Welsh rose" or "snail creep" motif, seen in the borders and corners of the central medallion, is a commonly used pattern in Welsh quilts. *Collection of Judy Greenwood.*

QUILTING

Left Feather Wreath Cushions by Amy Emms, Weardale, England, 48 x 48cm/19 x 19in. These cushions were quilted by the eminent British quilter, Amy Emms. Born in 1904, Mrs Emms was taught to quilt by her mother. She became a teacher herself, inspiring new quilters throughout her entire life. When she retired, Mrs Emms was honoured by the Queen of England who awarded her an MBE (Member of the British Empire) for her outstanding contribution to the craft of North Country quilting. The design used on these cushions is a traditional feather wreath.
Private collection.

Above Framed Quilt by Mrs Stewart, circa 1910, Bowburn, County Durham, England, 242 x 208cm/95 x 82in. A unique variation of a wholecloth quilt, this example is made of cream cotton sateen framed with a floral-patterned chintz. The reverse is pink sateen, also with a printed border. The central quilted medallion is complemented by large corner leaves connected with a hammock border. The frame is quilted with a running feather design.
Collection of Beamish, North of England Open Air Museum.

FABRIC AND COLOUR

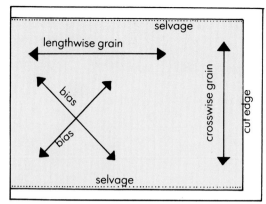

1 Fabric Selvages are the finished edges of fabric. Lengthwise grain runs parallel to the selvages and has little stretch. Crosswise grain runs perpendicular to selvages and has slight stretch. Bias runs at a 45° angle to selvages and has the maximum stretch.

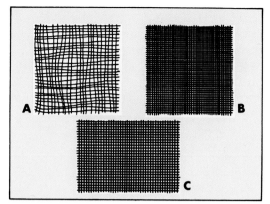

2 When buying fabrics for quiltmaking, check density of the weave by holding fabric up to light. A loose weave (A) will allow padding to migrate to the surface; a tight weave (B) will make fabric difficult to sew and quilt. Select fabrics with a medium weave (C).

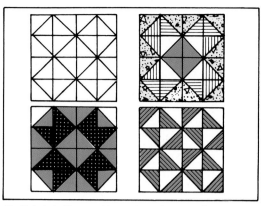

3 Fabric is the most important element of patchwork, quilting and appliqué. Designs come to life when made up in fabric, and the careful positioning of fabrics can make the same pattern appear totally different.

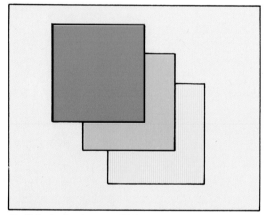

1 Value is the degree of lightness or darkness of a colour and is almost more crucial to the success of a design than colour itself. Designs can be changed depending upon placement of fabrics of different values; use assorted light, medium and dark values.

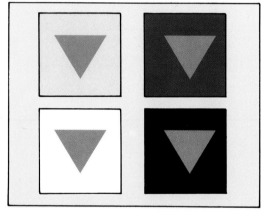

2 Values can appear to change depending upon the fabrics surrounding them. The same value of grey is used for all triangles shown in the illustration. Note how triangles appear darker on light backgrounds and lighter on dark backgrounds.

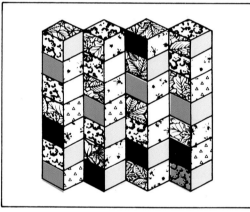

3 Careful manipulation of values can create depth in your work. Dark-value fabrics appear to recede and can be used to define light-value fabrics, which seem to advance. Optical effects can be achieved by careful placement of light and dark values.

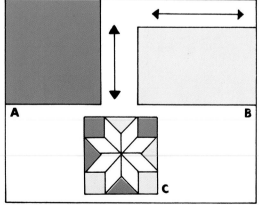

Solid-colour fabrics will create bold, sharply defined designs. Some solids, particularly those with a sheen, will vary slightly in colour when viewed from different angles (A & B). Always position pieces with grain running the same way to prevent mistakes (C).

1 Prints Patterned fabric is commonly taken to be a hallmark of quiltmaking, and the use of prints will add a traditional feel to your projects. For a successful result, use a combination of small-, medium- and large-scale prints in your work.

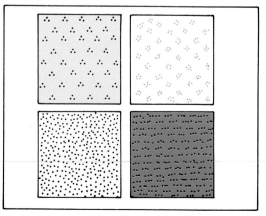

2 Small-scale prints will look solid from a distance, but will add sparkle and texture to a design. If you find that a fabric arrangement looks a bit dull, try substituting a small-scale print for a solid.

3 Medium-scale prints are the most familiar fabrics available in shops and will vary from swirling all-over patterns to floral and geometric repeats. Do not use too many medium-scale prints in one design or the pattern pieces may appear to blend together.

4 The designs of large-scale prints will not always fit a template shape. However, they can create startling contrasts with small- and medium-scale prints. View the designs through plastic or window templates to find the best position; *see pages 34-35.*

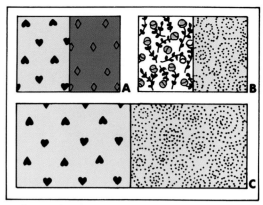

1 **Contrast** Strive to use fabrics that contrast well with one another, both in value and scale. Prints vary considerably in appearance, ranging from widely spaced motifs (A) to swirling compact designs (B). Combine the two for a memorable effect (C).

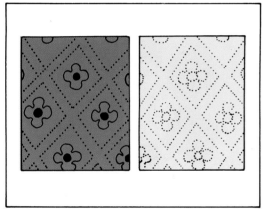

2 If you have difficulty locating light values of some fabrics, use the WS of the fabric as the RS. This will produce a subtle effect that will harmonize perfectly with the RS.

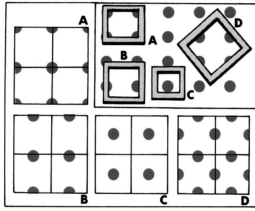

1 **Marking and cutting prints** Careful placement of templates on printed fabrics will result in some wonderful effects when pieces are joined. While it is better to cut straight edges on grain, you may wish to work on bias (D) for a particular look.

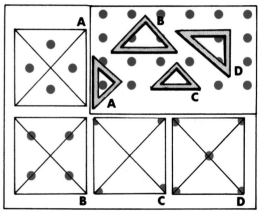

2 You can achieve a number of effects through precise positioning of triangular templates. However, cutting patterned fabrics this way will use up more yardage, and some quilters prefer the random appearance of less carefully planned pieces.

3 You can manipulate diamonds in many ways to achieve a multitude of different results. Experiment to find other design possibilities. Combine the diamonds to create stars, then use all the stars in one project for a striking and unusual effect.

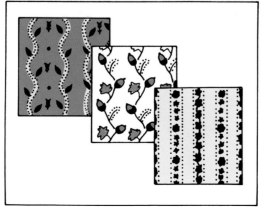

1 **Stripes** will add vitality and movement to a project, and can provide visual relief from busy prints. They do not necessarily have to be solid lines – any linear designs, such as the examples shown here, can be used in the same way as traditional stripes.

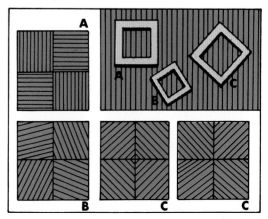

2 The same simple four-patch design can look entirely different if you vary the position of stripes. For an unexpected composition, cut some squares with stripes slightly askew to create tension and excitement (B).

FABRIC AND COLOUR

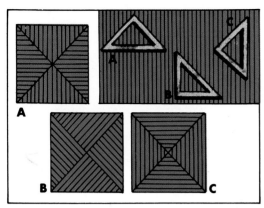

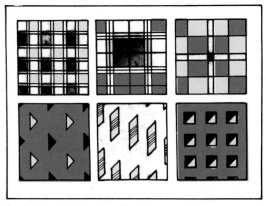

3 Stripes can create static or swirling effects if made up of triangles. They can also look particularly effective when used on pinwheel designs and other patterns that suggest motion.

4 Diamond shapes assume an entirely new character when cut from stripes. Try alternating striped and solid diamonds to create other effects. Careful cutting and extra yardage are required to make the most of a striped fabric.

Geometric prints Plaids and bold geometric prints can add unexpected richness and vitality to an otherwise static design. Many of the old patchwork quilts freely utilized checks, plaids and geometric fabrics in unexpected combinations.

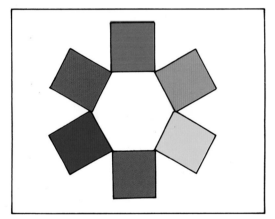

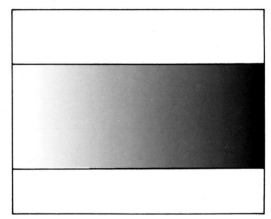

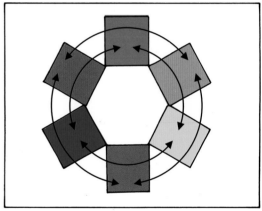

1 Colour There are 3 primary colours or hues from which all other colours are formed: red, yellow and blue. Green, orange and purple are secondary colours. Hues between primary and secondary colours are called intermediates.

2 A monochromatic colour scheme uses various tints and shades of one colour. A tint is formed by adding white to a colour; a shade by adding black. Neutrals (white, black and gray) can be added to a monochromatic colour scheme without changing it.

3 An analogous colour scheme uses 3 adjacent colours on the colour wheel in any tint or shade. Using only primary and secondary colours will result in a vivid design; for a quiet and restful look, make your selection from adjacent intermediate colours.

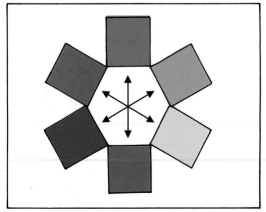

4 A contrasting colour scheme uses complementary colours – those that are opposite one another on the colour wheel. Using a colour with its complement makes the colour appear richer and more intense. The colours need not be pure: use any tint or shade.

5a A 2-colour scheme will have a clean, spare look. Use a combination of light and dark colours, or any colour with white or black. White will make an adjacent colour appear saturated and vivid; black will clarify the colour and make it appear to glow.

5b A 2-colour scheme of high contrast, such as white and black, will cause an optical illusion. The eye cannot determine which is the background colour and which is the foreground, because there is a consistent interplay between them.

PREPARATION OF FABRICS

1 Washing Always pre-wash fabrics to prevent shrinkage and bleeding in a finished project. Sort fabric into light and dark piles; wash separately in warm water with fabric softener or mild soap; do not use detergent if fabrics are clean. Hang to dry.

2 If you suspect that a fabric may "bleed", soak a scrap in a bowl of warm water for one hour. If dye runs, soak entire fabric in solution of 3 parts cold water to 1 part white vinegar. Test again with a fabric scrap. Discard if fabric still bleeds.

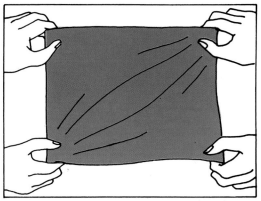

3 After fabric has dried, straighten the grain by grasping opposite corners with your hands (this process is best accomplished by 2 people). Pull fabric alternately from opposite corners a few times. Steam-press fabric to remove any wrinkles.

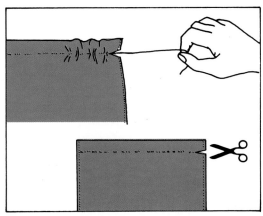

4a Next straighten raw edges. If fabric is not tightly woven, use scissors to clip about 6mm/¼in into selvage just below raw edge. Spread cut edges apart; grasp a crosswise thread. Pull thread gently across fabric; cut along line formed. Cut off selvages.

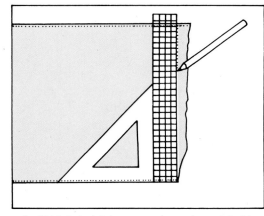

4b If fabric is tightly woven, use a ruler and drafting triangle to draw a straight line across fabric. Place triangle exactly on selvage, with ruler against triangle. Draw line across fabric. Also draw cutting lines along each selvage edge. Cut along marked lines.

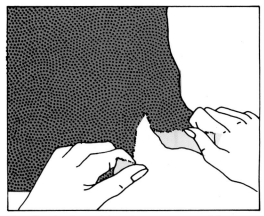

4c Tearing is a quick and easy way to straighten raw edges, but must be done with caution. Clip into selvage about 2.5cm/1in from end. Tear firmly and swiftly to other selvage; cut selvage. If you tear too slowly, fabric may split along lengthwise grain.

Storing fabric After fabrics have been prepared, separate into groups by colour. Fold and store on shelves, or in boxes. If you have space, divide pieces into prints and solids. Small remnants of fabric can be rolled and stored attractively in small wicker baskets.

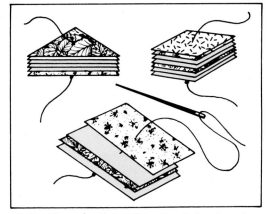

1 Organizing and storing cut pieces Cut all the pieces for a project at one time. To prevent confusion between different-sized pieces and to aid in finding them when you need them, stack in like groups and string together on thread, knotted at one end.

2 Alternatively, you can store like pieces in clear plastic storage bags. Keep the template for each piece in the same bag in case you need to cut more shapes and for easy reference.

EQUIPMENT

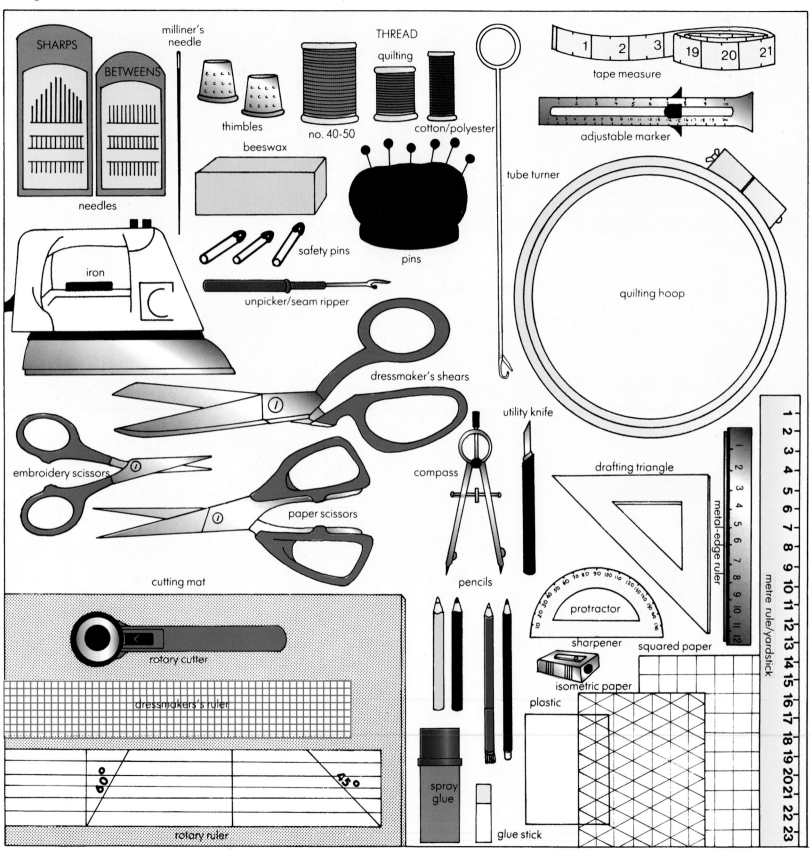

SHARPS

BETWEENS

needles

milliner's needle

thimbles

beeswax

THREAD

quilting

no. 40-50

cotton/polyester

safety pins

pins

tube turner

tape measure

adjustable marker

quilting hoop

iron

unpicker/seam ripper

dressmaker's shears

embroidery scissors

paper scissors

compass

utility knife

pencils

drafting triangle

protractor

sharpener

isometric paper

plastic

squared paper

metal-edge ruler

metre rule/yardstick

cutting mat

rotary cutter

dressmakers's ruler

60°

45°

rotary ruler

spray glue

glue stick

You won't need to buy much special equipment for quiltmaking; if you are a sewer, you probably already own most of the items you'll need. However, when purchasing equipment for quiltmaking, choose the best that you can afford; it is not worth sacrificing the quality of your work for mediocre tools. Also, keep your equipment in good condition. Sharpen your scissors and change the blades on your utility knife and rotary cutter regularly. Discard burred needles and pins which may mark your fabrics, and keep your iron clean and pencils sharpened. These preparations will make all the difference between professional and inferior work.

SEWING NEEDS

Needles: Use sharps for all hand sewing, including piecing and appliqué work. Use betweens for all hand-quilting; size 8 is recommended for beginners. As you progress, you may want to switch to smaller betweens in order to make smaller stitches – size 10 is the smallest needle. For basting, try using a long, thin milliner's needle, which is excellent for holding many stitches at one time.

Thimble: If you have never used a thimble before, now is the time to start. A thimble is absolutely indispensible in quilting, where you'll need to push the needle through several layers of fabric. You'll find that once you become proficient at using a thimble for quilting, you'll begin using it for regular sewing as well. Select a metal thimble with a flat top that fits comfortably on the middle finger of your sewing hand. Some quilters also use a thimble on the index finger of the hand below the quilt – you may wish to try a leather thimble for this.

Thread: For hand sewing and quilting, use 100% cotton quilting thread which is very strong, or standard No. 50 cotton thread. Select a colour that matches the darkest fabric you are sewing. If you are using many different fabrics, select a neutral thread that will blend inconspicuously with all of them, such as grey or ecru. For machine sewing, use a No. 40 cotton thread or a polyester thread wrapped with cotton.

Beeswax: Run your thread over a small cake of beeswax to strengthen it and help it to glide smoothly through the fabric. Beeswax will also help to prevent the thread from kinking.

Pins: Choose narrow, fine dressmaker's pins which slide easily through the fabric. Do not use thick, burred or rusted pins which will leave holes or marks. Pins with coloured glass or plastic heads are easy to manoeuvre when you are pinning through thick fabrics. Safety pins are sometimes used to "pin-baste" the layers of a quilt together; use size 2 safety pins, which are large enough to hold all three layers but small enough to leave the fabrics unmarked.

Iron: It is best to use a steam iron for pressing because the steam will help to set seams and remove wrinkles. Keep the iron set up close to your work.

Unpicker/Seam ripper: This is an essential tool for removing machine-sewn stitches.

Tube turner: While not essential for quiltmaking, this is useful when making small projects that require loops.

Quilting hoop: Consists of wooden hoop composed of two rings; the outer ring is tightened by twisting a screw which draws two wooden blocks together. For hand quilting, use as large a hoop as you feel comfortable with; hoops sized 35.6-58.4cm/14-23in are suggested. A round hoop is best; although oval hoops are available, these do not keep an even tension across the work and are not recommended. An embroidery or quilting hoop can also be used when sewing appliqués onto a background fabric.

IMPLEMENTS FOR MEASURING, MARKING AND CUTTING

Scissors: You'll need three pairs of scissors. Dressmaker's shears, preferably with a bent handle, should be extremely sharp; use them only for cutting fabric. You'll also need a pair of scissors for cutting paper; never cut paper with your sewing shears as this will dull your blades. Embroidery scissors are used for clipping threads and seam allowances; these should also be very sharp.

Rotary cutter and mat: Once you have used a rotary cutter, you'll wonder how you ever lived without it. It is an excellent tool for cutting strips, straightening fabric edges, even cutting out a variety of geometric patchwork pieces. Choose a cutter with a large blade, and keep spare blades handy. Always cut on a mat specially designed for a rotary cutter to keep the blade sharp; the mat will grip the fabric and also help the blade to cut straight. A "self-healing" cutting mat is ideal, and can be bought in most art supply stores.

Rotary ruler: This is made of thick, clear plastic and is marked with straight and sometimes angled lines to aid in measuring. If you do a lot of rotary cutting, you'll be glad you invested in this ruler – it makes the whole process easier and more accurate.

Dressmaker's ruler: This is a clear plastic ruler marked with horizontal and vertical grid lines to aid in marking seam allowances; it is excellent for drawing accurate templates too.

Coloured pencils: Keep a variety of colours on hand, using lighter pencils to mark dark fabrics and medium pencils to mark light fabrics; pale blue usually shows up well on light fabrics, and white or yellow stand out on darks.

Chalk pencil: This is useful for marking quilting or embroidery lines that may need to be brushed away later.

Pencil: Use a regular lead pencil for drawing templates and designs and for marking templates on fabric. Special pencils for marking templates on plastic are also available.

Pencil sharpener: Keep all your pencils very sharp so that your fabric pieces can be accurately marked. A thick pencil line will cause confusion about where to cut and may lead to inaccurate piecing.

Metre rule/Yardstick: This is used with a drafting triangle to straighten edges of fabric yardage.

Tape measure: Used for measuring fabric yardage and scraps of fabric to determine whether you'll have enough for a project.

Adjustable marker: Used for making repeated small measurements, such as when sewing pleats and tucks.

TOOLS FOR TEMPLATE MAKING

Utility knife: Available from art supply stores, this is essential for cutting templates from sturdy material such as cardboard. Keep a supply of spare blades on hand and change them frequently.

Metal-edge ruler: Use this with a utility knife to cut templates from sturdy material.

Protractor and compass: Use a protractor when drafting templates with unusual angles (*see page 40*), or for marking notches along curved seams. A compass is necessary for drafting many geometric shapes as well as curved or circular templates.

Drafting triangle: Usually made of clear plastic, this is used to verify correct angles of templates. It is also used in conjunction with a yardstick or rotary ruler to straighten edges of fabric yardage.

Spray glue: While rubber cement can be used to glue your template shapes to cardboard, spray glue will allow you to reposition the pieces and place them flat on the board. It is much less messy and dries quickly; spray your template shapes on the WS over a sheet of scrap paper.

Glue stick: This is useful for appliqué work, where pieces must be temporarily secured to a base. Test your glue stick on a scrap of fabric before using.

Graph paper and plastic: Have a supply of squared and isometric graph paper on hand to enable you to accurately draw your templates. Keep a sheet of plastic available for making reusable templates.

TEMPLATES AND MARKING FABRICS

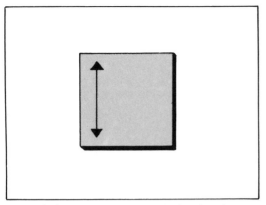

1 **Standard types** Templates used for hand sewing, appliqué work and quilting are cut to the exact shape of the piece and do not include a seam allowance. They are used to mark stitching lines on fabric, but not cutting lines.

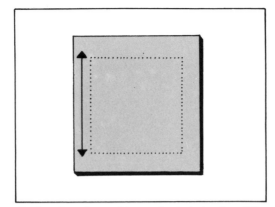

2 Templates for machine sewing include a 6mm/¼in seam allowance at all edges. Pencil line in illustration indicates original shape of piece before adding seam allowances; usually, this original shape will be a piece of graph paper glued to cardboard.

3 Window templates allow you to draw a seam line and cutting line at the same time; width of "frame" is 6mm/¼in. Large window templates need ladders (bars left in the template) to stabilize them.

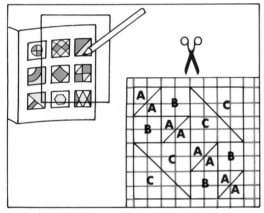

1 **Making templates** Trace a pattern from a book or magazine, or design one of your own. Enlarge design to correct size using a ruler, *see page 106*. Label the individual pieces of the pattern. Cut out one of each piece.

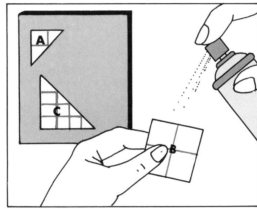

2 For making templates, choose a durable foundation that is easy to mark and cut, such as medium-weight cardboard. Spray-glue each pattern piece to the foundation, leaving 13mm/½in between pieces if making machine or window templates.

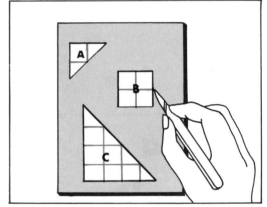

3 For machine and window templates, accurately mark a line 6mm/¼in beyond edge of glued shape. Holding a utility knife perpendicular to surface of cardboard, draw blade several times along edge of shape or on marked line to cut out template.

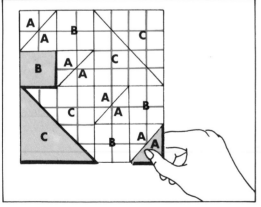

4 Confirm size of template by placing over same shape in your original drawing; templates must be accurate or mistakes will be compounded as stitching proceeds. Replace templates as they wear out and store in plastic bags or envelopes to protect them.

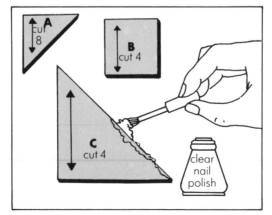

5 Label templates by letter, grain line and how many pieces to cut. If template needs to be cut in reverse or mirror image (*see page 55*) mark with a small R. Coat edges of templates with nail polish to prolong wear. Glue sandpaper to back to prevent shifting.

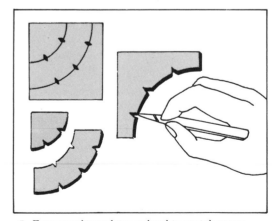

6 For curved templates or hard-to-match seams, mark notches on seam line of pattern before it is cut apart. Make templates as directed, then cut notches into templates with a utility knife. Notches are marked on fabric to help match pieces during sewing.

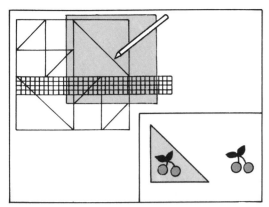

Plastic is an excellent medium for making templates: it can be used an infinite number of times, you can trace a pattern directly onto it without gluing, and it enables you to see exactly what a piece will look like when you are marking it on fabric.

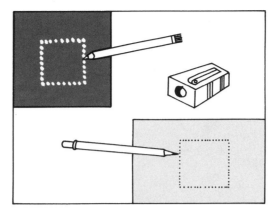

1 Marking fabrics Always mark patchwork pieces on WS of fabric, appliqué pieces and quilting patterns on RS. Use a white dressmaker's pencil or chalk on dark fabrics and a lead or pale blue pencil on light fabrics. Keep markers very sharp so lines are accurate.

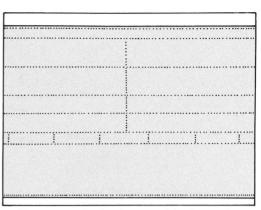

2 If you are cutting borders or sashing from a piece of fabric, mark those pieces on the WS before marking any patchwork pieces. Use a long ruler and a drafting triangle to measure carefully and accurately: be sure to add 6mm/¼in seam allowances.

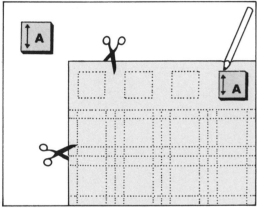

3 When marking around templates for hand sewing, position pieces at least 13mm/½in apart on WS of fabric. Some quilters mark the cutting lines (bottom). More experienced quilters do not mark these extra lines but cut pieces apart by eye (top).

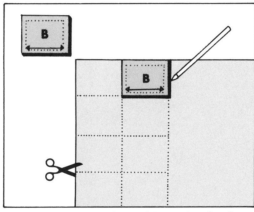

4 Because templates for machine sewing already include seam allowances, mark pieces adjacent to one another on WS of fabric for ease in cutting apart. Use very sharp dressmaker's shears or a rotary cutter, and cut exactly on marked lines for accuracy.

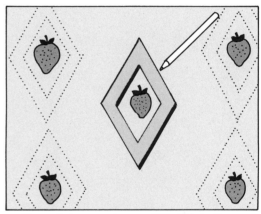

5 Place window templates on WS of fabric. For special effects, move the templates around until you find the most pleasing arrangement. Mark both the inner and outer lines if hand piecing; mark only the outer lines for machine piecing.

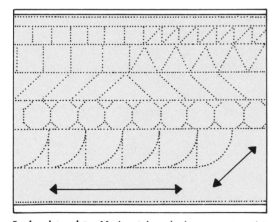

Patchwork templates Mark patchwork pieces one row at a time on WS of fabric, providing a mutual cutting edge if possible. The longest edge of each piece should always be on the straight grain of the fabric. Always mark curved edges on the bias.

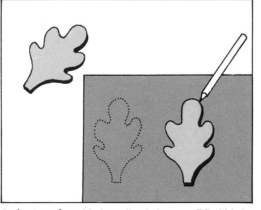

Appliqué templates Mark appliqué pieces on RS of fabric, leaving a 13mm/½in space between each one. Cut pieces apart by eye, leaving a 6mm/¼in seam allowance around all edges.

Quilting templates Make quilting templates in very sturdy material because they are often used for more than one project;plastic and heavy cardboard are best. Cut out interior spaces; draw overlapping lines on templates for later transference to fabric.

CUTTING FABRICS

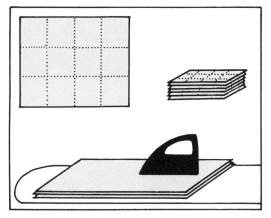

1 **Multiple cutting with scissors** Mark shapes on WS of one fabric. Begin layering fabrics on an ironing board, one at a time and WS up, aligning edges and grain line where possible. Steam-press between each layer. Place marked fabric, WS up, on top.

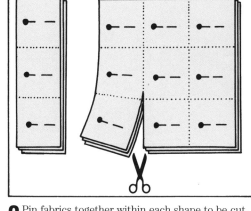

2 Pin fabrics together within each shape to be cut, without shifting or otherwise disturbing the layers of fabric. Using very sharp scissors, cut along the main lines, then cut out the individual shapes. Cut no more than 4-6 layers at a time to ensure accuracy.

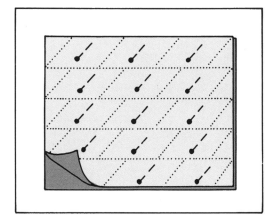

3 To cut mirror images *(page 55)*, mark requir-ed number of pieces (one direction only) on WS of one fabric; do not reverse template. Layer with second fabric RS facing. Pin layers together; cut pieces apart; remove pins. Mirror images automatically are cut.

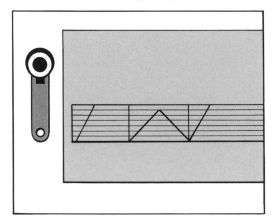

1 **Rotary cutting** is a fast and easy way to cut squares, triangles and rectangles. You will need a rotary cutter with a large wheel, a rotary ruler and a self-healing cutting mat. To prevent accidents, always close blade of cutter when you are not using it.

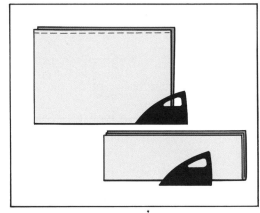

2 To prepare fabric, fold in half on straight grain matching selvages; steam-press layers together. Fold in half again, matching first fold to selvages, creating four layers; steam-press. Carefully pick up fabric without unfolding it and place on cutting mat.

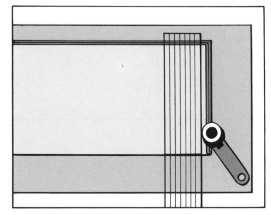

3 Place rotary ruler on fabric, aligning one of ruler's vertical grid lines with pressed folded edge of fabric (edge opposite selvages). Pressing down on the ruler with one hand, run cutter blade through fabric along edge of ruler to trim and straighten fabric.

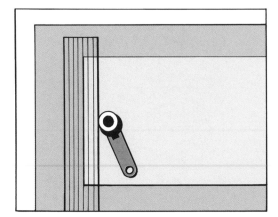

4 To cut strips, decide on width of strip required; add 13mm/½in seam allowance. Find this measurement on ruler. Turn fabric so straight edge is at left; place ruler with measurement line exactly on edge of fabric. Run blade along edge of ruler.

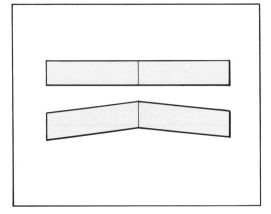

5 After cutting first strip, open it up to check your cutting. If cut correctly, strip should be perfectly straight (A). If ruler slipped slightly, strip will be angled near folds (B). Discard strip; re-trim fabric, making sure ruler is straight. Cut new strip as before.

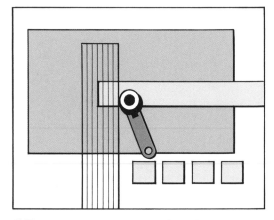

6 To cut squares, cut a strip to desired width of fin-ished square, plus 13mm/½in for seam allowances. Trim one edge of strip to remove folds. Then cut strip into sections, the exact same width as the strip. You will end up with perfect squares.

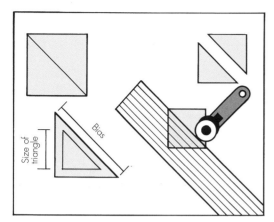

7 To cut half-square or right-angle triangles, cut a square to desired size of triangle, plus 2.2cm/⅞in for seam allowances. Cut square in half diagonally to make 2 triangles. Long edge of triangle will be on bias of fabric, 2 short edges on straight grain.

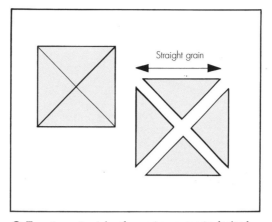

8 To cut quarter triangles, cut a square to desired size of triangle base (longest edge), adding 3cm/1 ¼in for seam allowances. Cut square diagonally in half, then in half again across opposite diagonal. Longest edge of triangle will be on straight grain.

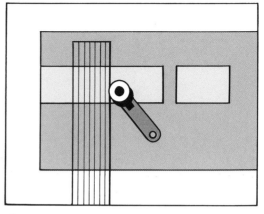

9 To cut rectangles, cut a strip to the desired depth of rectangle plus 13mm/½in for seam allowances. Trim one edge of strip to remove folds. Then cut strip into sections to desired width of rectangle.

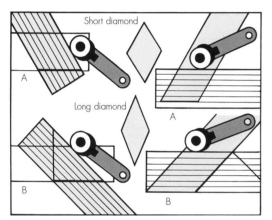

10 To cut diamonds, cut strip to width of diamond plus seam allowances. Place ruler on strip with 60° or 45° line on edge of strip; trim off end of strip as shown. Rearrange strip on cutting mat as shown; make second cut same width as strip.

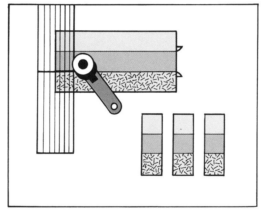

11 Patchwork can be quicker when you rotary-cut pre-sewn strips. First, cut strips of desired width using rotary cutter; stitch together. Press. Position ruler on strip at desired width, lining up a grid line on ruler with a central seam of the patchwork.

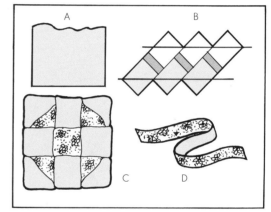

Other uses A rotary cutter is useful for neatening ragged edges of fabric after it has been washed (A); trimming offset edges of Seminole patchwork (B) or irregular edges of patchwork blocks (C); and cutting fabric strips for bindings, sashing and borders (D).

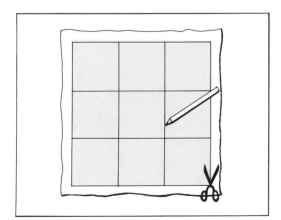

1 Quick Half-Square Triangles Using a pencil and ruler, carefully draw a grid of squares on WS of light fabric. Draw each square the desired finished size of the triangle plus 4.4cm/⅞in. Cut fabric along outer lines of grid.

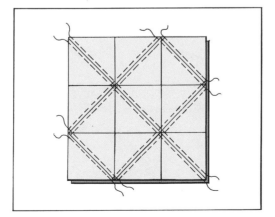

2 Draw a diagonal line through each of the squares as shown. Cut a contrasting fabric same size as marked fabric. Place fabrics together, RS facing; steam-press. Sew 6mm/¼in away from each side of each diagonal line; take care not to pucker fabrics.

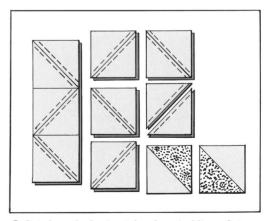

3 Cut along the horizontal and vertical lines. Cut squares in half along diagonal lines (between lines of stitching). Open triangles; press seams toward darker triangle. For every square drawn, you get 2 patchwork squares. Repeat for remaining squares.

Hand Sewing

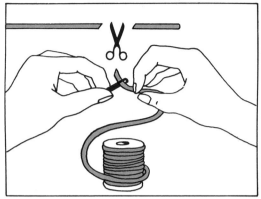

1 Threading a needle For easier threading, cut end of thread on the diagonal. Insert cut end through eye, first wetting end lightly if the plies have separated. Draw a length of thread through needle; tail should be about ¼ of total length.

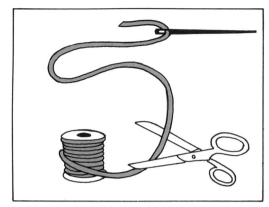

2 Measure the desired length of thread and cut off close to the spool. Use a 45.7cm/18in length of thread for most hand sewing; longer lengths can be used for basting.

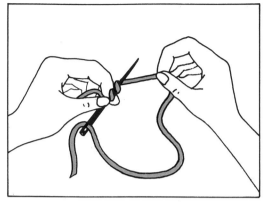

3 To knot the thread, wrap the end twice around the point of your needle, holding the end onto the needle with your other hand.

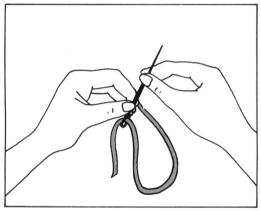

4 Holding onto the wraps with your fingers, slide them off the needle. Continue sliding the wraps to the end of the thread to form a knot. Clip off excess thread, close to the knot.

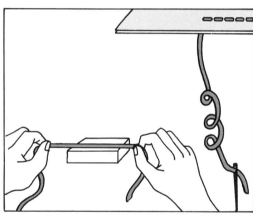

5 To prevent thread from knotting and kinking while you sew, run it over a cake of beeswax several times. If you find that the thread does kink as you are working, periodically allow needle and thread to hang straight down from the work to uncoil.

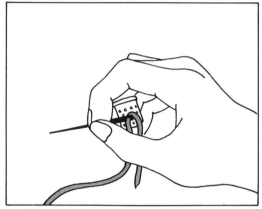

1 Technique Place a thimble on the middle finger of your sewing hand. Hold needle close to the point between your thumb and forefinger, with eye of needle resting against side of thimble. Try to hold the needle with a fairly relaxed grip.

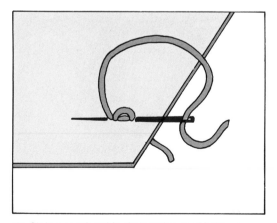

2 Sit in a comfortable chair with a good light source nearby. Try not to rush the work; rather develop a steady, even rhythm. Begin and end stitching either by working 3 small backstitches over one another, or with a sturdy knot; see next step.

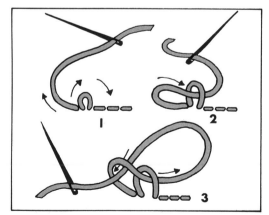

3 To make a sturdy knot, work a backstitch and pull thread through to form a loop (1). Insert needle through loop (2), then insert needle through second loop just formed (3). Pull thread tightly to form a knot. Clip away excess thread close to fabric.

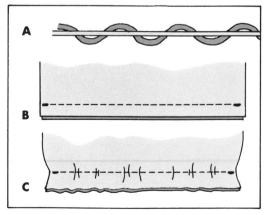

4 Keep the tension of your stitches even (A). Stitches should sit snugly on fabric surface and shouldn't be too loose (B) or too tight (C). To keep tension even, pull thread with same amount of force at end of each stitch.

HAND STITCHES

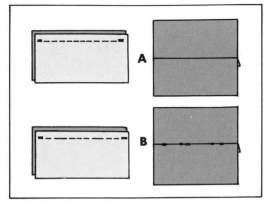

1 **Hand stitches** Sew same number of stitches per centimetre/inch (A), evenly spaced, but not too crowded. Too many stitches weaken seam by splitting threads in fabric. Uneven stitches will form visible gaps on RS when pieces are pressed (B).

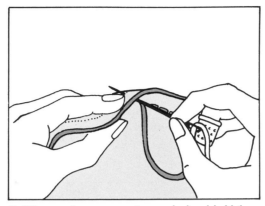

2 When sewing permanent seams by hand, hold the fabric pieces so that the sewing line is visible on the front and back as you work. Sew your stitches exactly on the marked lines so that pieces match up perfectly.

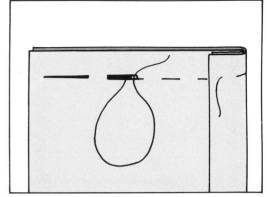

Basting is a temporary stitch used to secure pieces before sewing them together permanently. Use a long length of light-coloured thread that will contrast with the surrounding fabric for easy removal. Make running stitches about 6mm/¼in long, spaced 6mm/¼in apart.

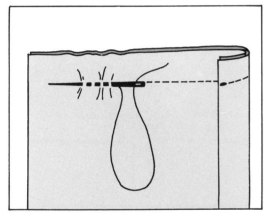

1 **Running stitch** This is the primary stitch used for sewing seams in patchwork and quiltmaking; it is also the basic quilting stitch. Make running stitches no longer than 1-3mm/¹⁄₁₆-⅛in and as straight and even as possible.

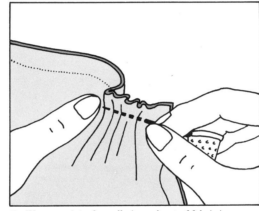

2 Weave point of needle in and out of fabric in a forward direction, grouping 4-12 stitches on the needle each time. Pull needle and thread through fabric to complete each series of stitches. Stitches will look the same on the front and back.

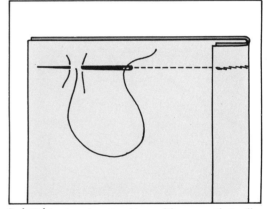

Backstitch is very strong and is used for seams that will receive stress. Make a 3mm/⅛in stitch, bringing needle point out 3mm/⅛in forward on seam line. Insert needle at end of last stitch; bring forward again. Stitches are continuous on RS, but overlap on WS.

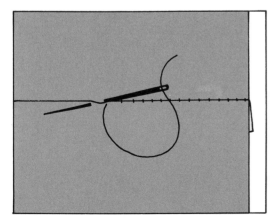

Slipstitch is used to secure a finished edge, such as an appliqué or binding, invisibly to another fabric. Catch a thread from under fabric with needle; at same time, catch a single thread on fold of fabric. Space stitches 3-6mm/⅛-¼in apart.

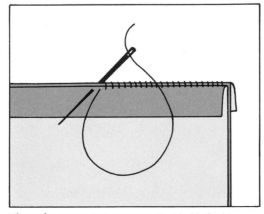

Whipstitch, oversewing or overcasting, holds 2 edges together with tiny straight stitches. Work from back to front, inserting needle at an angle through back and picking up 1 or 2 threads from each piece at a time. Work stitches 1-3mm/¹⁄₁₆-⅛in apart.

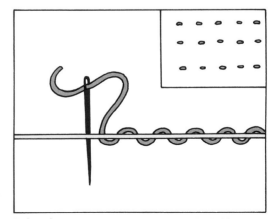

Stab stitch is used when sewing through thick fabrics or many layers where a running stitch would be too difficult, such as at seam crossings. It is also used in gathered patchwork; *see pages 70-71* . Hold needle perpendicular to fabric and work one stitch at a time.

MACHINE SEWING

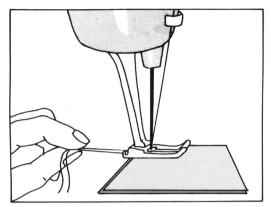

1 Technique Set machine at 10-12 stitches per 2.5cm/1in. Pin fabric pieces together smoothly with RS facing; insert edge under presser foot of sewing machine. Hold thread ends to keep them from being pulled into needle hole. Begin sewing.

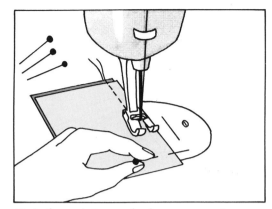

2 As the sewing proceeds, always remove pins as you come to them; do not sew over pins even though your machine may be equipped with a facility for this. If allowed to come into repeated contact with pins, the needle will form burrs, become dull and snag fabrics.

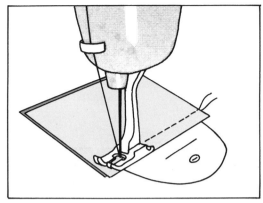

3a A 6mm/¼in seam allowance is standard in patchwork and quiltmaking; always sew with this size allowance when following directions in this book. Some presser feet are exactly 6mm/¼in wide on each side; if so, use edge of foot as a sewing guide.

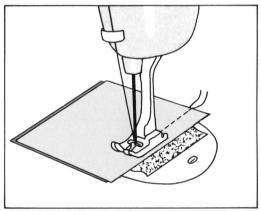

3b If you cannot use the presser foot as a guide, measure 6mm/¼in away from needle and mark throat plate of sewing machine with a piece of tape to act as a guide. Test that your guide is absolutely accurate before beginning a project.

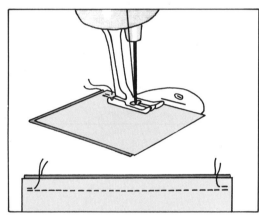

4 Backstitching is a quick and easy way to secure the beginning and end of machine sewing. Begin stitching a little way in from edge of fabric, reverse to edge, then continue stitching forward. At end, reverse several stitches back from edge. Clip threads.

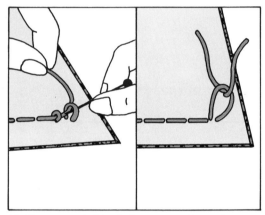

5 To secure stitching before you reach an edge, stop stitching at required point; cut threads, leaving long ends. Pull top thread to draw up loop of thread from other side; use a pin to help coax thread through. Tie ends into a knot.

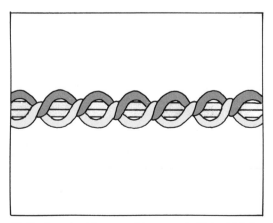

1 Tension must be correct to prevent stitched fabrics from puckering. Threads from needle and bobbin should cross each other exactly in middle of fabric. If fabric puckers, the problem is usually with thread coming from needle (upper tension).

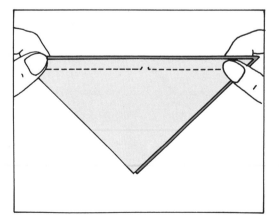

2 To test upper tension, cut 2 triangles with longest edges on bias. Thread machine with different colours in bobbin and needle; stitch bias edges. Grip ends of stitching; pull. If needle thread breaks, tension is too tight; if bobbin thread breaks, it is too loose.

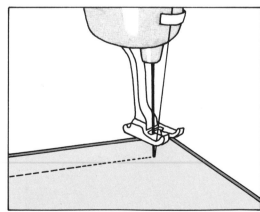

Turning corners Stitch to within 19mm/¾in of corner, change to finer stitch; continue to corner. Stop exactly at corner point with needle in fabric; lift presser foot and pivot fabric to new position. Sew small stitches for 19mm/¾in; resume regular stitches.

MACHINE STITCHES

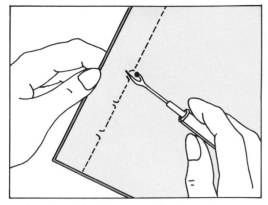

1 **Removing stitches** Use an unpicker/seam ripper to remove lines of machine stitching; never remove stitches by roughly pulling the edges of the fabric apart. Use sharp edge of implement to cut one stitch every 13mm/1/2in on one side of fabric.

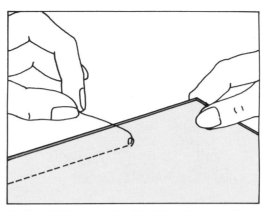

2 Turn fabric over and pull out thread on opposite side; the thread should lift easily away from the fabric. Clean up bits of thread from first side before you resume stitching.

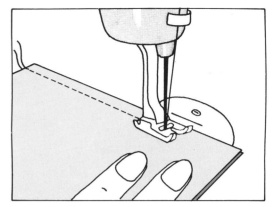

1 **Machine stitches** Straight stitch is the standard machine-sewing stitch. To begin, turn hand wheel to lower needle into fabric edge. Stitch forward slowly at an even speed, guiding fabric by hand. Reduce speed at end of seam. Do not go over edge.

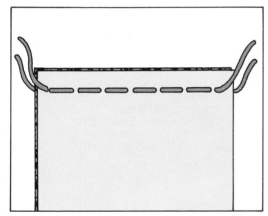

2 Basting stitches are long, temporary stitches that are easy to remove. Set machine at longest stitch and guide fabric slowly through machine, being careful to keep line of stitching straight. Do not backstitch or basting will be difficult to remove.

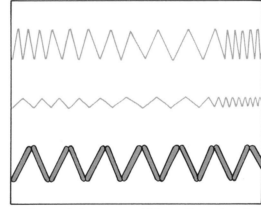

3 Zigzag stitches are not widely used in patchwork and quilting except decoratively to simulate embroidery or for special effects. Use a zigzag foot on your sewing machine. Experiment with different stitch widths and lengths on fabric scraps.

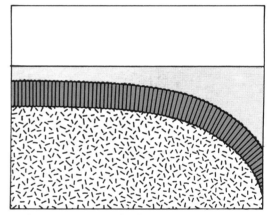

4 Satin stitch, a very closely-worked zigzag stitch, is used for machine appliqué work. Use an embroidery foot if you have one; this will enable you to see the fabric more easily. Experiment with satin stitch at various angles and curves on scrap fabric.

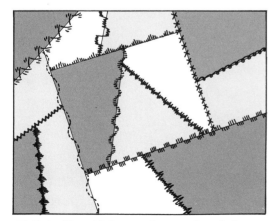

5 Embroidery stitches vary from one brand of machine to the next. Consult your manual to find the different embroidery stitches that your machine can sew. Use machine embroidery thread and stitch on RS of fabric. Test stitches on scrap fabric first.

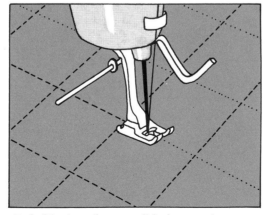

6 Quilting is easily accomplished on a sewing machine; use a medium-length stitch. For straight machine quilting, attach a quilting foot which moves over thick fabrics easily. Use a gauge to keep spacing even between rows of stitches.

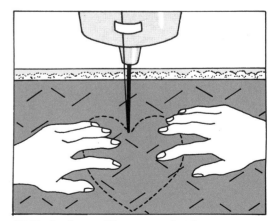

7 For freeform quilting, remove foot from your machine; lower foot lever as usual to engage top thread tension. Drop the feed dogs if possible. Keeping fabric stretched taut with your hands placed on each side of needle, stitch slowly, guiding the work evenly.

PRESSING

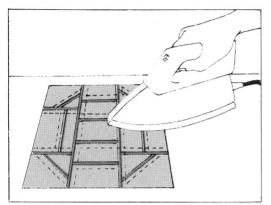

1 **Pressing** is the application of heat, pressure and moisture to fabric to remove wrinkles and set seams. To press, lift iron and set it down again in appropriate position rather than sliding it over fabric. Slight dampness is needed to flatten seams or edges.

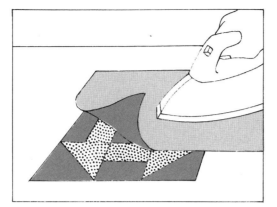

2 Use a press cloth on RS to prevent fabrics from glazing (acquiring a shine that cannot be removed). Press cloth should be of similar weight to fabrics being pressed. Press *with* grain of fabric whenever possible; do not stretch fabrics off grain.

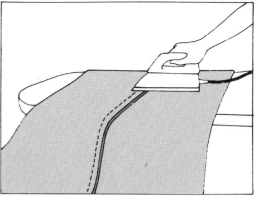

3 Ironing is different from pressing in that the iron is firmly propelled across the fabric to smooth wrinkles and remove puckers. Iron quilt backings and fabric for wholecloth quilts; iron RS of patchwork only after it has been pressed gently on the WS.

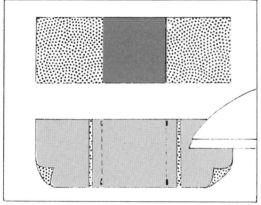

1 **Seams** Always press seam allowances to one side, not open as for dressmaking. Seams pressed to one side are stronger and will serve to hold the filling inside a quilt. If possible, press seams towards darker fabric and away from areas you wish to quilt.

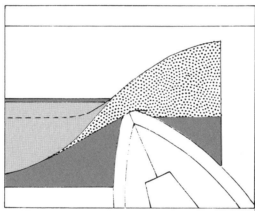

2 When pressing small patchwork pieces, it is sometimes easier to press from the RS. Place light fabric patch WS down on ironing board. Open pieces and press iron over light patch toward dark patch, smoothing dark patch to RS and setting it in place.

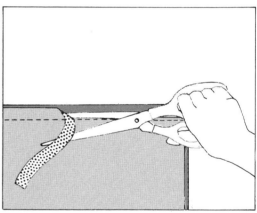

3 If you cannot avoid pressing a dark fabric toward a light one, trim seam allowance of dark fabric so it is slightly narrower than light one; otherwise a dark shadow will show on RS. When machine piecing, trim dark allowance before joining to another piece.

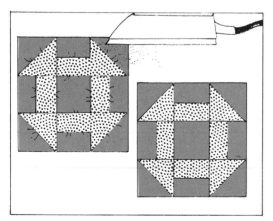

1 **Fabrics** Cotton is highly recommended for patchwork because slight wrinkles or puckers will disappear with the steam from a hot iron. Synthetic fabrics are not so forgiving and must be ironed with a cooler iron; thus, your stitching must be more exact.

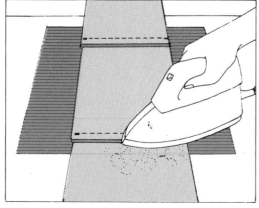

2 Steam any napped or pile fabrics to prevent them from flattening; to press a seam on WS, place self fabric or a thick towel underneath seam on RS. Press glazed chintz and polished cotton on RS without a press cloth and with little or no moisture.

Pressing embroidery Place embroidered fabrics face down on a thick towel and steam-press gently. Never press embroidered surfaces on the RS or stitches will flatten and lose texture.

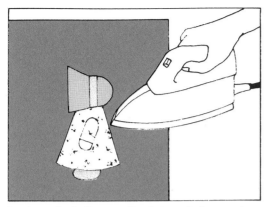

Pressing appliqués Press appliqué pieces before turning raw edges to the WS. After appliqués have been sewn to the background, press very gently. Over-pressing an appliqué may leave an impression of the seam allowances on the RS and cause glazing.

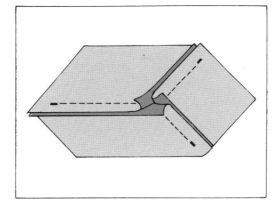

1 Pressing set-in seams To press a hand-sewn set-in seam or any seam where 3 corners meet at one point, swirl the seam allowances to reduce bulk in the middle. Steam-press gently on WS and then on RS, using a press cloth.

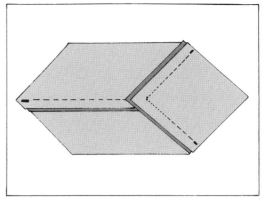

2 To press a machine-sewn set-in seam, press the 2 seam allowances of the set-in piece toward the other 2 pieces, folding the third seam allowance to one side as shown. Steam-press gently on WS and then on RS, using a press cloth.

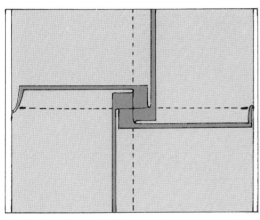

1 Pressing a 4-seam join For a hand-sewn 4-seam join, swirl all the seam allowances in the same direction to reduce the bulk where they meet in the middle. Steam-press gently on WS and then on RS, using a press cloth.

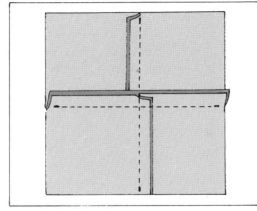

2 In machine sewing, every seam must be pressed before it is crossed by another. To reduce bulk where seams cross, press seam allowances in opposite directions. After seamed pieces have been joined, press new seam to one side, toward darker fabric.

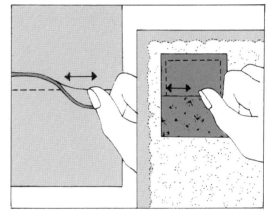

Finger pressing is a quick, temporary way to crease fabrics in a desired position; it is also used when fabrics are sewn to padding and cannot be pressed with an iron. Run a thumbnail several times over area you wish to press until it holds the fold.

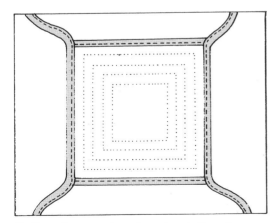

Blocking will correct skewed patchwork. To make a reusable blocking mat, cut a 40cm/16in square of sturdy fabric; draw concentric squares in useful sizes with waterproof pen. Bind edges; allow 30cm/12in ties to extend beyond square on 2 sides.

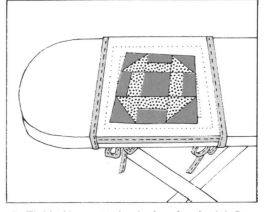

2 Tie blocking mat to ironing board so that it is firm and taut and marked squares are true. Pin skewed patchwork WS down onto mat in several places along each edge and at corners; align edges with one of the marked squares so all corners are at right angles.

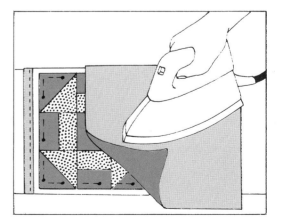

3 Cover block with a damp cloth and gently steam-press edges of block until straight. Try not to press down on pins, rather steam over them and press between them. Allow to dry thoroughly, then press centre of block, using steam as necessary.

I have found nothing so desirable for summer covers as the old fashioned scrap quilt, of which our mothers and grandmothers were so proud. They... are almost as easily washed as a sheet and can with very little trouble be kept sweet and wholesome, and last for years... Every young girl should piece one quilt at least to carry away with her to her husband's home, and if her lot happens to be cast among strangers, as is often the case, the quilt when she unfolds it will seem like the face of a familiar friend, and will bring up a whole host of memories, of mother, sister, friend, too sacred for us to intrude upon. *From* Beds, Bed Clothing and Bedmaking *written in 1888 by Annie Curd for Good Housekeeping.*

2

PERFECT PATCHWORK

PERFECT PATCHWORK

Though patchwork has generally been considered a utilitarian craft, one of the earliest examples appears to have combined function with decoration: wall paintings in Thebes created around the time of Ramses III suggest the use of ornamental patchwork in a chevron design on the sails of a boat.[2] However, patchwork originally developed to fill a specific need—to provide warmth in an economical way.

Up until the time that fabrics were commercially manufactured, all textiles were precious: fibres had to be harvested, spun into thread and woven into cloth by hand—therefore not even the smallest scrap was wasted. When clothing became unusable, untattered portions were saved and combined with other fabrics to create bedcoverings. Leftover scraps from making new clothes were utilized too. Later, as textiles and time became more plentiful, random arrangements of patches became more structured and simple geometric designs emerged. As these new arrangements were admired, they were also copied and changed, creating more designs. It's easy to imagine how quiltmakers became eager to devise their own patterns, showing off their creative and technical skills at the same time.

The most popular early style of organized patchwork was the medallion quilt where a central motif was surrounded by borders of fabric, pieced work, quilting or appliqué; *see page 159*. Mosaic patchwork, the piecing of one or more geometric shapes to create an all-over pattern, followed closely behind the medallion in popularity. Another favourite fashion was to make strip patchwork, where long strips of fabric were joined together. The strips themselves were sometimes pieced too; *see page 159*. Much later, after patchwork had been brought to America, block-style quilts evolved: single geometric images were assembled in block form and repeated across a quilt; this has since developed into the most popular quilt style. *See page 157* for the four basic styles of block quilts.

PATCHWORK IN ENGLAND

While the earliest patchwork quilts were probably made of wool because that was the most readily available fabric, the oldest surviving example of English patchwork was made with pieces of chintz imported from India. Dated 1708, it can be seen at Levens Hall, near Kendall in Cumbria. Because East Indian cottons were hard-wearing and generally colour-fast when washed, the late 18th-century patchwork that has endured is usually made of cotton. (*See page 112* for a discussion of the importation of chintz from India during the 18th century.) Although the Levens Hall quilt is the oldest, it is far too sophisticated and well designed to have been the first; whoever made this quilt had either made many similar ones or had been taught by someone else who had. It is frustrating

to think of the rich tradition of quiltmaking that must have preceded the making of this quilt, but of which we have not the slightest shred of evidence. It is because quilts were considered such an essential part of life during those early years that they were not elevated to a level that would have encouraged people to save and cherish them.[3]

The making of patchwork was widespread in England during the 19th century. Children, men, even friends and relatives were regaled to contribute their share toward whatever work was in progress.[4] National events were recorded in elaborate patchwork quilts, and many of these are well-preserved today. However, quilts were mostly constructed for family use and were never meant to be seen outside the home except perhaps on washing days.

Piecing patchwork over paper templates is traditionally English. This method developed when people had more time to piece intricate designs that are difficult to join with straight seams, such as hexagons and diamonds. Papers that have not been removed from antique quilts are usually a reliable way of dating a quilt that consists of fabrics spanning a wide time scale; *see Mosaic Quilt on page 9*

AMERICAN PATCHWORK

In America, patchwork became a veritable institution. Patchwork quilts were undoubtedly brought with the colonists from England; indeed the earliest patchwork quilt in America is believed to be of English origin. The quilt is a medallion-style Mariner's Compass surrounded by an expanse of triangles known as the Broken Dishes pattern; it is dated 1726 and can be found in Montreal's McCord Museum. There are very few quilts dated before *c.* 1800 that have survived, but this doesn't mean that they weren't made. Most probably, these quilts were used until they were in tatters, and then found another life as a filler in a new quilt.

Throughout the 19th century quilts were made by the hundreds, quite often to commemorate special events in quilters' lives. Births, marriages, friendship, coming-of-age and political events such as America's Centennial were all reasons for celebration, and what better way to celebrate than to make a quilt? The block style of patchwork became the symbol of American quiltmaking, and block names mirrored the attitudes, pastimes and places where the patterns were pieced. Often the same design would have several different names, depending upon where and when it was made.

It was in the early 20th century that the traditional American patchwork quilt developed into a national obsession. Fads in designs came and went, but that didn't detract from the fact that everyone was making quilts. Quilts were on view at fairs and prizes were given to those deemed meritorious. Magazines such as *The*

Ladies' Home Journal, House Beautiful, Good Housekeeping, and *The National Stockman and Farmer* as well as many national newspapers featured articles on patchwork and provided patterns to copy. During the 1940's–60's, quiltmaking declined and manufactured bedcovers were considered much more acceptable to modern life than antiquated patchwork quilts. Quilts were still quietly being made, but their time had definitely passed. Not for long.

The revival of patchwork quilting during the 1970's and 80's has reached incredible proportions. Hundreds of quilt shows, seminars, articles and books are being produced and evaluated by men and women eager to add to their knowledge and acquire new ideas. No longer is patchwork associated with little old ladies and maiden aunts, but with people of all ages and economic levels.

MAKING A PATCHWORK PROJECT

The methods outlined in this chapter are considered to be the best ways of accomplishing the various patchwork techniques. They are not the only ways to do patchwork, and you may be quite successful in working another way. Don't feel that you have to change your old methods; it can take a great deal of time to relearn a technique that you have been performing a certain way for many years. However, keep an open mind to see if you can improve your patchwork by trying something different.

How do you begin to make a patchwork project? The first step is to select a design that you like. There are over 50 different patchwork designs in this chapter from which to choose, and there are many books that provide other wonderful patchwork patterns (*see Patterns in the Bibliography*). Or you can devise your own original design. You must then decide on the size of the project that you are planning to make. Small projects like baby quilts or wall hangings are excellent for beginners because they will give you the satisfaction of completing something quickly.

When selecting a patchwork design, the number of pieces will determine how long it takes you to finish your project. If a design has four pieces, it will take half the amount of time needed to piece an eight-patch block, which will take half again as much time as a sixteen-patch block. Beginners should avoid designs with too many pieces, but if you find a patchwork block that you love which is made of many pieces, look at your finished design in a different way. Instead of making eight small blocks, double the size of the block and make four large ones; *see page 155* for an appliqué quilt that was made this way. The piecing will then take half the time. For a really quick and very dramatic result, enlarge a favourite block of the full size of the quilt; see the single block quilt on *page 155*.

PATCHWORK DESIGNS: FOUR AND FIVE PATCH

Four Patch: Windmill

Crosses and Losses

Big Dipper

Four Patch: Old Tippecanoe

Hovering Hawks

Eight Hands Around

Five Patch: Handy Andy

Jack in the Box

Cross and Crown

SEVEN AND NINE PATCH

Seven Patch: Bear's Tracks

Prickly Pear

Autumn Leaf

Nine Patch: Shoo-fly

Jacob's Ladder

Churn Dash

Nine Patch: Beggar's Block

Weathervane

Steps to the Altar

STARS

Evening Star

Northumberland Star

The Feather-Edged Star

Variable Star

Guiding Star

54-40 or Fight

Virginia Star

LeMoyne Star

Milky Way

REPRESENTATIONAL DESIGNS

Little School House

Bowtie

Ship

Flower Pot

Wild Goose Chase

Pieced Basket

Little Beech Tree

Maple Leaf

Palm Leaf, Hosannah

CURVILINEAR DESIGNS

World Without End

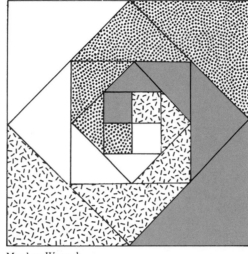

Monkey Wrench

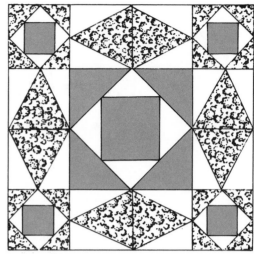

Storm at Sea

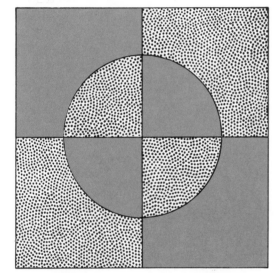

Rob Peter to Pay Paul

Drunkard's Path

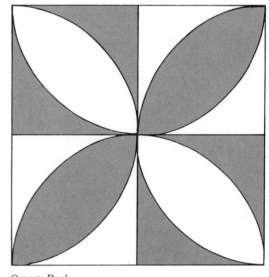

Orange Peel

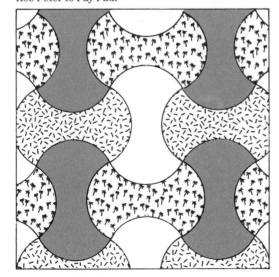

Double Axehead

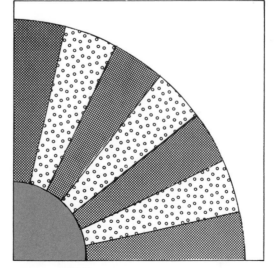

Grandmother's Fan

Mariner's Compass

HAND PIECING

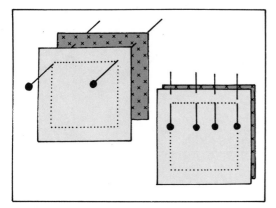

1 **Technique** *See pages 34-35, 38-39* Sewing lines are marked on WS; stitches are worked from corner to corner on marked lines. Hold pieces RS together, matching edges. Insert pins in corners; repeat along seam, matching marked lines. Secure pins.

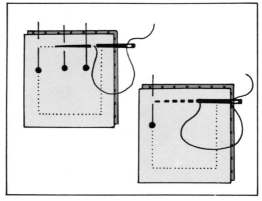

2 Thread a "sharp" needle, knot end and insert through fabric 3mm/⅛in from corner on marked line; make a backstitch into corner as shown or work 3 backstitches. Sew running stitches across seam on marked line, working 8-10 stitches per 2.5cm/1in.

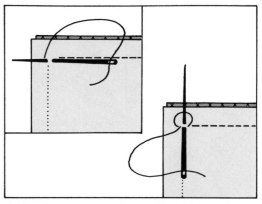

3 Continue to sew evenly spaced running stitches across seam, checking the back occasionally to make sure that stitches are exactly on marked line. At opposite corner, make a knot (*see Technique, step 3 on page 38*) or work 3 backstitches to secure.

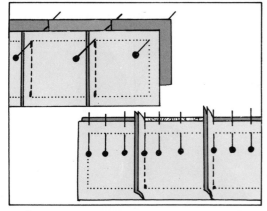

1 **Joining rows** Hold sewn pieces together with RS facing, matching seams. Insert a pin exactly through seams and corners on each piece. Also insert pins through marked seam lines, matching carefully. Secure pins.

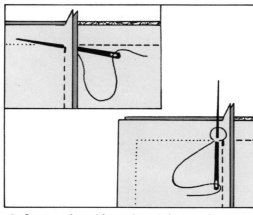

2 Sew together with running stitch. At each seam, knot or backstitch thread as in step 3 above, then insert needle through seam allowance to other side. Knot or backstitch again, and continue sewing. Seams should not be sewn to patchwork but left free.

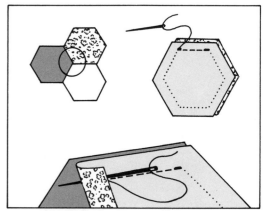

1 **Joining multiple seams** To join 3 patches, first sew 2 pieces together with running stitch as described above, making a knot or 3 backstitches at each corner. Open pieces, but do not press. Insert needle through corner of sewn seam to RS of fabric.

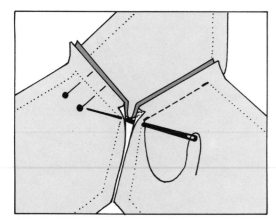

2 Insert point of needle through marked corner of third piece from RS. Pull needle and thread through to WS, securing the 3 pieces together at corner. Align edge of new piece with one of the first pieces; pin together.

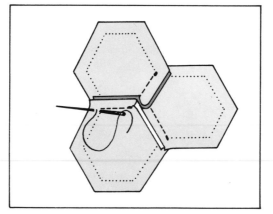

3 Work a knot or 3 backstitches at beginning of seam. Sew running stitches along new seam to opposite corner; secure thread. Return to centre. Pin remaining 2 edges together; knot or backstitch at centre. Sew to end of seam; secure thread.

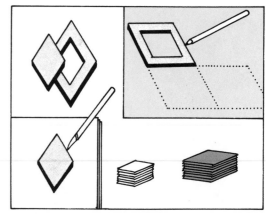

1 **Piecing over papers** Select pattern. Make 2 templates: one for hand piecing (A) and one window template (B); *see pages 34-35*. Use (A) to cut shape from papers; cut 2 or 3 at a time using a utility knife. Use (B) to mark and cut pieces from fabric using scissors.

MACHINE PIECING

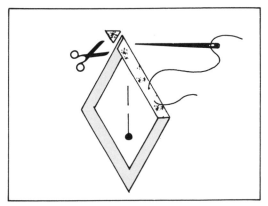

2 Centre a paper on WS of fabric shape; pin. Fold one seam allowance over paper without creasing paper. Beginning in middle of seam allowance, make a basting stitch through fabric and paper; leave 6mm/¼in thread end free. Trim tails (corners).

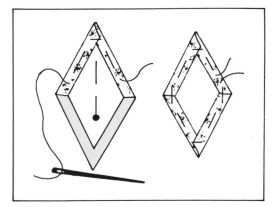

3 Fold adjacent seam allowance over paper forming sharp corner. Baste over corner to secure, bringing needle up in middle of next seam allowance. Repeat for remaining edges. Cut thread, leaving end free; remove pin. Press gently. Repeat for all patches.

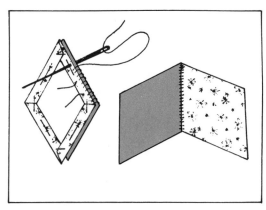

4 To join 2 patches, place RS facing, matching corners. With matching thread, whipstitch edges together from corner to corner, backstitching at each end. Make 16-18 stitches per 2.5cm/1in; do not catch papers in sewing. Stitches will barely show on RS.

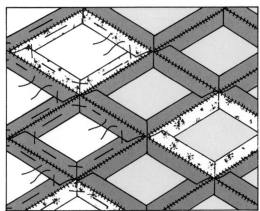

5 When all pieces are joined, turn patchwork to WS. Remove basting from each piece by pulling loose thread end, then lift each paper out individually; do not "shake" papers out as some might remain. Papers can be reused. Gently press finished patchwork.

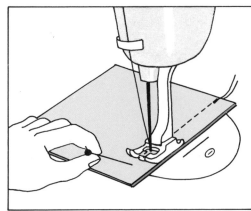

1 **Machine piecing** *See pages 34-35, 40-41* Sewing lines are not marked on fabric. Sew 6mm/¼in seams using presser foot or tape as a guide. Pin pieces RS together, matching edges. Feed fabric through machine; remove pins as you sew.

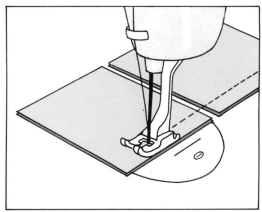

2 Sew pieces together in a chain to save time and thread. Provided that pieces are handled carefully, it is not necessary to backstitch at each edge. When chain sewing, always place the same piece on top and sew from the same edge to prevent mistakes.

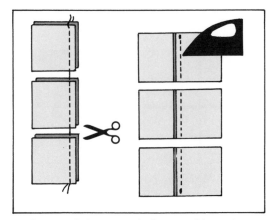

3 Remove chain-sewn units from machine and cut apart. Press seams of each patchwork unit to one side before joining to another unit; have an iron set up nearby to save time. Continue joining pieces by chain sewing until patchwork is complete.

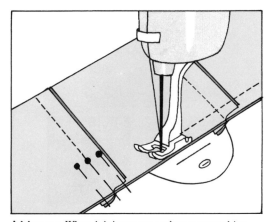

Joining rows When joining rows, make sure matching seam allowances are pressed in opposite directions to reduce bulk and make matching easier. Pin pieces together directly through stitching, and to the right and left of the seam; remove pins as you sew.

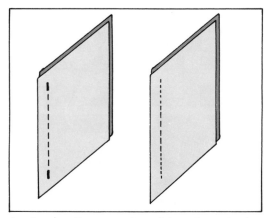

Securing edges To secure edges of pieces for setting-in (*see page 58*), either backstitch by reversing machine stitching, or sew tiny stitches at beginning and end of row. It is best to sew these pieces individually rather than by chain sewing.

DRAFTING PATCHWORK PATTERNS

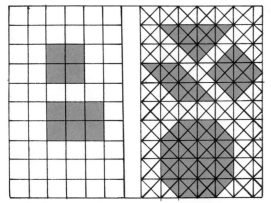

1 Graph paper Patchwork patterns can be drawn on 3 types of graph paper. Squared paper will accommodate squares and rectangles. Mark diagonal lines on squared paper to draw isosceles triangles, rhomboids, "hung" squares, and octagons.

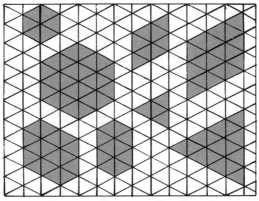

2 Draw hexagons, diamonds and equilateral triangles on isometric graph paper, which is available in most art supply shops.

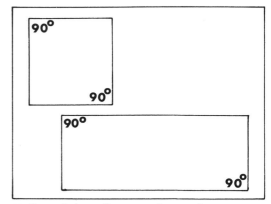

1 Geometric shapes Squares and rectangles are indispensable shapes in patchwork. It is important to draft the patterns with accurate 90° angles and measure edges carefully. Otherwise, errors will be very obvious when pieces are sewn together.

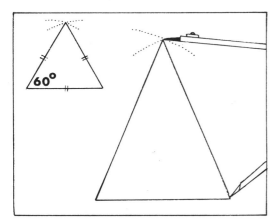

2 To draft equilateral and isosceles triangles first draw base to desired length. Using compass, delineate a point from each end of base to same measure for equilateral triangles, or to longer or shorter measure for isosceles triangles; join points.

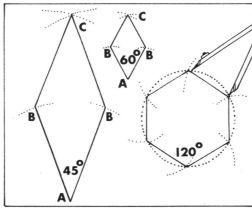

3 For long diamond, draw 2 sides to desired length at 45° angle (60° for short diamond) – AB. Set compass at AB; mark point C from each B; join points. For hexagon, draw circle. Use compass at same setting to mark 6 points on circumference; join points.

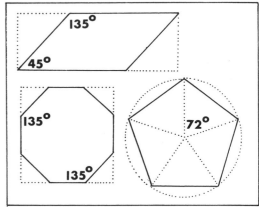

4 For a rhomboid, draw a rectangle: remove a triangle from 2 corners. For an octagon, draw a square: remove each corner. For a pentagon, draw a circle: draw line from centre to edge; draw 72° angle to circumference. Repeat 4 times; join points.

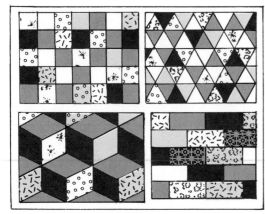

1 Types of patchwork One-patch designs are made from a single shape repeated in an all-over pattern. The earliest patchwork patterns were one-patch. They appear simple, but care is required in selecting fabrics and colours to best accentuate pieces.

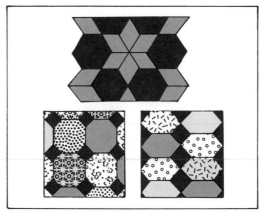

2 Two-patch designs utilize 2 shapes that combine to create a repeated pattern. Hexagons and diamonds, octagons and squares, and hexagons and squares are good combinations. Designs are intricate and must be pieced by hand, usually over papers.

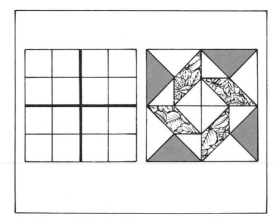

3 Many traditional quilts are constructed from square blocks of patchwork. Pieces comprising four-patch blocks can always be divided in multiples of 4, no matter how many pieces are used to create the design; this one is called Windblown Square.

JOINING PATCHWORK PIECES

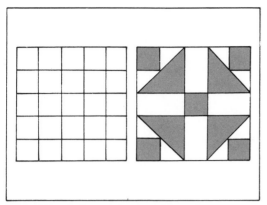

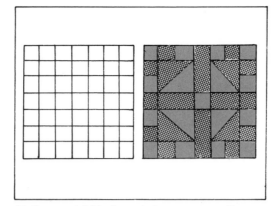

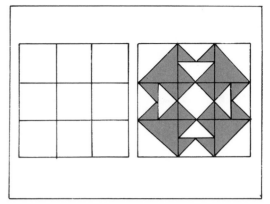

4 Five-patch blocks are actually composed of 25 individual squares. Each square may not always be evident, as in this example called Grandmother's Choice; but if you draw lines across the block, you will find that it can be neatly divided into 25 squares.

5 Seven-patch blocks are not very common; they are actually composed of 49 individual squares. Seven-patch designs often have a central cross dividing the block into 4 squares, as in this example called Lincoln's Platform.

6 Nine-patch blocks are very common; together with four-patch blocks, they form the basis of most traditional patchwork patterns. The 9 squares comprising this type of block may not always be immediately apparent, as in this design called T-Block.

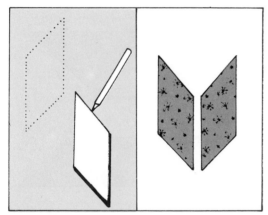

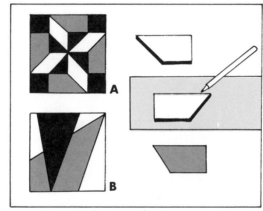

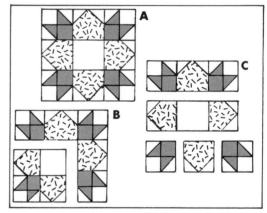

Mirror images Some patchwork designs utilize pieces that must be cut in the mirror image or reverse of one another. When marking such pieces on WS of fabric, mark around template, then turn template over to its reverse side to mark the second shape.

One-way shapes Some shapes are only correct when used in one direction, such as the piece for Clay's Choice (A), or for asymmetrical designs (B). Mark one-way shapes in reverse on WS of fabric; when pieces are cut, they will then be turned the right way.

1 Joining pieces Illustrations 1-9 show method of joining and machine-piecing a block called Weathervane (A). It is simpler to piece straight seams; avoid setting pieces in at a 90° angle (B), when they could be joined more easily with straight seaming (C).

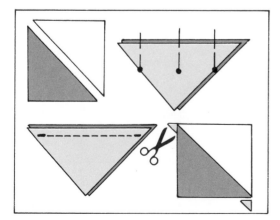

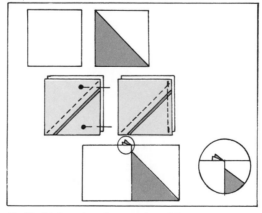

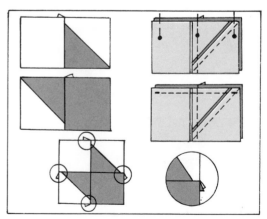

2 Analyse patchwork blocks to determine the order in which pieces are sewn together. Work from small units to large ones. In this block, join all small triangles first to form squares; pin, then sew together. Press seams to one side; clip off tails (corners).

3 Next join a pieced square to a plain square. Because of the seam allowance, stitching crosses triangle 6mm/¼in away from edge of block. When pieces are pressed open, point of triangle appears to float; this will result in a perfect point.

4 Join 2 pieced rectangles to form a corner square. Pin pieces together, matching seams carefully. Stitch, then press open. Now all triangle points seem to float; points should be exactly 6mm/¼in away from edge of fabric. Repeat for all corner squares.

JOINING PATCHWORK PIECES

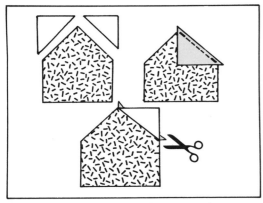

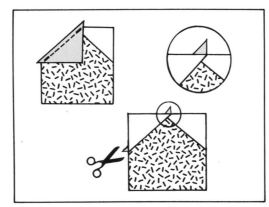

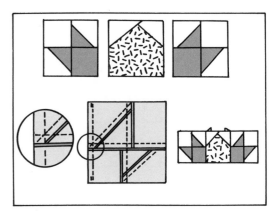

5 Next sew 2 triangles to each pentagon shape to complete the remaining pieced squares. Stitch diagonal edge of first triangle to top of pentagon; press to the right side and clip off the tails which form. Side edges should align exactly.

6 Sew second triangle to opposite side of pentagon in same manner; press open and clip off tails. Pieces should align exactly at top and sides as shown; if not, remove stitches and repeat until correct. Note: point of pentagon floats 6mm/¼in away from edge.

7 Next join squares comprising top and bottom rows of block. Pin pieces together, matching point of triangle to side seam of pentagon; stitch. Note: stitching crosses exactly over point of triangle; a perfect point results when pieces are pressed open.

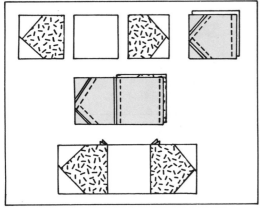

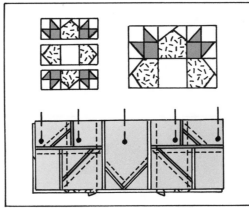

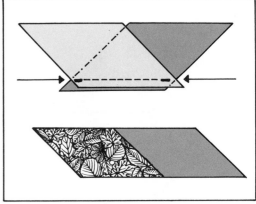

8 For middle row, sew a pieced pentagon to each side of the centre square. Press seams in direction opposite seams of top and bottom rows – in this case, toward sides. In this way, bulk will be reduced when rows are sewn together; seams will be easier to match.

9 To complete block, join rows, matching seam allowances and seams of triangles and pentagons. Pin, then stitch together carefully, making a 6mm/¼in seam. Open to make sure that all seams match perfectly, then steam-press gently.

1 **Offset seams** Patches with oblique angles, such as triangles, rhomboids and diamonds, must be sewn together with corners offset so edges align perfectly. Angle indicated by arrows should be exactly 6mm/¼in above edges to be joined.

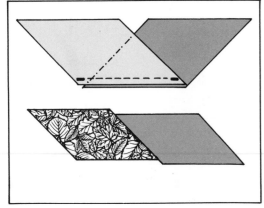

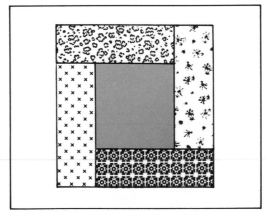

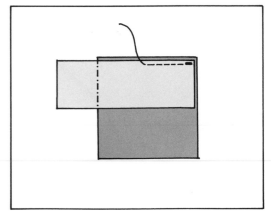

2 If patches are joined with corners matching, edges will not be in alignment when pieces are pressed open. If misalignment occurs, remove stitching and start again, this time offsetting corners as shown in step 1.

1 **Right-angle seams** Because straight seam sewing is always easier than turning corners, some quilters avoid piecing blocks which appear to have right-angled seams. Whenever you encounter such a design, follow steps 2-5 for easy straight seams.

2 Place first piece over centre with RS facing, matching one edge and allowing opposite edge to hang over. Stitch pieces together from middle of seam toward the matching edges. Press pieces open.

EIGHT-SEAM JOIN

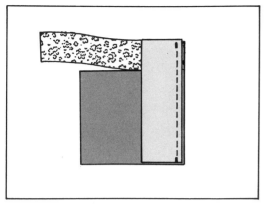

3 Place second piece over the centre and first piece along the straight edge just formed. Stitch together and press open. Repeat in same manner for third piece.

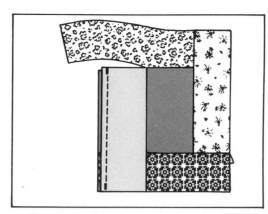

4 Place fourth piece along remaining edge. Stitch together and press open. "Hanging" edge of first piece is now even with the rest of the block.

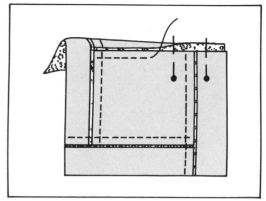

5 Pin block to hanging edge of first piece, then sew remainder of seam. Press open for a perfect corner, easily sewn in a straight line.

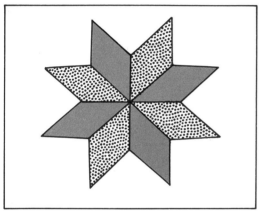

1 **Eight-seam join** Some of the most attractive patchwork patterns contain pieces that meet in a multiple join, such as the eight-seam join in the middle of LeMoyne Star. It is not too difficult to match up the pieces if you work slowly, carefully and accurately.

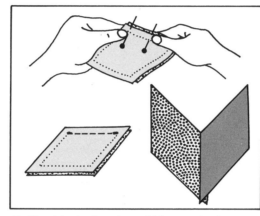

2 First join the 4 sections which comprise the eight-seam join. Hold 2 pieces RS facing, with edges matching; stitch together from corner to corner. Make 4 sections in this manner.

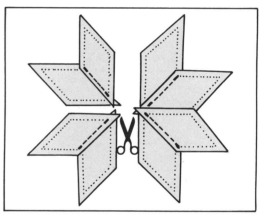

3 Next sew 2 pairs of sections together to form each half of the design. Clip off the tails that form in the centre.

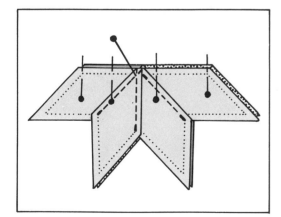

4 To join halves, insert a pin exactly through centre seam on WS of one piece, 6mm/¼in away from edge to be joined; same pin should be inserted through RS of other piece at same point. Pin remainder of seam as shown, keeping centres aligned. Stitch seam.

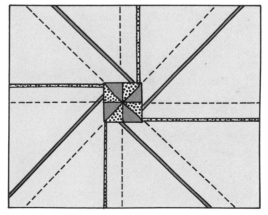

5a If you are sewing by hand, fold all the seam allowances in the same direction, then swirl the seam allowances in the middle to reduce bulk before pressing. Steam-press gently. The back of the pieced design should look like this.

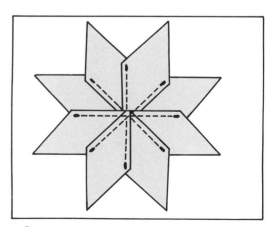

5b If you are sewing by machine, press the seam allowances flat as shown in step 3, then stitch the final seam and press in one direction. Back of pieced design should look like this. Stitching passes directly over point of diamond, and all seams match.

SETTING-IN

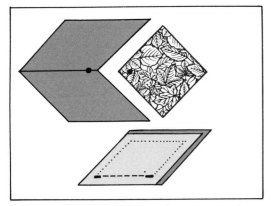

1 **Setting-in** is required when you have to sew a piece into an angle. The pieces are united exactly at the areas indicated by the dots. When sewing the pieces which form the angle, end stitching 6mm/¼in from edge; backstitch or knot end.

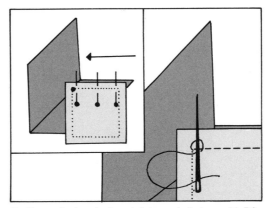

2 To sew by hand, pin patch to angled piece with RS facing, matching corners (dots) exactly. Stitch seam following arrow, removing pins as you sew. Knot or backstitch thread at corner to secure.

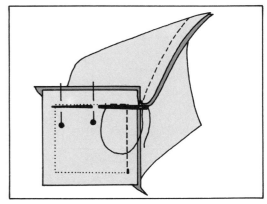

3 Swing adjacent edge of patch to align it with other edge of angled piece. Insert pin in corner, matching dots, then pin remainder of seam. Stitch seam, removing pins as you sew; knot or backstitch at end. *See page 43* for pressing instructions.

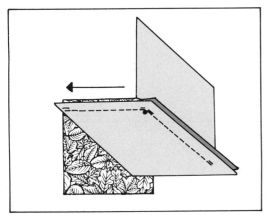

4 For machine sewing, pin one angled piece to one edge of patch with RS facing, matching corners. Stitch from corner to end of seam following arrow. Break thread.

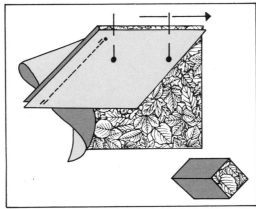

5 Swing adjacent angled piece to other edge of patch and pin. Stitch from corner to side edge. There should be no puckers or wrinkles on RS of work if seam has been sewn correctly. Clip off any tails. *See page 43* for pressing instructions.

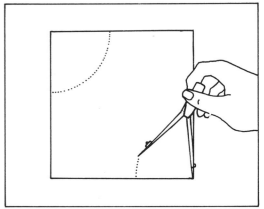

1 **Drafting a curved-seam pattern** Cut paper pattern of desired size. Use a compass to draw curves on the pattern. Curves may also be drawn freehand for a random effect, but this is recommended only for more experienced sewers.

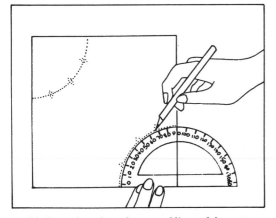

2 Mark notches along the curved lines of the pattern at regularly spaced intervals. Use a protractor to position notches evenly apart. Notches are used as guides for pinning and sewing curved edges together.

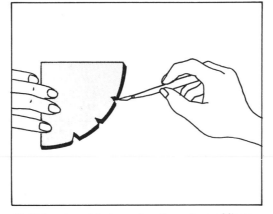

3 Make a template for each pattern piece, adding a 6mm/¼in seam allowance if making machine or window templates; *see pages 34-35*. Using the tip of a utility knife, cut out the notches along the curved edges.

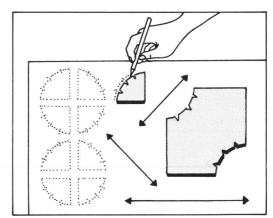

1 **Cutting and piecing** Curved edges should be placed on or near the bias with straight edges on the straight grain of fabric. If possible, position templates to provide a mutual drawing and cutting edge. Mark notches carefully.

CURVED SEAMS

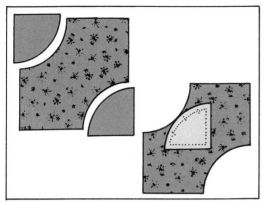

2 When cut pieces are arranged on a flat surface, edges appear to match one another perfectly. But when pieces are placed with RS facing for sewing, curves bend in opposite directions. Easing and pinning are required for a perfect fit.

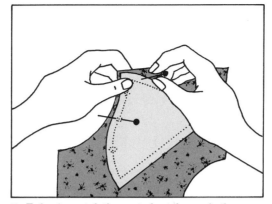

3 To begin, match the central notches on both pieces and pin together. Next, turn the pieces to align the straight outer edges and pin. Then, match the other notches and pin, smoothing and easing pieces to fit.

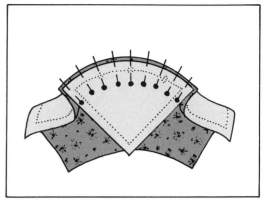

4a Use as many pins as necessary. Because curved edges are cut on the bias, pieces will fit together smoothly. Illustration shows convex edge fitted into a concave one.

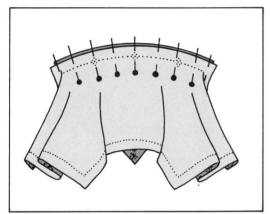

4b Some quilters prefer easing the concave edge into the convex one. Try both ways to determine which method is preferable for you.

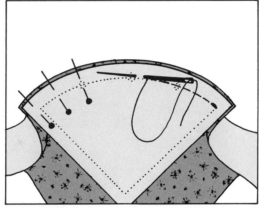

Sewing curves by hand *See pages 38-39, 52.* Knot or work 3 backstitches at corner. Work running stitches exactly on marked line to opposite corner, removing pins as you go; secure thread end. Check back of work to ensure stitches are exactly on marked line.

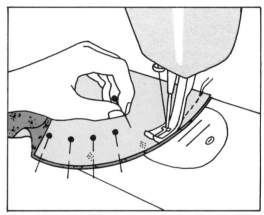

Sewing curves by machine *See pages 40-41, 53.* Sew 6mm/¼in seam. Stitch the seam slowly, making 12-14 stitches per 2.5cm/1in; remove each pin just before sewing over it. Backstitch at beginning and end of seam.

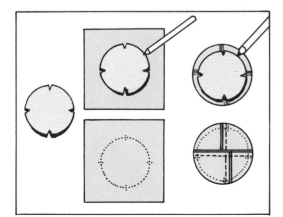

1 **Setting in a circle** Make a circle template of desired size with notches dividing circle into 4 equal quarters; *see pages 34-35.* Use template to mark stitching line in centre of fabric frame and on circle to be inset; be sure to mark all notches.

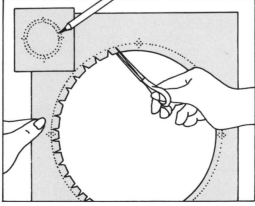

2 Mark cutting line on frame 6mm/¼in within marked stitching line; cut out opening along inner marked line. Clip curved edge just to stitching line.

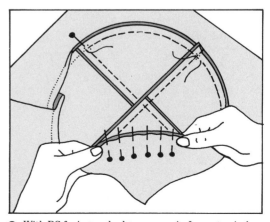

3 With RS facing and edges even, pin frame to circle at each notch. Working on one quarter at a time, pin frame to circle, easing frame smoothly to fit. Stitch pieces together 6mm/¼in from edges. Repeat for each quarter until finished. Press inset circle toward frame.

AMISH PATCHWORK

The word "Amish" conjures up many images: somber and austere clothing, horses and buggies, rich farmland and a distinctive style of patchwork quilt. The Amish are a misunderstood culture, often ridiculed by those who lack the patience to try to understand their philosophy. Simple plain living within a loving and supportive community, guided by the precepts of the Bible, are the foundations of their world. The Amish live in a cultural haven of their own making, a bastion against what they see as the modern dissolute society around them. They claim that they live "in" the world, but are not "of" the world, and dismiss any non-Amish people as the "English".

The Amish religion has its roots in the Anabaptist movement which followed the Reformation. For the same reason that many early settlers moved to America – to avoid religious persecution – the Amish left their German homeland and settled in Lancaster County, Pennsylvania, in 1727. The Amish settlers adopted simple dress, virtually unchanged today, in an effort to set themselves apart from the rest of the world and be recognized by their co-religionists. Although they have adapted somewhat to modern times, the strict Amish still live without electricity, automobiles, buttons, indoor plumbing and other conveniences that would negate their concept of "plainness". Even today, some heavily populated areas of Pennsylvania, Ohio, and Indiana are eerily dark and silent when night falls because there are no electric lights, machines or cars.

The Amish are a hardworking people who delight in honest toil. Because they do not use electricity, their work is limited to the time between the rising and setting sun. The seasons also regulate their routine. During the summer and autumn, when there is so much to be done on the farm and in the garden, there is little time for needlework. The winter, however, is the time for piecing quilts. Every woman in the family participates, from the small girls who thread needles to the old grandmothers who can no longer carry on hard labour, but who can still cut and piece beautifully. Sharing the work in this way, each family has pieced tops ready for quilting in spring and early summer at quilting bees, or frolics – social events that are eagerly anticipated. The Amish lead a thoroughly communal life, and get together whenever there is a barn to be raised, a family problem to solve, an event to celebrate – or a quilt to be finished. Several quilts can be completed in one day. Such frolics are always accompanied by wonderful meals, laughter and deep feelings of fellowship.

THE QUILTS

It is easy to recognize antique Amish quilts because they are as simple and compelling as the people who made them. Stark geometric shapes, glowing woollen fabrics and glorious quilting are probably the three most easily identified elements of an Amish quilt. Powerful solid colours in unlikely combinations are found in many examples, attesting to the ingenuity and creativity of women who love colourful gardens yet dress themselves in subdued fabrics. Squares, rectangles and triangles are the basic shapes used in Amish quilts, and the large spaces lend themselves beautifully to flowing lines of quilting, always worked by hand.

Since 1860, Amish quilts have been pieced on a sewing machine – treadle, not electric! Because the components have straight edges, the actual piecing is easy; this is why no instructions for making the quilts are given here. If you wish to make one of the Amish quilts illustrated on these pages, follow the basic instructions for drafting patterns and piecing patchwork on *pages 52-58* ; the patterns for the simple geometric shapes can be drafted on graph paper to whatever size you choose.

The designs shown here represent traditional Amish quilts from two regions of the United States: Lancaster County, Pennsylvania where the oldest styles can be found; and the Midwest, specifically Ohio and Indiana – home of the more progressive Amish.

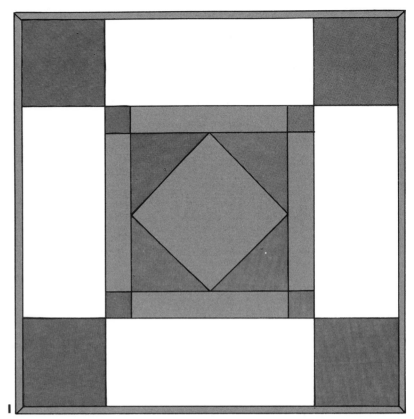

1

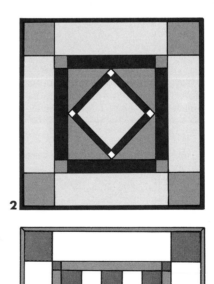

2

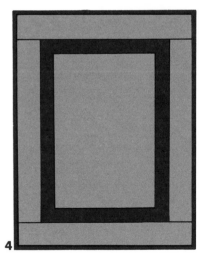

4

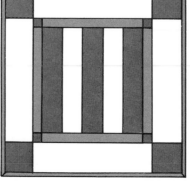

3

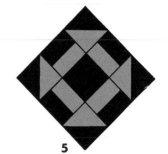

5

6

7

1 **Centre Diamond:** This is the oldest and plainest of the Lancaster County quilt designs. An elaborate medallion, such as a feather wreath encircling a star or basket, was usually quilted in the middle.

2 **Diamond in a Square:** An adaptation of the Centre Diamond, this style was often worked in a selection of visually startling colours. The binding was usually a contrasting fabric.

3 **Bars:** Another traditional Lancaster County design, a Bars quilt was an excellent way to utilize long scraps of fabric. Variations on this theme can also be found: often the bars were split with a contrasting fabric; at other times they were pieced with patterns such as Wild Goose Chase and Nine-Patch.

4 **Plain:** Found only in Ohio, Plain quilts are deceiving upon first appraisal because of their unpretentious appearance. However, study them a little more closely and the elaborate quilting will take your breath away. The colour combinations are also quite dramatic. These quilts are generally rectangular.

5 **Hole in the Barn Door:** This single block is typical of those used by the Midwestern Amish of Ohio and Indiana. In a quilt, blocks would be "hung"" (turned sideways) and interspersed with plain squares.

6 **Lone Star:** By far the most impressive Lancaster County design, this underscores the importance of the sun and stars to a people who live without electric light. Lone Star quilts are often found in excellent condition because they were "best" quilts, used only for company or special occasions. Backgrounds were usually dark blue or black so as to set off the star and make it appear to glow.

7 **Sunshine and Shadow:** While the other Lancaster County designs required new pieces of fabric specifically for the quilt, this pattern made use of even the smallest scraps, which is why it was so commonly made by these thrifty people. The quilts were well planned to make the most of bright colours.

The Lancaster County Amish live in the most disciplined way, and this is reflected in their quilting. Because the Amish settled in this area first, the designs born here represent the essence of the classic Amish quilt style. In many cases, the patterns are composed of large unbroken expanses of fabric, thus requiring the purchase of material specifically for making a quilt, rather than the reuse of old fabrics.

The Midwestern Amish lead somewhat less restricted lives, and their quilts mirror their more enterprising attitudes – they have adopted patchwork patterns commonly used by the "English" and they are more willing to use patterned fabrics rather than solids. Baby Blocks, Bear's Paw, Ocean Wave and Hole in the Barn Door are some of the favoured block designs. Black is commonly used for the backgrounds, and black thread is often used in the quilting.

Sadly, the patterns illustrated have largely been abandoned by contemporary Amish quilters; instead they are now making American-style patchwork quilts (which require less hand quilting) for commercial purposes. Nevertheless, these are the designs most likely to be seen in any museum exhibition of antique Amish quilts, and are well worth copying by quilters wishing to create simple yet bold quilts.

QUILTING PATTERNS

The most impressive feature of an Amish quilt is undoubtedly the quilting itself. A density of 18 and 20 stitches per inch is not uncommon on some of the early quilts; this was made possible by the use of thin wool fillings. More recent quilts which use polyester padding are thicker and the quilting stitches are larger. But no matter what the size of the stitches, the patterns are wonderful and imaginative: feathers, ferns, flowers, baskets and stars are just some of the images rendered in the intricate quilting. Wide borders lend themselves perfectly to the quilting stitches, and twists and cable patterns are common. A few typical Amish quilting designs are given on *page 137*

CATHEDRAL WINDOW

To those who have never tried it, the Cathedral Window pattern looks like an intricate, unsolvable puzzle. But however complicated the finished result may appear, it is amazingly simple to construct. The name Cathedral Window derives from the stained glass appearance of the finished pattern. *See photograph on page 10.*

You can do the entire design by hand, making it easy to carry around and work on at odd times. Those interested in a quicker outcome can perform much of the work on a sewing machine, although the last step must be worked by hand. Technically, Cathedral Window projects are not "quilts" as there is no backing or padding, nor is any actual quilting involved. However, the result can be very warm because it is composed of many layers of fabric.

THE ESSENCE OF THE DESIGN

Cathedral Window is composed of folded and refolded squares of plain fabric. The folded squares are sewn together to form the "frame" of the window. A square of contrasting fabric (the "window" itself) is then placed over the stitched seam. It is therefore necessary to assemble two blocks in order to make one Cathedral Window. The fold of the frame is rolled over the window and slip-stitched invisibly in place, hiding all raw edges. The resulting pattern appears to be circular, although no curved seams are ever cut.

Because there is no set pattern to follow – only squares to be cut – the quilter must determine how many blocks will be needed to complete a project. The chart gives several finished block sizes and the number of blocks you can cut from a metre/yard of fabric.

Finished block size	Square for frame	Square for window	Frame squares per metre/yard
14cm/5½in	30.5cm/12in	8cm/3¼in	12
12cm/4¾in	25.4cm/10in	7cm/2¾in	12
10cm/4in	23cm/9in	6.4cm/2½in	20
9.5cm/3¾in	20.3cm/8in	5.7cm/2¼in	20
7cm/2¾in	15cm/6in	3.8cm/1½in	42

VARIATIONS

Add a contrasting fabric to the frame before making the final fold; see last illustration on facing page. The frame need not be made from only one solid fabric – use a variety of solids to make secondary designs such as borders, squares or circles. Or use a print for the frames and a solid fabric for the windows. Cut out motifs from printed fabrics, such as birds, flowers, animals or figures, and centre each one in a window. This is particularly appreciated when the project is for a child.

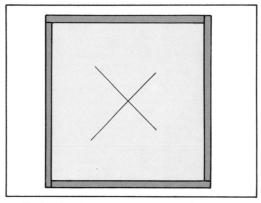

1 **Hand sewing** Cut true squares on straight grain from solid fabric; finished block is about one half size of original square. Press raw edges 6mm/¼in to WS. Bring opposite corners together; press fold lightly each way to indicate midpoint.

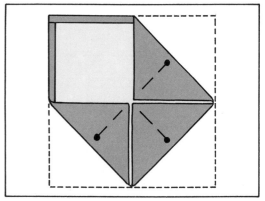

2 Fold each of the corners to midpoint; press and pin in place. Corners should align exactly in the middle.

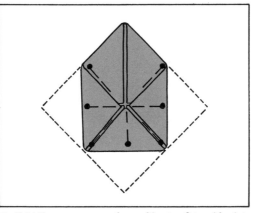

3 Fold the new corners formed in step 2 to midpoint; press and pin in place. The pins from step 2 should lie in the spaces between the new folds.

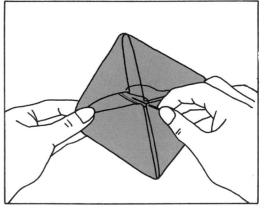

4 Using a double strand of thread in needle, sew corners together securely and neatly by making a sturdy double cross-stitch over midpoint. The stitches may go through all layers of block, but will show on the back. Remove all pins.

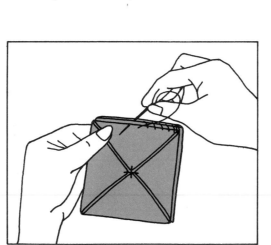

5 To join 2 blocks, place together with smooth, unfolded sides facing. Whipstitch along top folds, catching only a few threads with each stitch; stitch securely at corners. Open and press flat. Rows are joined in the same way.

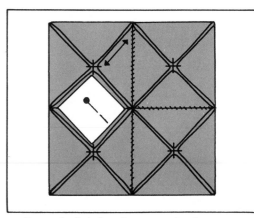

6 To cut the "windows", measure the distance indicated by the arrow; cut one true square to this size for each window. Place a window square on the diagonal over a seam as shown; pin in place.

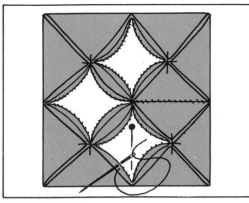

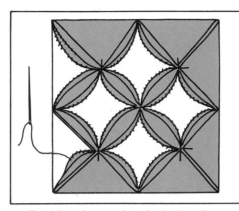

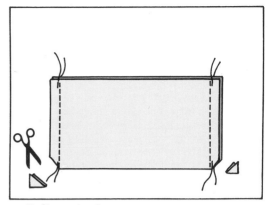

7 Roll top fold of "frame" over raw edge of window; slipstitch invisibly in place. Folds are on the bias so edges will curve naturally. Continue around entire window, stitching folded edges together at each corner.

8 To add windows to the sides (optional), cut window squares in half on the diagonal, forming 2 triangles. Pin one triangle between 2 folds. Roll folds over triangle as in step 7. Hem remaining raw edge of triangle if desired.

1 **Machine sewing** Cut true squares on straight grain from solid fabric; finished block is about one half size of original square. Fold in half with RS facing; stitch a 6mm/¼in seam along each side edge. Trim corners.

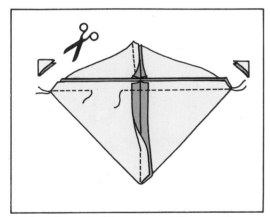

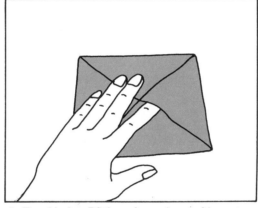

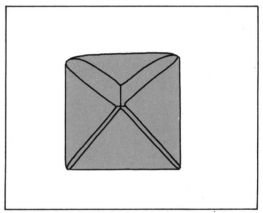

2 Open "pouch" without turning RS out; re-align top edges so seams match in the middle, RS facing. Finger-press seams open and pin together. Stitch across top edge, leaving an opening for turning. Trim corners.

3 Turn block to RS through opening, pushing out corners carefully. Smooth one seam allowance at opening beneath the other. Press block carefully. Opening does not need to be stitched closed.

4 Fold each of the corners to midpoint; corners should align exactly in the middle. Press carefully to form creases, then release. Do not stitch corners together in centre.

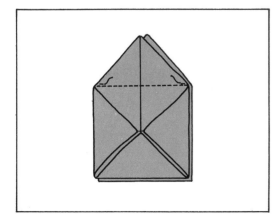

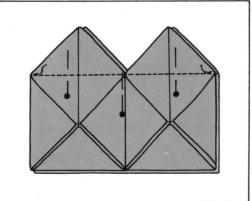

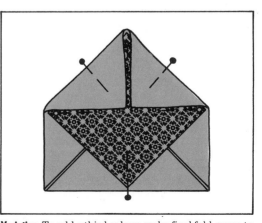

5 To join 2 blocks, place together with smooth, unfolded sides facing. Raise same corner flap on each piece and pin together, matching pressed creases. Stitch along crease, backstitching at each corner to secure. Open and press flat.

6 Join rows as in step 5; be sure to match seams and creases carefully. Backstitch at all corners and across all seams. Follow steps 4, 6, 7 and 8 of *Hand sewing* to complete the pattern.

Variation To add a third colour, make final fold, press to form creases and release. Cut a square of fabric to size of square formed by creases; baste in place. Continue with remaining steps. Fabric will be revealed when frame is sewn to window.

CRAZY PATCHWORK

Considered one of the earliest forms of piecing, Crazy Patchwork is composed of a random arrangement of fabric pieces sewn to a base; the edges of the patches are covered with embroidery. Crazy patchwork is usually not quilted because of the difficulty of sewing through many layers of fabric; projects are often simply tied and lined.

The original Crazy quilts were completely utilitarian. Worn blankets were replaced with pieces of discarded clothing, usually woollen, so as not to waste even the smallest fragment of material. Eventually the entire foundation was covered with these irregular patches, resulting in a "crazy" appearance. The effect was probably unintentional, dictated by the needs of a thrifty lifestyle.[5]

Crazy Patchwork changed dramatically in the 1880s when it became overwhelmingly popular in Britain and America. In keeping with the ornate decorative style of this period, women turned the Crazy quilt into a medium for displaying their needlework skills as well as their collections of rich fabrics, beads, ribbons, lace and memorabilia; anything that could be sewn to a surface was used. Political and sentimental messages shared space with prize ribbons, ties, scarves, hat bands and fabrics from cherished old clothes. The embroidery was the crowning glory of each quilt. In addition to the intricate stitches which covered the edges of the patches, motifs of every imaginable shape were lovingly stitched – from gossamer spiders' webs to flowers, birds, animals and people. Embroidered signatures and dates turned most Crazy quilts into treasured family heirlooms. Although quilts predominated, Crazy Patchwork was also found on sofa and piano covers, cushions and other household furnishings.

MAKING A CRAZY QUILT

Some Crazy quilts consist of an all-over pattern of patches, completely random in shape and size and arranged in no particular order; these are rather unwieldy to construct because of the large size of the foundation. A solution is to make Crazy quilt blocks. You can then sew the blocks directly to one another, or intersperse them with sashing, patchwork or plain blocks.

Mix large and small pieces and use fabrics of the same general quality – your project will only be as strong as the weakest fabric. The finished piece must be dry-cleaned, not washed, if fibres are mixed within the same project.

Although planning and stitching a Crazy Patchwork quilt is relatively simple, take care to smooth the patches in place without stretching them or the base. If adding Crazy Patchwork to clothing or blocks where the finished size is important, cut the foundation larger than you need, then trim the finished piece to size; this is necessary because the embroidery will often cause the fabric to "pull in" a bit.

EMBROIDERY STITCH DETAILS

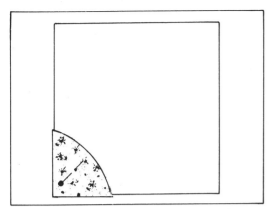

1 Technique There are 3 methods of applying Crazy patches to a base. For all methods, begin by placing the first patch, RS up, on one corner of base; pin or baste in place. Base can be any fabric compatible in weight and fibre content with patches.

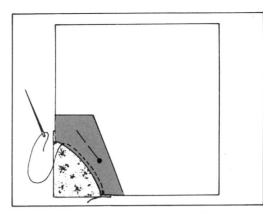

2a To construct Crazy Patchwork by the traditional hand method, place second patch on base so that it overlaps first patch by about 13mm/½in; pin. Work row of running stitches through all layers, close to raw edges of second piece; backstitch at each end.

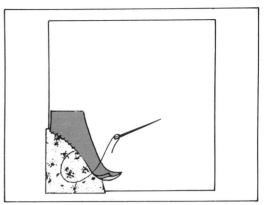

2b For a neater hand finish, press raw edge of second patch 6mm/¼in to WS, then place over first patch, overlapping edges by about 6mm/¼in. Slipstitch pressed edge in place.

2c For a simple machine method, place second patch over first patch, RS facing and with raw edges approximately matching. Stitch together with a 6mm/¼in seam. Smooth second patch to RS and press gently.

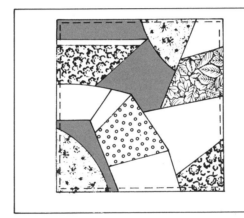

3 Continue with chosen method until entire foundation is covered. During construction, be careful not to stretch patches or foundation, so as to keep the work flat. Trim any uneven side edges to match base, then stitch close to edge all around.

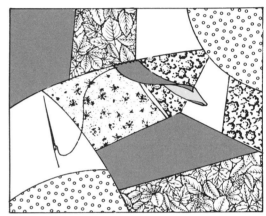

4 Check work carefully upon completion – foundation should not be visible. If any gaps occur, stitch a new piece over the area to cover. If using methods 2b or 2c, press all raw edges of new piece to WS and slipstitch in place.

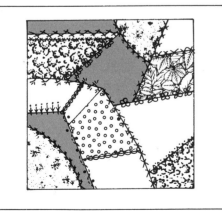

5 Using silk, cotton or novelty embroidery threads, or crewel wool if working with heavy fabrics, embroider fancy stitches over every seam. Follow basic stitch details on *the facing page,* combining stitches to create original arrangements.

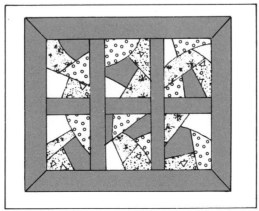

1 Crazy quilts Arrange Crazy blocks side by side or join with sashing as shown. Stitch blocks together to form the quilt top, adding a border if desired. Line project for added stability, tying layers together at strategic points; *see page 149.*

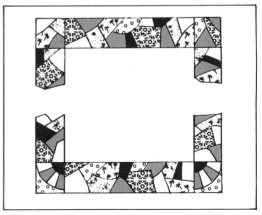

2 Enliven a plain quilt by adding a Crazy border. Use Crazy Patchwork for the entire border as shown at the top of the illustration, or intersperse with patchwork blocks as shown at the bottom.

DOUBLE WEDDING RING

The Double Wedding Ring has long been the traditional pattern to make in celebration of a marriage or special anniversary. The curved pieces connect and overlap at regular intervals to form an overall design of interlocked circles. The variegated pieces in each curved arc are said to symbolize the ever-changing state of married life. And as the name suggests, the intertwined circles have an unmistakable resemblance to wedding rings.

This pattern first appeared in America in the late 19th century, but it wasn't until around 1920 that it caught the imagination of American quilters. The design has retained its appeal through the years and has travelled the Atlantic to become just as fashionable in Europe.

Double Wedding Ring has never been considered an easy pattern to execute – in fact, quilters have been warned away from attempting it because of the supposed difficulty in sewing the curved seams and matching the corners. While it is not suggested that a complete beginner choose this as a first pattern, there is no reason why a quilter of modest experience should not give it a try. Full-size templates for a 28cm/11in-diameter circle are given on *page 97*. The step-by-step instructions that follow are intended to guide even the most apprehensive quilter through the procedure with relative ease.

If an entire quilt seems a little ambitious for the first attempt, try making one complete circle into a cushion; *see page 171*. Those who are still a bit nervous about the patchwork have another option. Piece only the ovals, then appliqué the pieces onto a wholecloth background – this is a perfectly acceptable way of achieving a similar effect.

CHOOSING FABRICS

There is no doubt that Double Wedding Ring is a very impressive design, but much of the drama depends upon the choice of fabrics. Eight different fabrics are needed for the rings. These can blend or contrast with one another, but they should be exciting fabrics because they provide the focus of the design. The rings should harmonize with the background.

Traditionally a solid fabric – usually white or ivory – is used for the background, giving the maker the chance to do some fancy quilting in the large central area of each ring. If you prefer simple outline quilting, select a print fabric instead, but choose a quiet print rather than a bold, splashy one; the rings should not have to compete with a busy background. If pale colours are chosen for the rings, select a dark fabric for the background to achieve a luminous effect.

A narrow bias binding is used for this design; *see pages 166-168*. Do not use purchased binding; rather, choose one of the fabrics used in the quilt and make your own.

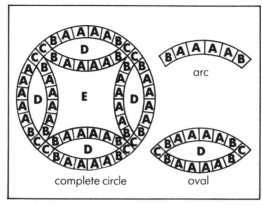

1 **Cutting and piecing** You need only 5 templates to make the Double Wedding Ring. The following pieces are required to construct one complete circle: A-32, B-16, C-8, D-4, E-1. D and E are cut from the background fabric.

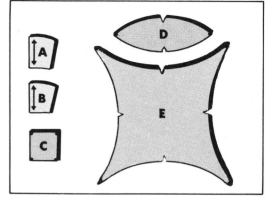

2 Trace pieces A-E on *page 97* and make a template for each; *see pages 34-35*. Mark grainline on A and B. Mark corner points on C, D and E. Using the tip of a utility knife, cut out a notch in the centre of each curved edge of D and E.

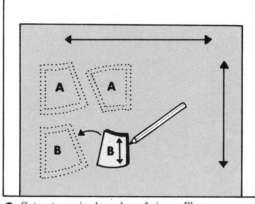

3 Cut out required number of pieces. Place one straight edge of each A and B piece on straight grain of fabric; for each arc, reverse one B piece to obtain its mirror image before marking and cutting. Mark all notches and corner points on WS of pieces.

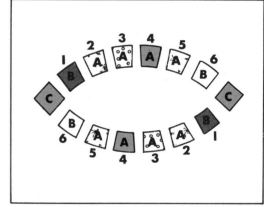

4 Arrange A, B and C pieces as they will be sewn together; join pieces in same order for each arc unless making a scrap quilt. Plan design so that Cs are the same on each oval, but different on adjacent ovals; see *Joining* illustration, step 4 on facing page.

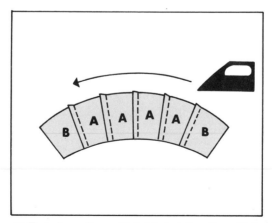

5 To make each arc, stitch 4 As together, then stitch a B and reversed B to each end. Turn to WS and press gently so as not to stretch bias edges. Press all seams in same direction. Construct 7 more arcs to make one complete circle.

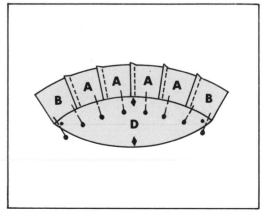

6 Next construct each oval. Pin D to one arc, matching central notch of D to inner central A seam of arc. Turn pieces to align each end; pin. Pin remainder of seam; stitch from corner to corner. Repeat 3 more times to make 4 partial ovals.

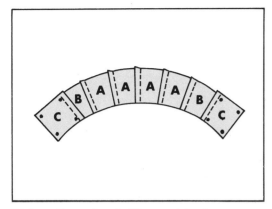

7 Sew a C to each end of the remaining 4 arcs, making sure that C fabrics are the same on each arc. Press seams of C toward B.

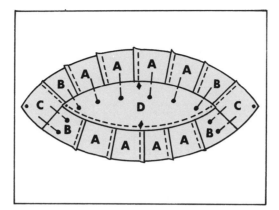

8 Sew an A-B-C arc to remaining edge of D, matching central notch of D to inner central A seam of arc. Turn pieces to align outer edges of C and B; match corner points of C and D. Pin; stitch. Press D seams toward arcs. Make 3 more ovals in same way.

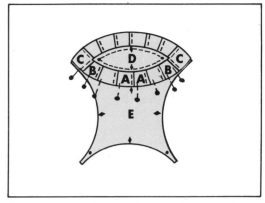

9 Pin one oval to E, matching central notch of E to outer central A seam of oval. Turn pieces to align each B-C seam to corner point of E; pin. Pin remainder of seam; stitch from point to point in a smooth curve. Press E seam toward arc.

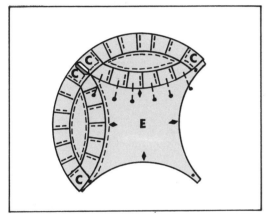

10 For second and fourth ovals, C pieces should be different from Cs on first and third ovals. Pin second oval to E on edge adjacent to first oval; pin to match edges of C pieces at one end and corner points at the other. Stitch in a smooth curve.

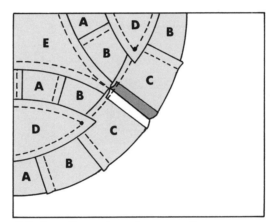

11 Press E seam toward arc; press C seam allowances open. Continue adding third and fourth ovals to E in same manner until circle is complete. For fourth oval, match edges of C pieces at each end.

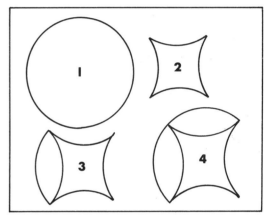

1 **Joining** A Double Wedding Ring quilt is comprised of 4 basic components, repeated any number of times: 1 is a complete circle; 2 is an E piece; 3 is an E piece with an oval sewn to one edge; 4 is an E piece with 2 ovals sewn to adjacent edges.

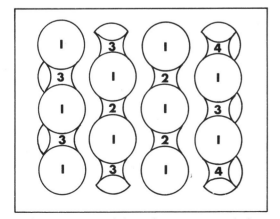

2 Sew components 1-4 together to create vertical rows; sew rows together to complete quilt top. Careful matching and pinning are required when sewing components and rows together. For different size quilts, add or subtract components and rows.

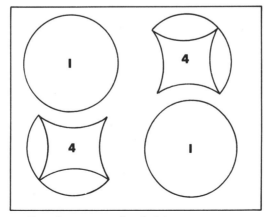

3 To make a very small quilt, join components 1 and 4 as shown. This size is ideal for a novice to try.

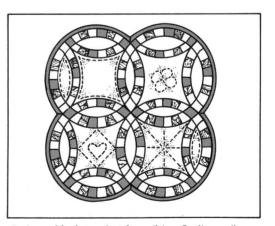

4 Assemble the project for quilting. Outline-quilt each arc, or quilt a fancy design on each E piece as shown; a full-size quilting pattern is given on *page 136*. Add a narrow bias binding; *see page 136* for instructions on binding angled edges.

FOLDED STAR

Folded Stars are composed of rectangles or circles of fabric which are folded into triangular shapes and arranged on a base; they are then sewn in place by hand in a variety of ways. Known in Great Britain as Somerset Patchwork, this delightful variation is not technically patchwork at all because the pieces are not actually fitted and seamed together. Folded Stars look intricate, but are so easy to make that you can complete one in a short time.

The secret of making successful Folded Stars is in the fabric selection. First, try to use only 100% cotton fabrics as they will hold creases well and save time in assembly. Folded Stars are constructed from a minimum of 20 triangles and you should prepare all the triangles before beginning; if you use polyester fabrics, the creases may not hold long enough for you to complete your arrangement, which means that you'll have to press the pieces twice.

Fabrics in each round should be highly contrasting, both in colour and pattern. The worst mistake you can make is to try to be subtle – it won't work. The fabric in each round should sparkle when placed next to subsequent rounds. This is an excellent way to test your sense of colour and contrast. If you have trouble with colour, stick to two or three dissimilar hues such as red, white and black.

Do not use large-scale prints which would become unreadable when folded into small pieces. Tiny prints can be very effective because they add depth and dazzle to what might otherwise be a static colour scheme. Experiment and have fun with Folded Stars. Make your samples into pot holders, cushions, wall hangings, Christmas ornaments – even quilts. Folded Stars can also be framed like paintings.

As a variation, try using ribbons instead of rectangles of fabric. Simply cut the ribbons into 6.4cm/2½in lengths and fold into triangles. Mixing satin, cotton and grosgrain ribbons in one star will add texture and character.

When finished, Folded Stars are round owing to the way in which they are put together. However, through experimentation, you can come up with a variety of different shapes such as squares, rectangles and octagons, depending upon how many triangles you fit into each round. Play with your triangles before sewing them to the base; you'll be amazed at how many variations you can design. If you decide to take advantage of the round shape, bind the edges with bias binding; *see pages 166-167*. Then use the star as an appliqué. If you prefer to frame the star with fabric, see *Finishing* on the facing page. Press the edges of the star and frame gently; avoid pressing the star itself or it will flatten and lose its textured quality.

Because of the many layers involved in making a Folded Star, finished stars are too thick to quilt, although you can make up for this by quilting the background frames instead.

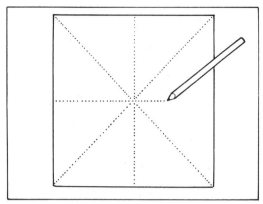

1 Technique Cut a square base from lightweight fabric or interfacing; base should be slightly larger than desired finished size. Lightly pencil 2 diagonal and 2 vertical lines on base to indicate centre of square and placement of folded triangles.

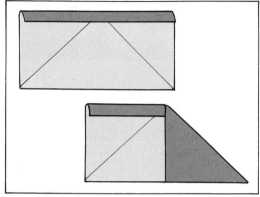

2 Cut fabric rectangles 6.4 × 3.8cm/2½ × 1½in. Turn one long edge 6mm/¼in to WS and press. Fold top edges to centre of rectangle along fine lines; press, forming a triangle. Prepare a large number of triangles beforehand to save time.

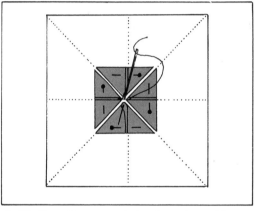

3 For Round 1, arrange 4 triangles on base with folded sides uppermost; match angled sides of triangles to diagonal base lines. Pin in place. Hand-stitch centres of triangles to centre of base; baste around outer edges of triangles; trim corners.

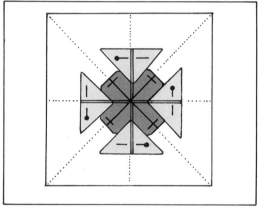

4 Round 2 requires 8 triangles of the same colour. Pin 4 triangles to base, aligning fold of each triangle with a horizontal or vertical base line; overlap Round 1 as shown. Position points of triangles about 13mm/½in away from centre of base.

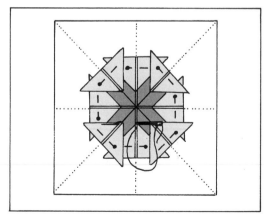

5 Pin 4 more triangles to base, aligning fold of each triangle with a diagonal base line; overlap Round 1 as shown. Stitch each triangle point in turn securely to base, working around base in a circular manner. Baste outer edges of Round 2 in place and trim corners.

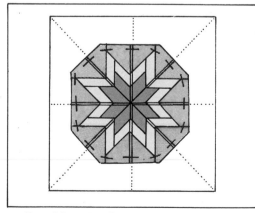

6 Round 3 requires 8 triangles of the same colour. Pin each triangle to base, overlapping every triangle in Round 2; position points of Round 3 about 13mm/½in away from points of Round 2. Stitch points to base; baste outer edges in place and trim corners.

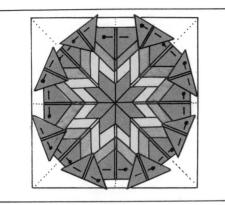

7 Round 4 requires 16 triangles. Pin 8 triangles to base, overlapping Round 3; position points 13mm/½in from points of Round 3. Pin 8 more triangles to base so that points touch star points of Round 2. Stitch points to base; baste outer edges; trim corners.

8 Round 5 and subsequent rounds require 16 triangles each. Pin triangles to base, overlapping triangles of previous round. Stitch points, baste edges and trim corners. Add rounds in same manner until star is desired size. Trim edges to form a circle.

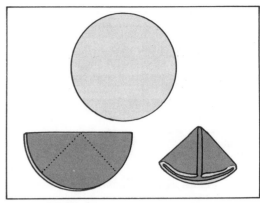

1 **Variation** Triangles and base can also be cut from circles. To make triangles, trace 6.4cm/2½in circle pattern on *page 93*; make template and cut from fabric. Fold fabric circle in half and press, then fold sides down on dotted lines to form triangle. Press.

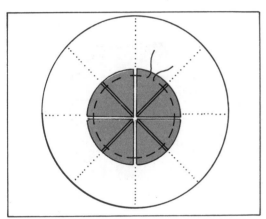

2 Cut circular base slightly larger than desired finished size of star. Lightly pencil 2 diagonal and 2 vertical lines to indicate centre and placement of folded triangles. Position Round 1 on base as shown; hand-stitch points, then baste outer edges to base.

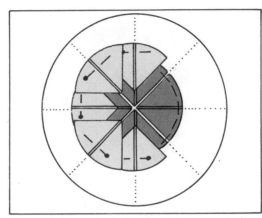

3 Round 2 requires 8 triangles of the same colour. Pin triangles to base, aligning folds with marked base lines. Position points of triangles about 13mm/½in away from centre of base. Stitch points and baste outer edges to base.

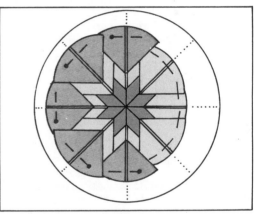

4 Round 3 requires 8 triangles of the same colour. Pin triangles to base, overlapping every triangle in Round 2; position points of Round 3 about 13mm/½in away from points of Round 2. Stitch points and baste outer edges to base.

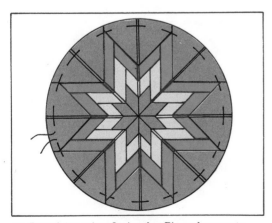

5 Round 4 requires 8 triangles. Pin and secure to base as for Round 3. Round 5 and subsequent rounds require 16 triangles; overlap each triangle of Round 4, then pin 8 triangles to base so points touch star points of Round 3. Trim base to match star.

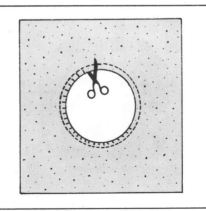

1 **Finishing** For frame, cut a square from coordinating fabric. Mark diameter of star (minus 13mm/½in), centred on WS of frame; stay-stitch marked line. Mark 6mm/¼in seam allowance within circle. Cut out circle on inner line; clip curves.

2 Fold and press seam allowance of frame to WS along stay-stitching. Position WS of frame on RS of Folded Star; pin and baste pressed edges of frame to star all around opening. Slipstitch frame to star using matching thread. Remove basting. Press gently.

GATHERED PATCHWORK

First developed in England in the middle of the 19th century, Gathered Patchwork can be considered an early example of the "quilt-as-you-go" method. The procedure incorporates the techniques of piecing and quilting into one operation and the resulting work has a texture and dimensionality that is difficult to achieve in other forms of patchwork. There are few surviving examples of Gathered Patchwork quilts because this was not a conventional technique.

While Gathered Patchwork is more time-consuming to construct than ordinary patchwork, the final quilting step is eliminated, which saves much effort when the piecing is finished. You can make complete quilts using this technique; however, the combination of plain patches with gathered ones is particularly effective, each enhancing the other. In her book *Traditional Quilting*, Mavis Fitzrandolph features a lovely hexagon, triangle and rhomboid quilt made in Gathered Patchwork *c.* 1850. Only the white hexagons are gathered; the red triangles and rhomboids are flat, serving to reinforce the textured appearance of the rest of the quilt.[6]

Although Gathered Patchwork has traditionally used the hexagon as the basic shape, you can translate the technique into any other geometric shape, such as the octagon illustrated here.

Gathered Patchwork consists of three layers held together initially with pins and basting stitches, then with simple running and stab stitches. The top fabric, larger than the base, is pleated over a mound of padding to impart surface relief. The base is usually not seen, so you can use a plain unbleached fabric such as calico/muslin. Hand sewers who prefer working over papers can use them for preparing the base, but not the top.

The middle layer is the padding. Formerly, carded wool was used for this layer, but wadding/batting or loose stuffing make excellent modern-day substitutes. The padding should not exceed 13mm/½in in thickness. Prepare several pieces at one time to ensure that the same amount of padding is added to each patch.

The top or gathered layer can be any cotton or cotton-blend fabric, solid or print. It is the same shape as the base, but should be 13-25mm/½-1in larger at each edge, depending upon the amount of texture desired.

You can sew Gathered Patchwork by hand or machine. Work with large pieces for easier handling; anything smaller than 7.6cm/3in across is very difficult to manipulate.

If the entire project is hand-sewn with only gathered patchwork pieces, no backing is necessary because there are no visible raw edges. Machine-sewn Gathered Patchwork or projects with a mixture of gathered and plain pieces need a backing to hide the raw edges.

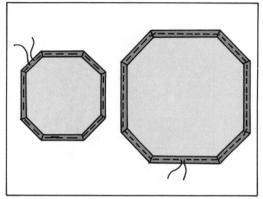

1 **Hand sewing** Prepare base and top pieces by pressing raw edges 6mm/¼in to WS; if working with paper, add to WS of base. Baste seam allowance of base in place. Sew small even running stitches close to fold all around top piece.

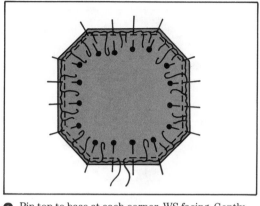

2 Pin top to base at each corner, WS facing. Gently pull running stitches of top, gathering excess fullness so top matches base. Pin all around, adjusting gathers evenly.

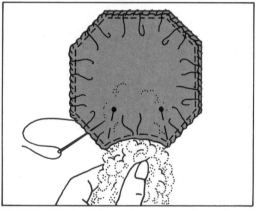

3 Whipstitch top to base at edges, securing gathers. Just before sewing last side, remove basting and paper (if using) from base. Insert padding between top and base, spreading it evenly across middle of patch. Sew last side closed. Remove running stitches.

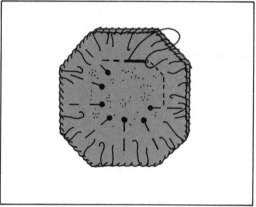

4 Smooth excess fabric of top toward middle of patch and secure with a circle of pins. Leaving a border of 13-25mm/½-1in, sew through all layers with a sturdy running stitch; stitching will echo exact shape of patch. Remove pins.

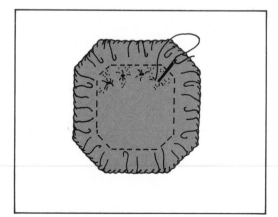

5 Using matching thread, sew stab stitches through all layers of central area every 6mm/¼in, working in a circle from outer edges toward centre. Each stitch forms a tiny furrow in top and padding. Pull all knots into padding to hide them; clip off excess thread.

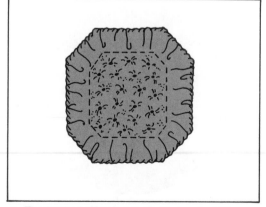

6 The finished effect is a puffy, textured middle area with flatter gathered sides – the stab and running stitches actually "quilt" the 3 layers together. You can join pieces with whipstitches as for normal hand sewing over papers; *see pages 52-53.*

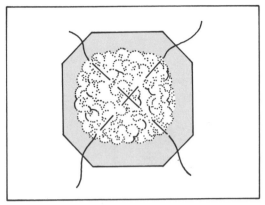

1 Machine sewing Spread padding evenly across middle of base on WS. Loosely baste in place with 2 diagonal lines of stitching.

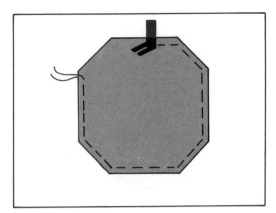

2 Machine-baste 6mm/¼in away from raw edges of top all around. Gently pull machine basting threads to gather top to same size as base.

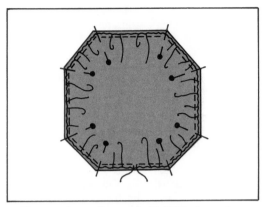

3 Pin top to base all around with WS facing and padding in between. Adjust gathers evenly. Machine-stitch close to raw edges, securing gathers; remove pins.

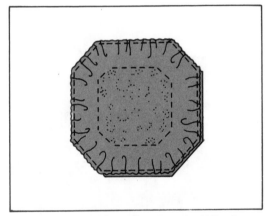

4 Smooth excess fabric of top toward middle of patch and secure with a circle of pins as in step 4 on facing page. Leaving a border of 13-25mm/½-1in, machine-stitch all around, echoing exact shape of patch. Clip thread ends. Remove pins.

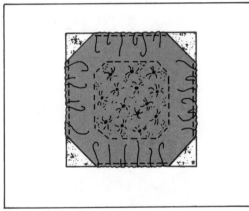

5 Work stab stitches in centre of patch as in step 5 on facing page. Prepare a number of pieces and sew together gathered sides facing, matching raw edges. Or sew plain fabric pieces to edges of gathered pieces to enhance textured effect.

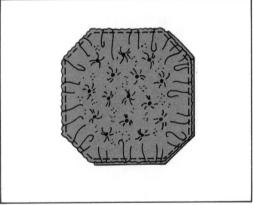

1 Variations Do not sew running stitches around the patch as in step 4. Instead, work stab stitches across entire piece for an all-over puckered effect.

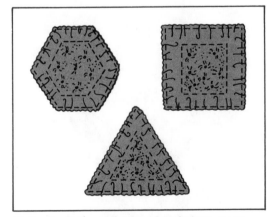

2 Try the Gathered Patchwork technique on any geometric shape. It is particularly effective on octagons, hexagons, squares and triangles. Remember to work with large shapes for easier handling.

3 Instead of using plain blocks in a quilt set, use Gathered Patchwork squares for a spectacular and unique result.

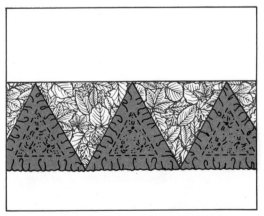

4 You can make borders more beautiful by adding gathered patches. Try combining a Gathered Patchwork border with a simple pieced top or a quilted wholecloth top.

HONEYCOMB

The Honeycomb – or hexagon – has been a remarkably popular pattern for over two hundred years. Derived from Middle Eastern mosaic designs, the Honeycomb is virtually a symbol of traditional English patchwork.

Because Honeycomb Patchwork requires extreme accuracy, the pieces are backed with carefully cut paper templates, and are usually hand-sewn together. The most common Honeycomb unit is a single rosette, comprising a central hexagon surrounded by six other hexagons in a different colour or pattern. You can create double and treble rosettes by attaching additional rows of colour. Honeycomb pieces can also be combined to form a variety of shapes, such as diamonds, stars or hearts.

The Honeycomb has answered to various charming names, most popular being Grandmother's Flower Garden. In England's West Country, the pieces are also quaintly described as sixes, optigons and octicians.[7]

When the straight sides of a Honeycomb piece are elongated, the design is called a Church Window because it evokes the image of a Gothic-style window; this shape is frequently combined with squares or diamonds. The hexagon takes on a more sinister appearance when the angled edges are elongated, which is why the resulting shape is called a Coffin.

While early Honeycomb quilts were quite disciplined in the use of colour and arrangement, modern quiltmakers are creating many exciting designs with this simple six-sided shape. The hexagon shape can be divided into three diamonds, for example, which can add a different dimension to a design.

The Honeycomb pattern was often the first design taught to children in the mid-19th century. Little girls were not allowed to play until they had cut and prepared a number of hexagons for sewing that evening. Also at this time, dowagers who disapproved of any nighttime meanderings by their servants encouraged them to create Honeycomb quilts during their only spare time – the evening! Thus, many Honeycomb quilts of this period feature the cotton dress prints worn by young girls and housemaids. These were scrap quilts in the truest sense because bits and pieces of material were hoarded for years until enough had accumulated to make a quilt.

In many instances when padding was unavailable or too expensive, the papers were deliberately retained to give a finished quilt added warmth. Patchwork pieces were backed with the paper ephemera of the time such as newspapers, letters and shopping lists. Today, many amateur "patchwork archaeologists" have attempted to piece together the life of an unknown quilter by using the scraps of information found on these backing papers. Papers have proven invaluable in dating antique Honeycomb quilts and projects.

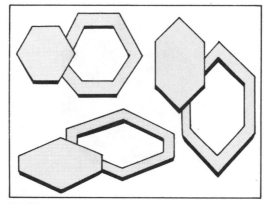

Templates Select the Honeycomb, Church Window or Coffin shape. Trace the desired pattern on *page 86* and make two templates: one for hand piecing and one window template; *see pages 34-35*. Technique that follows is the same for all shapes.

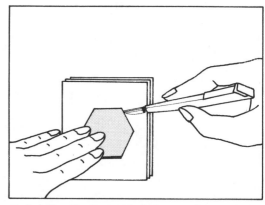

1 Technique Use the hand-piecing template to cut the shape from papers. Place 2 or 3 papers on a cutting board; position template on papers. Holding template firmly, trace around edge with a sharp knife. Cut all papers required for a project in this manner.

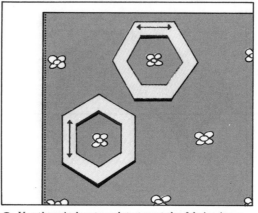

2 Use the window template to cut the fabric pieces. The straight edges of each hexagon may be parallel with the selvage or perpendicular to it. Use the window area of the template to position any fabric design to its best advantage.

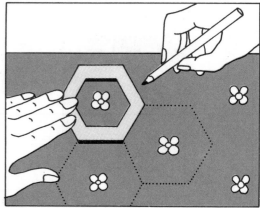

3 Mark the outer edge of the window template on RS of fabric. If cutting many hexagons from one fabric, mark additional pieces adjacent to the first so as to create mutual cutting lines. Cut out the pieces along the marked lines using scissors.

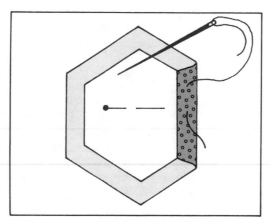

4 Centre a backing paper on WS of a fabric hexagon; pin. Fold one seam allowance over paper without creasing paper. Make a basting stitch through fabric and paper, beginning in middle of folded seam allowance. Leave a 6mm/¼in thread-end free.

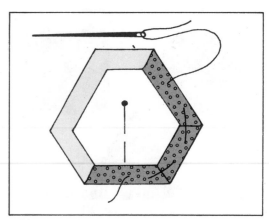

5 Fold adjacent seam allowance over paper in same manner, forming a sharp corner. Make basting stitch over folded corner to secure, bringing needle up in middle of next seam allowance. Repeat for remaining edges.

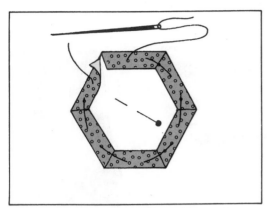

6 To finish final corner, slip excess fabric of last seam allowance beneath first seam allowance and baste in place. Cut thread, leaving end free; remove pin. Press gently. Prepare all patches in same manner.

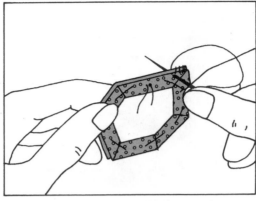

7 To join 2 hexagons, place RS facing, matching corners. Using matching thread, whipstitch folded edges together from corner to corner, backstitching at each end to secure. Make 16-18 evenly spaced stitches per 2.5cm/1in without catching papers in the stitching.

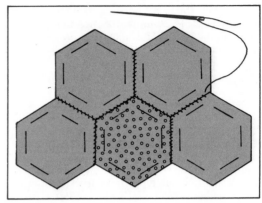

8 Join additional patches in same manner. Stitch entire length of each seam, backstitching at corners. Stitches will barely show as straight stitches on RS. Do not break thread when joining many patches at the same time, but use continuously.

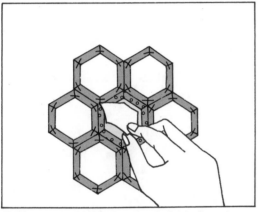

9 Remove papers when project is finished or when a patch is bordered on all sides by other patches. Remove basting from hexagon by pulling loose thread end, then lift paper out. Papers can be reused. Press finished patchwork gently and carefully.

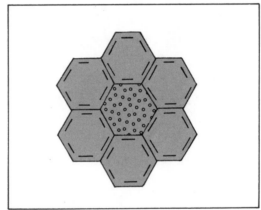

1 **Design possibilities** The single rosette is the most common unit and is the basis for countless designs. Use same fabric for each "petal" around a contrasting centre. Plan arrangement of rosettes carefully before joining to background hexagons.

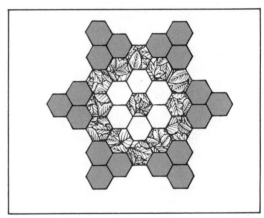

2 For a double rosette, add a row of contrasting hexagons around a single rosette; add a third row for a treble rosette. Add other units to create different shapes. The design illustrated here is a double rosette with triangles of hexagons forming a star.

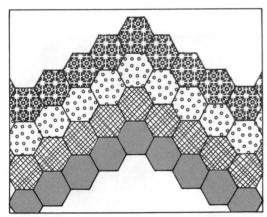

3 An excellent border design is called Ocean Wave. Place light and dark fabrics together as shown to accentuate the undulating pattern. Hexagons can also be arranged in straight lines for a striped border.

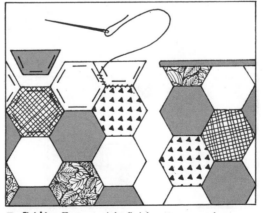

1 **Finishing** For a straight finish, cut prepared hexagons in half (or prepare half-hexagons using pattern on *page 96*) and insert in between pieces along each edge; whipstitch in place. Assemble quilt and bind with coordinating fabric; *see pages 166-167*.

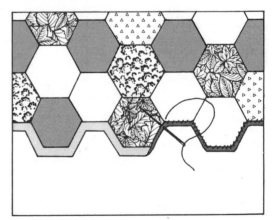

2 For a shaped edge, cut quilt backing slightly larger than project; trim edges of backing to correspond with edges of hexagons. Roll the backing over the patchwork, clipping at corners where necessary. Slipstitch in place, hiding all raw edges.

LOG CABIN

Log Cabin is the best-known form of patchwork; it is also very old. Primitive examples can be found in the British Museum in London, noted for its collection of Egyptian mummies – both human and animal. Some of the animal mummies are wrapped in what looks like Log Cabin patchwork, and although the pieces aren't actually stitched together, the resemblance to the Log Cabin pattern is striking.

One of the earliest Log Cabin quilts, a Barn Raising design, was made in England before 1830 by a woman named Mary Morgan, who later emigrated to the southern United States.[8] This shows that Log Cabin was not native to America as is commonly thought. However, there is no doubt that the pattern was named after an American tradition – building houses from logs.

Visually, the name is very apt: the central square is usually bright red, imitating the fire always glowing in the hearth of a cabin. The block is half dark and half light, representing the effect of sunshine and shadow on a house, and the design is "built" of strips of fabric like the logs used to construct a pioneer's home.

From about 1850 until the present day, Log Cabin patchwork has been very popular in Britain and America, and with good reason. Easy to construct, it utilizes narrow strips of fabric that are virtually unusable for other purposes. Plus the design possibilities are endless; not only are there hundreds of variations of the Log Cabin block, but there are also many different arrangements of the finished blocks.

There are two ways to assemble a Log Cabin block. In the first method, the strips are pieced in turn around the centre to build up the design. The advantage of this technique is that the finished block can be easily quilted because it basically consists of one layer of fabric.

The second and more widely used method is called press piecing. This entails sewing the centre to a base, then sewing all the strips to the base around the centre and pressing them to the right side. This technique provides stability for thin fabrics or materials of different weights and textures and is a natural precursor to the Quilt-As-You-Go method, described in detail on *pages 144-145*. Because of the extra layer, however, it is difficult to quilt.

Colour is particularly important in a Log Cabin block because one side of the square must be dark and the other side light; therefore, you will need equal amounts of light and dark fabrics. There must be a strong differentiation between light and dark, so save any medium shades for another quilt.

If you have many light fabrics, but few darks, simplify your work by using only one fabric such as black for the dark half. Or, if you have many darks but few lights, use one pale colour for the light half. While the central square can be any colour, use the same fabric throughout to act as a focus and provide a unifying factor.

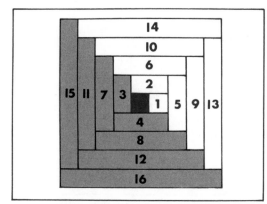

Basic Log Cabin Each block is constructed from the middle outward. Fabric strips are sewn around the centre with light fabrics on one half and darks on the other, separating the block into two triangles of colour.

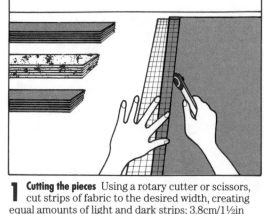

1 Cutting the pieces Using a rotary cutter or scissors, cut strips of fabric to the desired width, creating equal amounts of light and dark strips; 3.8cm/1½in strips are standard and will make finished 2.5cm/1in logs.

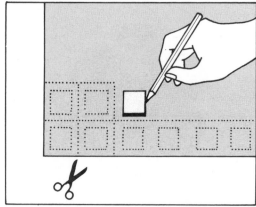

2 For the centre piece, choose a pattern (*see page 94*) and make a template; *see pages 34-35*. A square is illustrated here, but you can use any geometric shape. Cut all centres for one project from same fabric, adding 6mm/¼in seam allowances.

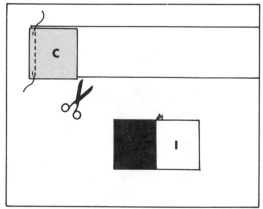

1 Piecing without a base With RS facing, sew the centre square to a light strip, backstitching at each end to secure. Trim away excess strip so it is even with edge of square. Always press seam allowances to one side, away from centre.

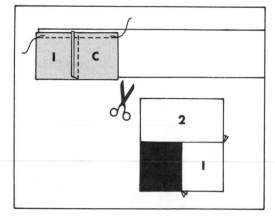

2 Select a light fabric for the second strip. Sew top edge of pieced centre to second strip with RS facing, backstitching at each end. Trim away excess strip so it is even with pieced centre, and press.

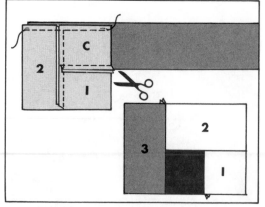

3 Select a dark fabric for the third strip. Sew left edge of pieced centre to third strip with RS facing, backstitching at each end. Trim away excess strip so it is even with pieced centre, and press.

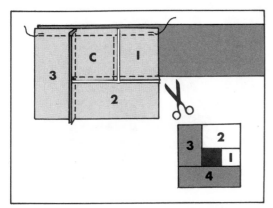

4 Select a dark fabric for the fourth strip. Sew bottom edge of pieced centre to fourth strip with RS facing, backstitching at each end. Trim away excess strip so it is even with pieced centre, and press.

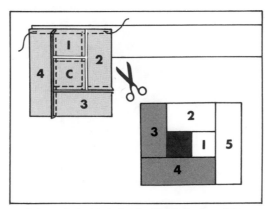

5 Select a light fabric for the fifth strip. Sew right edge of pieced centre to the fifth strip with RS facing, backstitching at each end. Trim away excess strip so it is even with pieced centre, and press.

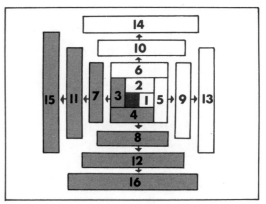

6 Continue adding each strip in turn around the pieced centre until block is desired size. Alternate between light and dark fabrics for each half of the block. Trim strips and press as described above.

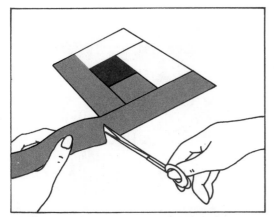

7 Alternatively, you can trim each strip before sewing it to the pieced centre. Simply place the strip next to the block in the correct position and cut to size. Sew the strip to the block as described above and press.

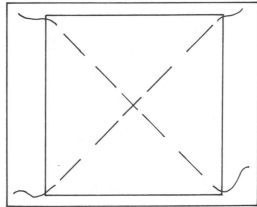

1 **Press-piecing** Base should be compatible in fibre content with logs you will use; cut base 13mm/½in larger than desired size. If logs are 3.8cm/1½in strips, cut a 24.2cm/9½in-square base. Draw or baste diagonal lines on base to indicate centre.

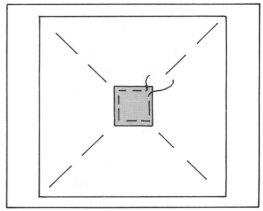

2 Place centre square RS up on middle of base, aligning corners with diagonal lines. Pin or baste in position. (Centre is illustrated in pale grey up to step 5 so that basting stitches are visible.)

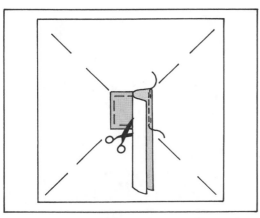

3 Select a light fabric for the first strip. Place strip over centre square; trim away excess strip so it is even with centre. Stitch together, RS facing, along right edge. Fold and press first strip to RS.

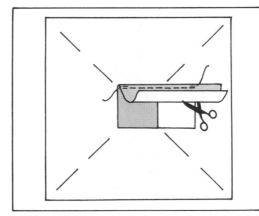

4 Select a light fabric for the second strip. Place strip over pieced centre; trim away excess strip so it is even with pieced centre. Stitch together, RS facing, along top edge. Fold and press second strip to RS.

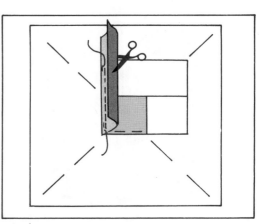

5 Select a dark fabric for the third strip. Place strip over pieced centre, aligning edges on left; trim away excess strip so it is even with pieced centre. Stitch together, RS facing, along left edge. Fold and press third strip to RS.

LOG CABIN

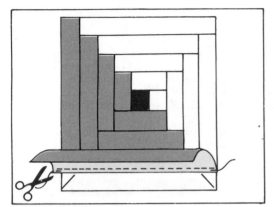

6 Continue adding strips to base in this manner, working in a clockwise direction around pieced centre until base is covered. Trim away loose threads on WS and press carefully before joining to other blocks.

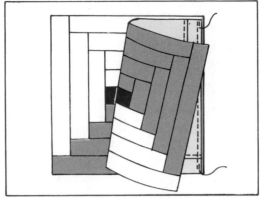

Joining Log Cabin quilts are quick to make because they do not require sashing or a border. Decide upon a set; see *Sets* below or make up a set of your own design. Sew finished blocks together with RS facing and edges even to create desired pattern.

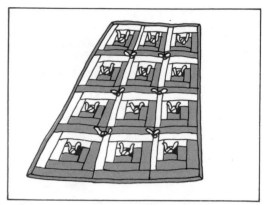

Quilting Assemble the pieced top for quilting; *see page 139*. If blocks have not been pieced on a base, quilt logs along seam lines. If blocks have been press-pieced, tie the layers together at centres and corners; *see page 149*. Add a simple binding to finish.

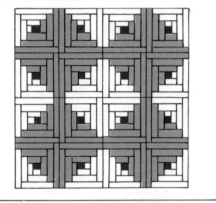

1 Sets There are hundreds of arrangements for Log Cabin blocks; 4 of the best-known examples are illustrated here. While only 16 blocks are shown for each, simply add extra blocks to create a larger quilt. This design is called Light and Dark.

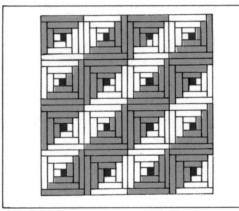

2 Straight Furrow is a very dramatic arrangement whereby the diagonal strips of dark and light resemble the furrows made in soil by a farmer's plow.

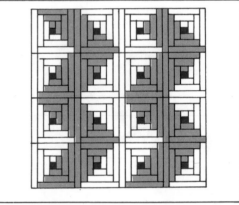

3 Streak of Lightning: the zigzag effect created by turning the blocks as shown certainly resembles jagged lightning bolts in the sky. Make this in blue and yellow for a spectacular result.

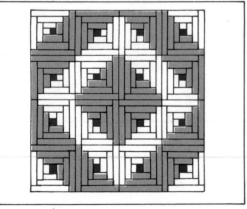

4 Barn Raising: light and dark concentric diamonds enclose a dark middle square. Illustration shows only the 16 central blocks; at least 36 are needed to make this design. Continue adding blocks to create diamond effect.

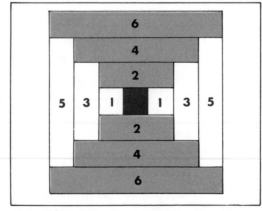

1 Log Cabin variations To construct Courthouse Steps, piece the block on opposite rather than adjacent sides of centre square, dividing block into 4 sections of colour. When setting blocks together, join dark edges to form a spool pattern.

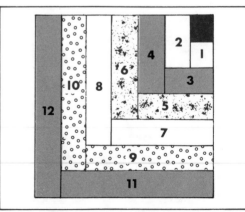

2 To construct Echo or Chevron Log Cabin, place the "centre square" in one corner and build the design outward from that corner. Add strips in rows; make each row a different fabric as shown, or divide the block diagonally into light and dark halves.

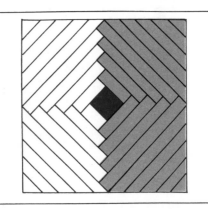

3 Off-Centre Log Cabin requires strips of 2 different widths. The division between light and dark appears curved, resulting in wonderful effects when blocks are joined. *See page 94 for construction details.*

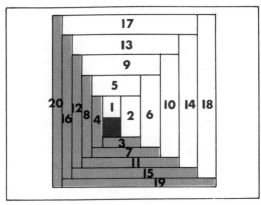

4 Hung Centre Log Cabin has the centre square turned on point; it must be constructed on a base. Add strips around centre as for basic Log Cabin until base is covered. Trim away strips extending beyond base. *See page 94 for construction details.*

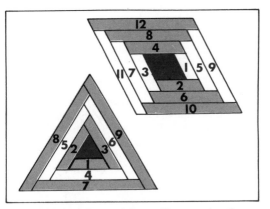

5 Triangle and diamond shapes illustrate that the Log Cabin technique can be used with any geometric shape in the middle. Add strips around centre until block is desired size. *See page 94 for templates and construction details.*

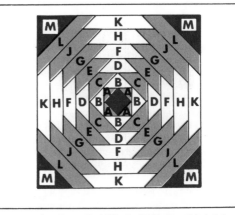

1 **Pineapple** Also called Windmill Blades, this intricate Log Cabin variation is for experienced quilters. Trace the full-size patterns on *page 95* for a 30.5cm/12in block and make templates; *see pages 34-35.* Cut required pieces as directed on patterns.

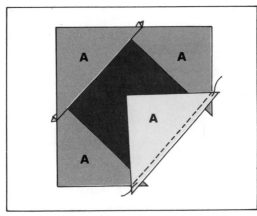

2 Design is assembled in rounds; always press seam allowances away from centre. To begin, sew 2 dark A triangles to opposite sides of centre; press, then stitch remaining A triangles to centre as shown. Press.

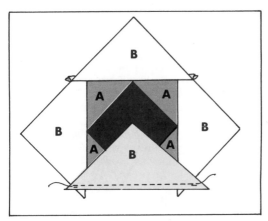

3 Sew 2 light B triangles to opposite sides of pieced centre; press, then stitch remaining B pieces to centre as shown. Press.

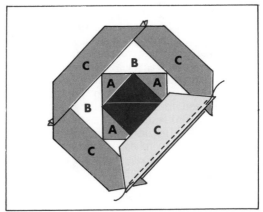

4 Sew 2 dark C pieces to opposite sides of pieced centre; press, then stitch remaining C pieces to centre as shown. Press.

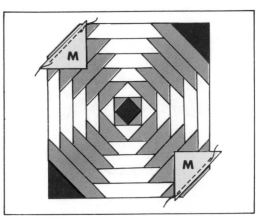

5 Continue adding pieces to pieced centre in rounds, working in alphabetical order. Accuracy is important, as is the careful placement of light and dark, so take your time to get it right. To finish, sew corner M pieces to centre as shown.

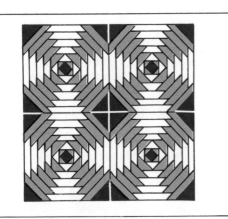

6 Join Pineapple blocks without sashing to create a dazzling effect. At least 4 blocks must be constructed because the complete design is evident only after blocks are sewn together.
Outline-quilt each seam and add a simple binding.

PUFF PATCHWORK

Puff Patchwork does not resemble any other form of piecing. On first observation, one is struck by the three-dimensional quality of the work. The immediate impulse is to reach out and stroke the surface, which undulates between the plump pouches of fabric and the deep furrows between them. Although very modern in appearance, Puff Patchwork has been around for quite some time. In his book *The Pieced Quilt*, Jonathan Holstein features a superb woollen Puff quilt from Maine, dated *c.* 1875.[9] The design is also known as Biscuit Patchwork.

Traditionally, Puff Patchwork consists of one shape – the square – repeated many times. The finished project is not actually quilted. A pouch, formed by joining two different-sized fabric pieces, is filled with loose stuffing which traps a layer of air. This creates a warm yet lightweight covering. Puff quilts are usually lined, then tacked or tied at strategic points.

It is possible to create an almost limitless number of designs, depending upon the order in which the different-colour puffs are sewn together. Any patchwork pattern based on the square can be adapted to this technique – Nine Patch, Sunshine and Shadow and Irish Chain are ideal examples. You can create sashes and borders by repeating puffs of the same colour in horizontal and vertical rows. Plan your design on graph paper to determine the exact number of puffs required in each colour and the finished size of the project; puffs usually pull in somewhat when finished, so allow for this shrinkage if making a project of a specific size. If you enjoy working from a graph, you'll have a great advantage in that books of counted cross-stitch and tapestry/needlepoint charts will become valuable sources of quilt patterns.

Perhaps the most popular method of constructing Puff Patchwork is to use up odd pieces of fabric to make a scrap quilt. To design a scrap Puff quilt prepare all the puffs first, then arrange them on a flat surface to achieve a good mix of colours and prints.

ADAPTING TRADITIONAL DESIGNS

While the square is the traditional shape used in Puff Patchwork, you can substitute any geometric form. Simplicity is the key, however. Let the colours and fabrics make the design statement, rather than some complicated arrangement. It might be fun to try making a simple wall hanging in Puff Patchwork using one of the patchwork designs shown on *pages 47-52* ; see *Design possibilities*, step 3 on the facing page. Enlarge the pattern so that the wall hanging consists of only one block with a plain border. Make each separate patchwork piece into a puff. The assembly is identical to that used for traditional patchwork, but the result will be highly unusual. Translate this into a quilt, making your wall hanging composition the central medallion, surrounded by borders of puffs.

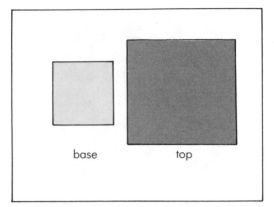

1 Technique Base is desired size of finished square plus 6mm/¼in all around; use any sturdy pre-shrunk fabric because it will not show when project is finished. Cut top 2.5-3.8cm/1-1½in larger than base; the larger the top, the bigger the puff.

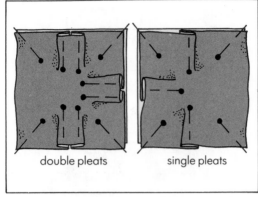

2 Place top and base together WS facing, matching corners; pin. Make double or single pleats along 3 sides of top to ease in excess fabric. Pin, then stitch in place by hand or machine, making a 3mm/⅛in seam. Remove pins.

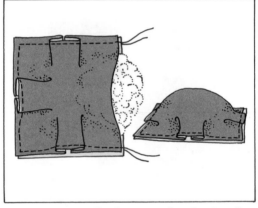

3 Insert loose stuffing into open edge of each puff, using same amount for each one for a uniform appearance. Pin open edges together making double or single pleats; stitch closed 3mm/⅛in from edges.

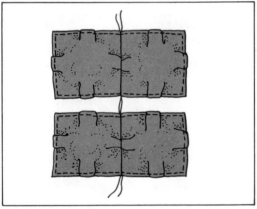

4 Stitch 2 puffs together with RS facing; if using a sewing machine, chain-sew puffs to save time. Puff projects are assembled in rows. Add required number of puffs to each original pair to complete each row.

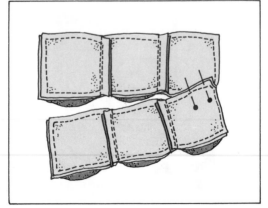

5 Join rows by pinning together with RS facing, matching seams carefully; finger-press seam allowances in opposite directions for easy matching. Stitch together by hand or machine.

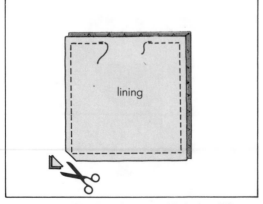

6 When Puff Patchwork is assembled, place RS up over lining fabric; cut lining to size. Pin lining to patchwork with RS facing; stitch all around, leaving large opening for turning. Clip corners. Turn to RS, fold raw edges at opening inside and slipstitch closed.

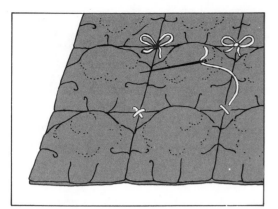

7 To secure lining to top, tie together at corners of each puff, making a bow or knot on RS or WS of project; *see page 149.* Or sew backstitches or cross-stitches at each corner.

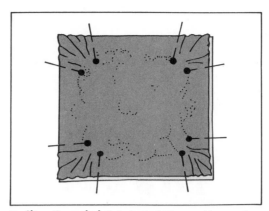

1 **Alternative method** Cut pieces for top and base as in step 1 of *Technique.* Pin top to base; ease in excess fabric at each corner. Stitch pieces together all around by hand or machine and remove pins. Join squares and rows as in steps 4 and 5.

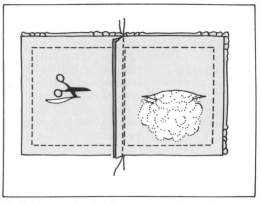

2 Using a small pair of scissors, carefully cut an opening in the backing only of each puff. Gently insert stuffing through the opening, using same amount of stuffing for each puff.

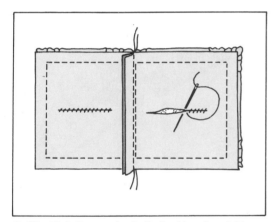

3 Slipstitch the opening in the backing closed. Line and tie project as directed in steps 6 and 7 of *Technique.*

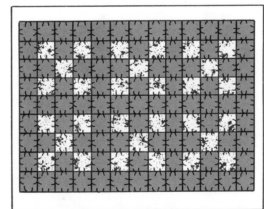

1 **Design possibilities** Plan your design on graph paper to determine the required number and colour of puffs. Make patchwork blocks in puffs; such as the Nine-Patch pattern shown. Create sashes and borders by joining puffs of same colour in rows.

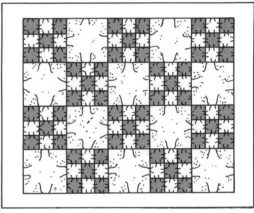

2 Try translating all-over designs such as Irish Chain into Puff Patchwork. This example combines 2 sizes of puff squares to reproduce the traditional patchwork pattern.

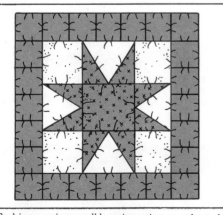

3 Fashion a unique wall hanging using an enlarged patchwork block made from puffs and surrounded with a border. You can make any geometric shape into a puff; just remember to make the top patch 2.5-3.8cm/1-1 ½in larger than the base.

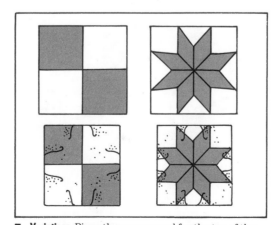

1 **Variations** Piece the square used for the top of the puff. The design can be simple, such as the Four-Patch shown here (left); or a little more complex, such as the LeMoyne Star (right).

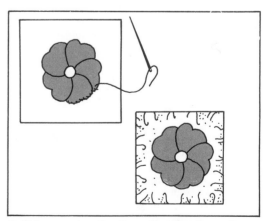

2 Before constructing the puff, appliqué a motif onto the middle of the top patch. Repeat the same appliqué throughout the project, use a variety of different motifs, or intersperse appliquéd puffs with plain puffs.

SEMINOLE PATCHWORK

From the time that North America was colonized, the native American Indians were continually forced to move south and west to avoid land conflicts. Some tribes, including the Seminoles, moved into southern Florida. In the 1830s, pressured by encroaching white settlers and the United States government to move west to Oklahoma, a small group of Seminole and Miccosukee Indians retreated deep into the Florida Everglades. There they lived in virtual isolation for many years, because this swampy area was not considered a desirable place to colonize by the white settlers. The Seminoles adapted to their new environment and proceded to establish a culture based on hunting and trading. About 1900, traders supplied Seminole women, who had always been adept with a needle, with hand-cranked sewing machines. This led to the birth of Seminole Patchwork.

Although intricate in appearance, with some patches no larger than 3mm/⅛in, Seminole patchwork involved a method of piecing that not only eliminated the need for templates, but made the work quick and easy to do. The technique consists of sewing fabric strips together, cutting the strips into sections, then sewing these sections together again in different combinations. This means that no small pieces ever need to be handled, even though the finished result may be composed only of tiny patches. It also means that the work must be done on a sewing machine. The intricate pieced bands thus constructed are used to decorate clothing and small craft items.

This technique is still being practised by the descendants of the original group of Seminoles who stayed in the Florida Everglades. They now live on the Immokalee Seminole Indian Reservation. There the women work to produce patchwork items for sale.

Seminole Patchwork does not have a long history, nor do the designs have any deep meaning; most patterns are not even named. The women record their designs for posterity by making a sample and sewing it to another sample and so on, until a long strip of patterns is formed; from this strip, designs can be copied or changed. Colour is important to Seminole Patchwork. Vivid hues of yellow, red and turquoise are often set against black for dramatic effects. While any fabrics can be used, beginners should work with contrasting solids. Prints will blend together, which is not desirable: the more distinct the seam lines, the more effective the patterns.

No measurements are given with the instructions because Seminole Patchwork can be worked in any size. However, ratios of strips are given for most patterns. For example when strips are numbered 1, 2 and 3, strip 2 is twice the width of strip 1, and strip 3 is three times the width of strip 1. Where no numbers are given, all strips are the same width.

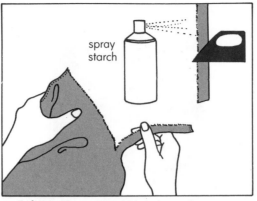

1 Technique Tear strips of fabric from selvage to selvage on grain; if you cut the strips, make sure that they are on grain. To save time, cut several layers at once using a rotary cutter; *see pages 36-37*. Lightly spray-starch and press each strip after tearing.

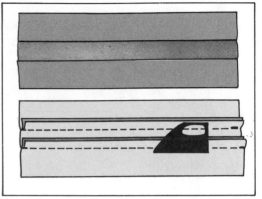

2 Sew any number of strips together. Strips can be any width, but all must be the same length. After sewing, press seam allowances to one side.

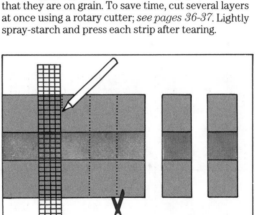

3 Using a soft-lead pencil or fabric marker and a clear plastic ruler marked with a grid, draw parallel lines across pieced strip. Cut strip into sections along each marked line using scissors or a rotary cutter.

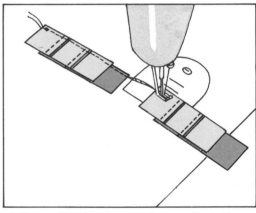

4 Sew sections together in pairs according to the design you have chosen. When joining sections, seam allowances should face in opposite directions to reduce bulk. Chain-sew the pieces to save time and thread.

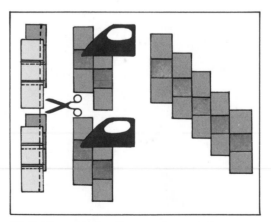

5 Cut the pairs of sections apart, open and press. Chain-sew the pairs together; open and press lightly. Continue sewing sections together in this manner until pieced band is complete. Press very gently so as not to stretch pieced band.

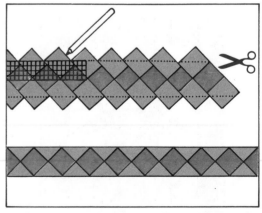

6 Place plastic ruler over pieced band; draw straight line at each outer edge as shown. Trim away excess fabric. There is always a 6mm/¼in seam allowance above and below main design (top), but designs will be shown without seam allowance (bottom).

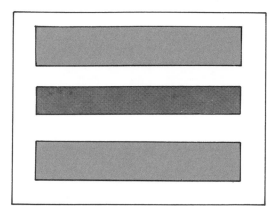

7 For greater flexibility in the ultimate use of the pieced band, cut outer strips slightly wider (6mm/¼in) than inner strips. This will give you a larger area at each edge for the seam allowance, which can always be trimmed off later if you don't need it.

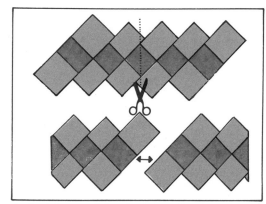

8 Straighten angled ends of pieced bands as follows: draw straight line in middle of pieced band, dividing one motif exactly in half; cut along line. Sew remaining angled edges together, matching seam allowances. Outer ends of band will now be straight.

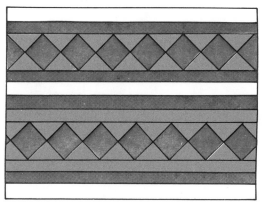

9 Edging strips are used to finish off pieced bands, make bands wider, or create special effects. Sew straight strips to each edge of pieced band, sewing band and strips together evenly. Note how use of 2 strips (bottom) makes diamonds appear to float.

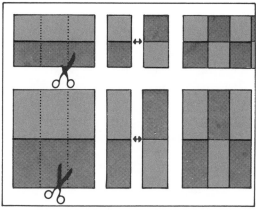

1 **Straight repeats** Sew any number of strips together, cut into sections and rejoin on straight grain in various combinations. Shown here are strips of same width, cut and sewn with colours alternating to form a checkerboard of squares and rectangles.

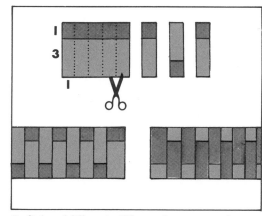

2 Strips of different widths can be sewn together to create a variety of designs. Cut 2 strips in a ratio of 3:1 and sew together. Cut apart (width: 1) and turn the sections so colours alternate. Sew together. Pattern on right shows same design in reverse colours.

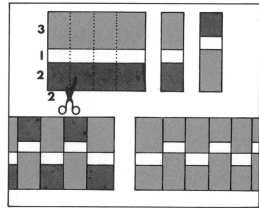

3 Sew 3 strips in a ratio of 3:1:2 together and cut apart (width: 2). Turn sections so colours alternate. Sew together again to form a pattern of rectangles moving across middle of pieced band. Pattern on right shows same design in only 2 colours.

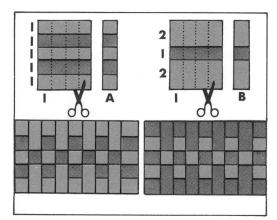

4 Combine 2 or more different pieced sections. For A, sew 5 strips of same width together and cut apart (width: 1). For B, sew 3 strips in a ratio of 2:1:2 together and cut apart (width: 1). Sew A and B together alternately. Design is in reverse on right.

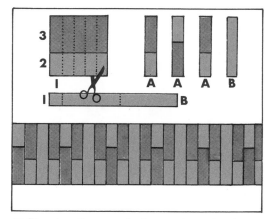

5 Pieced sections can also be sewn to unpieced strips. For A, sew 2 strips in a ratio of 3:2 together and cut apart (width: 1). For B, cut unpieced strips same height and width as section A. Sew A and B together alternately as shown to form pattern.

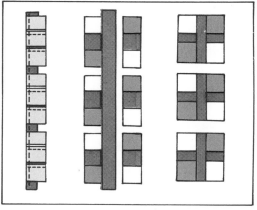

6 For speedier sewing, do not cut unpieced strips into sections; sew pieced sections to strip as if in a chain. Press. Sew other pieced sections to opposite edge of strip; press, then cut strip apart for complete pattern.

Seminole Patchwork

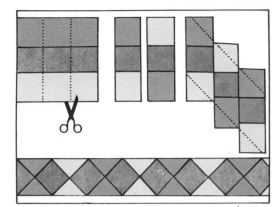

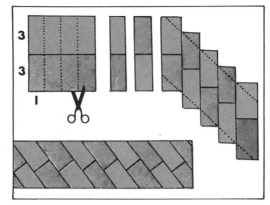

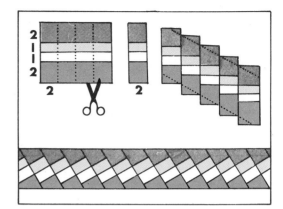

1 **Offset repeats** Sew any number of strips together, cut into sections, and offset sections as shown. Rejoin in various combinations. Shown here are 3 strips of the same width cut, offset and sewn, with colours alternating, to form diamonds.

2 Create a lightning bolt effect: sew 2 strips of the same width (3) together, cut into sections (width: 1) and offset by 6-13mm/¼-½in. Sew several bands together for an impressive result.

3 An easy way to offset pieces is by matching the staggered seamlines. Sew 4 strips in a ratio of 2:1:1:2 together and cut apart (width: 2). Offset the sections, matching seams as shown; sew together.

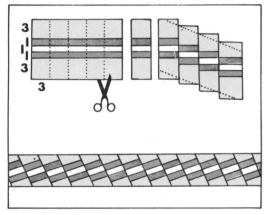

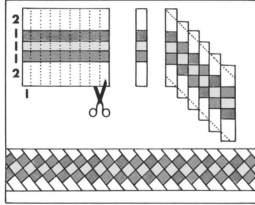

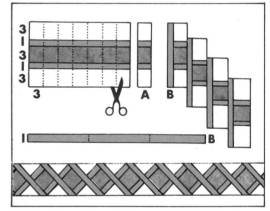

4 Narrow strips can make a design appear more intricate. Sew 5 strips in a ratio of 3:1:1:1:3 together and cut apart (width: 3). Turn the sections so that the colours alternate. Offset the sections, matching seams as shown; sew together.

5 Pieced bands can be as complex as you wish to make them. Sew 5 strips in a ratio of 2:1:1:1:2 together and cut apart (width: 1). Turn the sections so that the colours alternate. Offset and sew together, creating a complicated pattern of squares.

6 Pieced sections can be sewn to unpieced strips, then offset for dramatic results. For A, sew 5 strips in a ratio of 3:1:3:1:3 together and cut apart (width: 3). For B, cut unpieced strips (width: 1) same height as section A. Sew each A to a B. Offset and sew together.

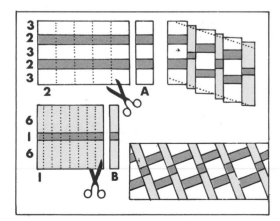

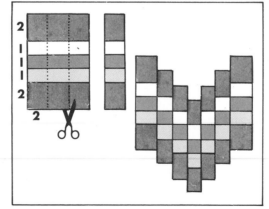

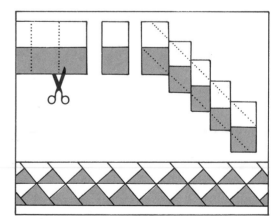

7 Combine 2 or more different pieced strips. For A, sew 5 strips in a ratio of 3:2:3:2:3 together and cut apart (width: 2). For B, sew 3 strips in a ratio of 6:1:6 together and cut apart (width: 1). Offset and sew A to B as shown.

Corners Seminole Patchwork can be shaped by the manner in which the pieces are joined together. To create corners, stagger the pieced sections as shown in the diagram, and sew together. Continue to add pieces until desired size is reached.

Triangles Create perfect triangles: sew 2 strips of same width together and cut apart (width: same as one strip). Offset by 6-13mm/¼-½in. Trim the edges. Join several bands of triangles to form a traditional Pyramids design – but with half the work!

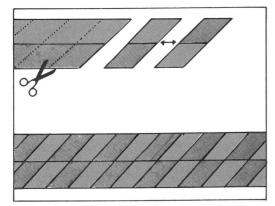

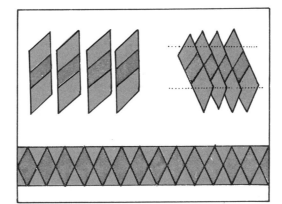

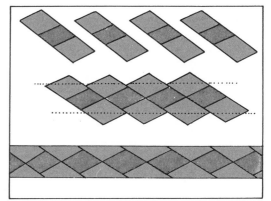

1 **Angled repeats** Sew any number of strips together, cut into sections at an angle, and rejoin. Match seams carefully; they may not always line up the way you'd expect. This design shows angled sections sewn together to form a skewed checkerboard.

2 Angled sections can be joined by aligning the uppermost points of each section. Vertical diamonds will result when 3 strips of the same width are sewn together, cut at an angle and rejoined with the top points of the sections aligning.

3 Angled sections can be offset to form horizontal diamonds. Sew 3 strips of the same width together, cut at an angle and offset, matching seams. Sew together, matching seams carefully to keep the row of diamonds straight.

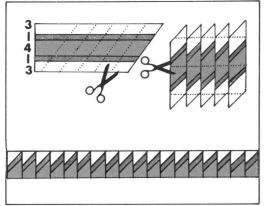

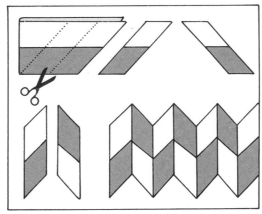

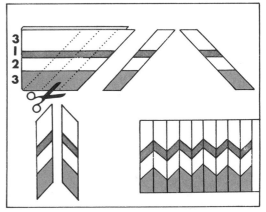

4 To save time, cut an extra-wide middle strip. Cut pieced band in half lengthwise; use each half as a separate band. Sew 5 strips in a ratio of 3:1:4:1:3 together; cut apart at an angle. Sew together with top edges aligning. Cut in half to make 2 separate bands.

1 **Mirror image** Before cutting, fold pieced strip in half, then cut into angled sections. Sections will be facing in opposite directions. Sew together, alternating colours, for a 3-dimensional effect.

2 Complex mirror images are fun to design. Sew 4 strips in a ratio of 3:1:2:3 together. Fold pieced strip in half, then cut angled sections to form mirror image pieces. Sew together as shown to create an effective zigzag pattern.

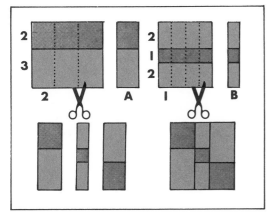

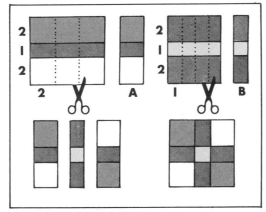

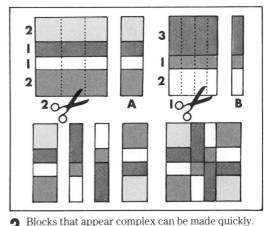

1 **Blocks** You can piece complete blocks with Seminole Patchwork. For A, sew 2 strips in a ratio of 2:3 together and cut apart (width: 2). For B, sew 3 strips in a ratio of 2:1:2 together and cut apart (width: 1). Turn A sections as shown; sew together.

2 For A, sew 3 strips in a ratio of 2:1:2 together and cut apart (width: 2). For B, sew 3 strips in opposite colours together in a ratio of 2:1:2 and cut apart (width: 1). Arrange sections as shown and sew together to create this traditional design.

3 Blocks that appear complex can be made quickly. For A, sew 4 strips in a ratio of 2:1:1:2 together and cut apart (width: 2). For B, sew 3 strips in a ratio of 3:1:2 together and cut apart (width: 1). Alternate A and B sections; sew together.

SHELL PATCHWORK

The Shell pattern existed before patchwork, as we know it today, was even conceived. The shape is seen in the tiles and floor patterns of historic European churches dating back many centuries. The earliest example I have found is in the Loire region of France in the abbey church of Cunault, which was built in the 11th-13th centuries. The floor tiles there are cut in a perfect Shell pattern in lovely shades of ivory and terracotta. The tiles are arranged in alternating horizontal and vertical rows of colour, with an effect that is both dramatic and serene. It is possible that a Shell quilt inspired the builders of Cunault abbey to use the pattern for tiles – but this will never be known.

Some of the earliest Shell quilts are to be found in England. The Victoria and Albert Museum, London, owns a set of bed hangings from the late 18th century. Before it was used in patchwork, the Shell pattern was a quilting motif called Mother of Thousands.

Shell Patchwork is not difficult, but that doesn't mean it isn't time consuming. The entire design is usually worked by hand, and great accuracy is required in assembly. The pattern is built up in overlapping rows which resemble Clamshells or Fishscales – terms by which the work is also known.

The finished project should have a backing; a layer of padding in between the pieced top and backing is optional. If the project is merely backed, you can tie the layers together at regular intervals; *see page 149*. If you are making a proper quilt (with padding), outline-quilt each of the shells to accentuate the design.

MACHINE SEWING

Those proficient in sewing curves can construct Shell Patchwork on a sewing machine.
1. Trace Shell pattern C on *page 96* and make a window template; *see pages 34-35*.
2. Mark the inner and outer lines on the WS of the fabric; cut out the shells along the outer marked lines. You can then assemble the patchwork in rows.
3. Referring to step 5 of *Technique*, pin the first row of shells to a board, folding the seam allowance at each side edge 6mm/¼in to WS.
4. Slipstitch the shells together at the folded side edges. Remove from the board.
5. Review *Sewing Curves on page 59*. For the second row, pin a shell into the first curved space with RS facing; match centre top of shell to slipstitched seam where the first 2 shells meet. Pin in place, easing fabrics carefully to fit.
6. Stitch the seam, remove the pins and press the seam allowance toward the first row. Continue in same manner across second and all subsequent rows until patchwork is complete.
7. Follow step 1 of *Finishing* to trim the top and right side edges. Insert the top patches into the bottom edge by machine. Attach the side pieces by hand, following step 3 of *Finishing*.

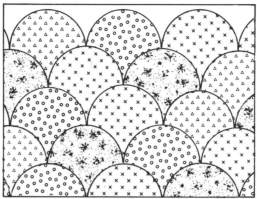

1 Fabric Because Shell Patchwork is an all-over pattern based on a single shape, it is important to select fabrics carefully in order to delineate each shell. Do not choose similar shades or prints, because these will obscure the edges.

2 Highly contrasting fabrics will show Shell Patchwork off to best advantage. You can arrange fabric shells in a random way, or order them into horizontal, vertical or diagonal rows.

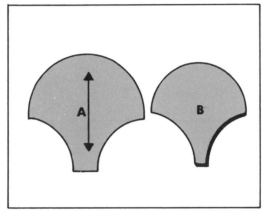

1 Technique Trace shell patterns A and B on *page 96* and make a template for each; *see pages 34-35*. Use pliable cardboard or thin plastic for B. Mark grainline on A. Use A to cut shells from fabric, placing grainline on straight grain of fabric.

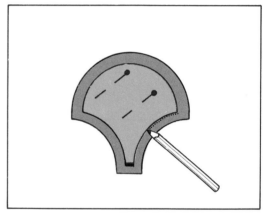

2 Centre template B on RS of fabric shell and pin securely, using 2 pins to prevent template from shifting. Using a pencil or fabric marker, lightly outline lower edges of B on RS of fabric.

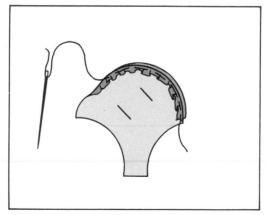

3 Turn shell over and fold convex upper edges to WS following curved edge of template. Make small pleats in fabric to form a smooth edge; do not gather. Baste edges in place without catching the template in your stitching.

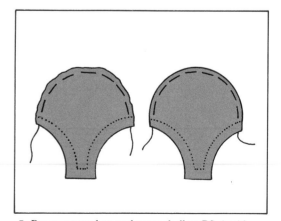

4 Remove template and press shell on RS. Avoid making large pleats which result in uneven, slightly jagged edges as in the shell on the left. Folded edges should be rounded and unwrinkled as in the shell on the right.

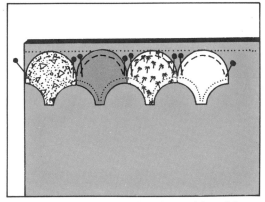

5 Use a large piece of cardboard or cork board for assembling the pieces; draw a straight line parallel to the top of the board to align first row. Pin row of shells to board RS up so that tops match line and side edges of shells meet.

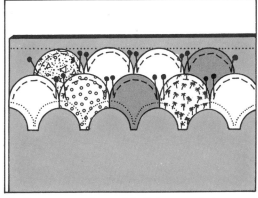

6 Stagger second row of shells in spaces between first row so basted tops overlap first row by 6mm/¼in; pieces will overlap exactly on lower marked outlines of first row. Pin in place. Side edges of shells should meet as they did in first row.

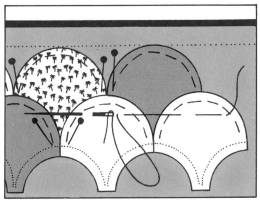

7 Baste rows together securely, removing holding pins from board as you go. Remove basted patchwork from board.

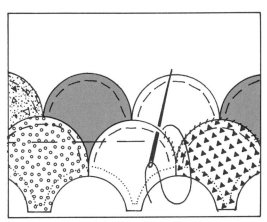

8 Slipstitch basted edges of shells in place, joining the 2 rows. Continue in same manner for additional rows until desired size is reached. Remove all basting along *stitched* edges only. Retain basting along unstitched areas at top and sides.

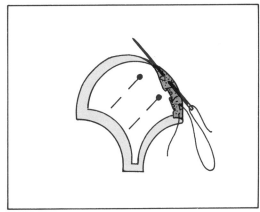

Alternative method Use template B to cut one backing from interfacing or fabric for each A shell. Pin B to WS of A, fold top edges of A over B and baste. Continue as instructed in steps 5-8 of *Technique*. Backings remain in project when it is complete.

Variation Arrange shells as shown to create delightful optical effects. Lap basted edges over marked lines as for traditional Shell Patchwork, then slipstitch securely in place.

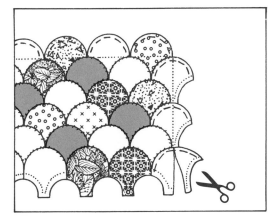

1 **Finishing** Use a ruler and pencil to draw straight lines across top and down right side edge of finished patchwork as shown. Carefully trim away excess fabric beyond lines; retain excess fabric pieces.

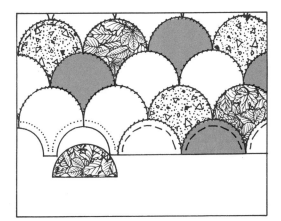

2 Use patches cut from top to fill in spaces along bottom edge, overlapping shells at bottom edge by 6mm/¼in. Slipstitch neatly in place. Remove basting from "filler" patches when bottom row is complete.

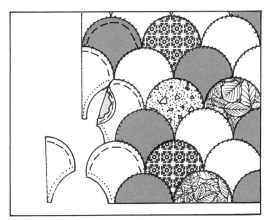

3 Use patches cut from right side to fill in uneven spaces along left side. Lap basted edge of filler patch over marked lines on patchwork; lap basted edge of patchwork over marked lines on filler. Slipstitch in place. Remove basting.

STRING PATCHWORK

Strings are the long, narrow, seemingly unusable pieces of fabric that remain after cutting out a garment. On their own, strings are simply too slender to be of much use in sewing, and many dressmakers discard them. However, sew several strings together and the result is a pieced fabric that can add a new dimension to patchwork quilting.

Because strings are usually not symmetrical, they are joined in a random way, giving the finished project an appearance similar to Crazy Patchwork; *see pages 64-65* . String Patchwork is quicker and easier to construct because it is worked entirely on the sewing machine and there is no need to add embroidery. Because of its spontaneity and the exciting combinations of fabrics and colours that can be achieved, this technique is ideal for teaching children how to sew.

String Patchwork utilizes fabric scraps to create intricate-looking designs that are actually very simple to make. There are two methods of doing this: making string fabric and sewing strings to a base.

String fabric is created by sewing strips of a similar length together to form a piece of material which can then be cut into a variety of usable shapes. String fabric is extremely versatile. You can use it in much the same way as an ordinary piece of uncut material – to cut patchwork and appliqué pieces, or as a background for an appliqué design. Borders, sashing, piping and ruffles can be made from string fabric; random shapes can be cut and resewn to invent original designs. You can also use string fabric to create more controlled designs; simply cut your strings from whole fabrics to a specific length and width and join them in a fixed order, then cut out the required shapes from this pieced fabric.

For more complex designs or patterns that require shaped templates, you can sew strings to a fabric or paper base. A fabric base should be lightweight and compatible in fibre content with the fabrics being applied to it. A paper base should be relatively soft for easy removal after sewing; old newspaper is ideal.

Remnants and scraps from quilting and sewing projects and used clothing should provide an interesting mix of patterns and colours for String Patchwork. Additional fabrics may be needed to add some drama to a colour scheme.

One hundred percent cotton fabric is recommended as it will hold creases well when pressed, although woollen fabrics can make dramatic String Patchwork designs too. Wash all fabrics before use. Place strings in a mesh bag to prevent fraying during washing. Carefully iron each piece, trimming off the frayed edges. Sort into groups by colour, then divide these colour groups into prints and solids. Arranging the fabrics in advance will show at a glance the available colours and prints as you sew.

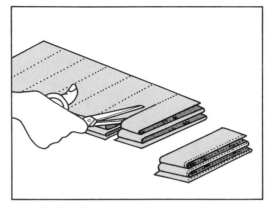

Cutting strings from whole fabric Carefully fold a length of fabric into several even layers. Use a pencil and ruler to mark a variety of even widths on the top layer. Cut through all layers on marked lines using scissors or a rotary cutter. Unfold and press.

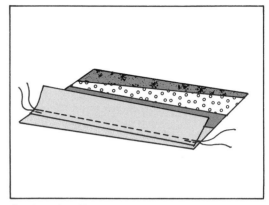

Rotating strings You can sew strings together at an angle to enliven a design. Adjust the position of a strip by moving the edges up or down; check the effect by folding to the RS. Sew in place when satisfied with the result.

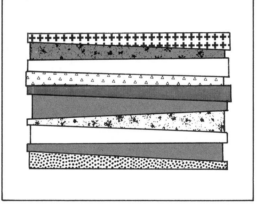

1 String fabric Select strings of a similar length; sew together with right sides facing, rotating fabrics to form interesting angles. Splendid visual effects can be achieved by sewing contrasting fabrics together. Press seam allowances to one side.

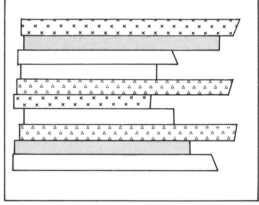

2 Wastage of fabric results when different lengths of string are sewn together as shown here. To make the best use of your fabric, prepare several pieces, each a different width. Note how uninspiring straight strings and repetitive fabrics look.

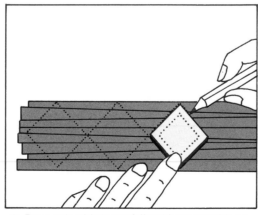

3 Press string fabric carefully without stretching it, then mark patchwork templates lightly on RS. The position of each template will dictate the angle of the strings. To assure accuracy, mark and cut only one layer of string fabric at a time.

4 Patchwork pieces cut from string fabric can be joined to produce a multitude of effects; rearrange pieces to find best composition. Part of the charm of String Patchwork is the random effect when pieces are combined; make no effort to match seams.

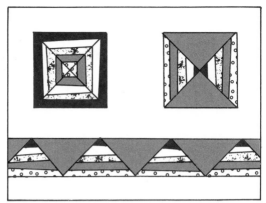

5 Secondary designs can be fashioned from leftover pieces of string fabric such as these triangles which remained after cutting the squares in step 3. Combine string pieces with ordinary fabrics to form blocks and borders.

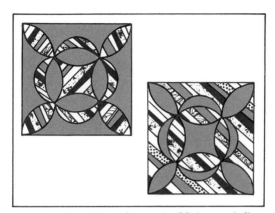

6 Cut appliqué pieces from string fabric to revitalize traditional patterns such as The Reel, shown here. Alternatively, position appliqués on a background of string fabric to produce an exciting composition.

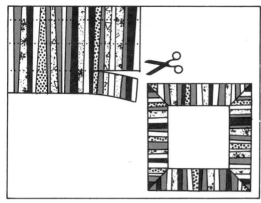

7 To make string borders, sashing, ruffles or piping, prepare a large piece of string fabric. Mark and cut the fabric into even strips of the required length and width, then proceed as if using ordinary fabric.

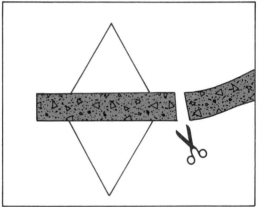

1 **Strings on a base** Cut a base from fabric or paper; mark seam allowance on WS. Centre first string RS up on RS of base. To avoid wastage, position each string so that excess extends from one side of base only; trim away excess string near base.

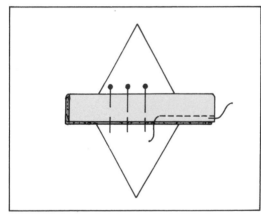

2 Position second string over first, RS facing; rotate second string if desired, then pin to secure both strings to base. Stitch strings together so that raw edges of both strings are well within the seam allowance.

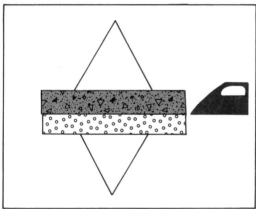

3 Fold second string to RS and press carefully. Turn template so that raw edge of first string is at the bottom.

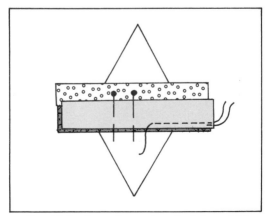

4 Sew third string to first as described above; fold to RS and press. Continue adding strings to base in this manner until the entire base is covered. Press carefully on each side.

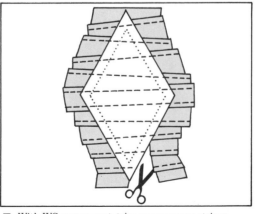

5 With WS uppermost, trim away excess strings, even with edge of base. Note marked seam allowance and stitching lines on base. Gently remove paper base, if using.

6 Use string-covered pieces together or in conjunction with ordinary fabric to create a variety of patterns. Note how the placement of strings on the same base can produce entirely different results in a finished design.

STRIP PIECING

The term Strip Piecing means different things to different quilters. In this book, it refers to a technique that simplifies an image into strips, which are then used to produce an abstract or pictorial design in fabric. Strip Piecing is usually worked on a sewing machine and requires little technical expertise other than the ability to sew a straight line. It can also be called free-form patchwork: templates are rarely if ever used, and the image is built up by adding rows of fabrics, changing them and substituting new ones rather than sticking to a rigid design drawn on graph paper. This is the method to try if you wish to evaluate your artistic capabilities; you may find that you prefer the freedom of this process to more conventional forms of patchwork.

Any image or picture can be translated into Strip Piecing, but it must be kept simple. Natural images such as landscapes and seascapes, flowers, animals, even city skylines will reproduce well in strips. Geometric designs may appear easier, but here your sense of colour and contrast will be tested. Whatever you choose to depict, keep the following hints in mind.

You will need a large variety of fabrics – solids, prints or a mixture of the two. Use prints sparingly, however, unless you want your strips to blend together; prints should enhance the visual excitement of a Strip Pieced design rather than overwhelm it. For subtle colour variations, combine fabrics of different weights and textures in one project – cotton, silk, velvet, corduroy, lamé and satin, for example. The same colour will look quite different in assorted fibres and weaves. Some quilt artists are hand-dyeing fabrics to create subtle gradations.

When you divide your drawing into rows, make each row a different width; using the same width through a whole piece will result in a static design. Pin your strips to a wall or arrange them on the floor and step back to study the strip widths and colour relationships. Use a reducing glass to make the strips appear as if they are already sewn together. Refrain from actually sewing until you are satisfied with your arrangement. Critically view your design. Do any colours seem wrong, either too vivid or too bland? If so, discard them and substitute more appropriate colours or prints. Are any sections very dull? Then add an unusual strip of fabric to make that area come alive. To create the illusion of depth, cut narrow strips for the areas you wish to recede, choosing fabrics with tiny prints or misty, greyed tones. Select wide strips and bold colours to advance other parts of the design.

Utilize quilting to delineate features such as mountain crevasses, veins on flowers, ocean waves or animal fur. Add a sense of movement to a geometric piece by quilting curved lines over a straight composition or straight lines across a circular one. Quilt receding areas in the same direction and leave other areas unquilted so they will advance.

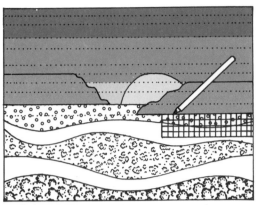

1 Technique Draw a simple picture on paper that is one quarter to one half the desired finished size of your piece. Rule lines of various widths across the drawing. When satisfied with your pattern, enlarge it to full size to use as a guide for cutting strip lengths.

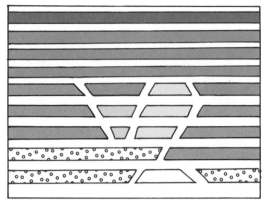

2 Cut strips from fabric to match your pattern; be sure to add 6mm/¼in seam allowance to each edge. Pin strips to a wall or arrange on floor following pattern as a basic guide. Study the fabrics and substitute new pieces to achieve best composition.

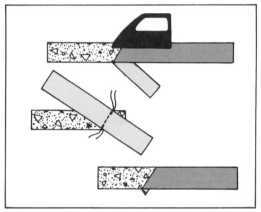

3 To join angled edges, place strip that is meant to advance visually over adjacent strip, folding at required angle. Press angle, then open top strip as shown; stitch along crease, backstitching at each end to secure. Trim off excess fabric and press.

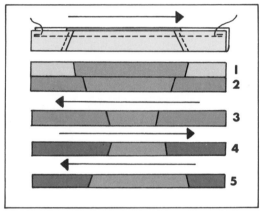

4 To join rows, stitch pieced strips together with RS facing and raw edges even, making a 6mm/¼in seam. To prevent strips from curving, stitch each row in direction opposite preceding one: stitch first row from left to right, second from right to left and so on.

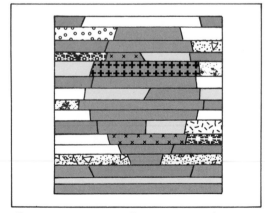

Abstract images are an excellent way to appraise your sense of colour and contrast. Do not be afraid to experiment with bold images, odd textures and unorthodox colour combinations. Insert an unexpected strip of fabric to catch the viewer's eye.

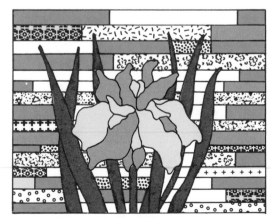

Appliqués To simplify your work and add texture, appliqué intricate shapes onto a Strip Pieced background. Lightly stuff appliqués for a 3-dimensional effect. Add details in embroidery.

Yo-Yo

Frivolous, fragile and feather-light, Yo-Yo quilts provide a welcome distraction from the more serious business of accurate piecing and careful stitching. Also called Suffolk Puffs, Rosettes and Bon-Bons, Yo-Yos are quick to prepare and assemble: they are perfect for quilters with plenty of scraps and not much time. With no padding or backing, Yo-Yo projects do not afford much warmth, nor can they really be considered proper quilts, but over the years they have found their own niche in the quilting world, and are mostly made into summerweight coverlets, shawls and wall hangings.

The technique is simple enough for a child to try, and would be an ideal way to introduce someone to patchwork. Circles of fabric are gathered and pressed into little "wheels" which are then slipstitched together. Trace one of the circle patterns on *page 93* or use a compass or any circular item you may have at home for a template – cups, glasses and other round containers are suitable. The circles should be at least 6.4cm/2½in in diameter because the finished Yo-Yo will be one-half the size of the original circle. For a uniform appearance, all Yo-Yos in one project should be the same circumference, although a project can be made from a mixture of different-sized Yo-Yos if they are all appliquéd to a backing.

All fabrics in one project should be of a similar weight and fibre content, but that's where the rules end. Experiment with all types of prints for unusual results – stripes, plaids and large-scale prints are particularly effective as Yo-Yos.

Because finished Yo-Yos are circular, not every edge is stitched, so that open spaces are formed between the pieces. For shawls and wall hangings, these spaces create an airy feeling, but if you wish to make a more durable and warm coverlet, sew the Yo-Yos to a base such as a blanket or sheet. Choose a backing fabric that is compatible in fibre content with the Yo-Yos.

By nature Yo-Yos are 3-dimensional. This feeling can be enhanced by making two Yo-Yos in different fabrics and sizes and sewing the smaller one over the bigger one.

Yo-Yos can be used as appliqués to simulate many circular shapes such as flowers, candy or popcorn. Use embroidery to emphasize a floral feeling; antique Yo-Yo quilts were often embroidered with a variety of stitches, almost in a Crazy quilt style. Work your stitches in contrasting threads over the gathered middle of the Yo-Yo or work French knots or straight stitches over the whole piece.

Padding can be added to Yo-Yos. Cut a circle of padding to one-half the size of the original circle. After sewing the edges of the circle, but before gathering, place the padding in the middle and gather fabric edges over it. Add a small circle of contrasting fabric over the padding before drawing the circle closed; or work embroidery stitches over the opening.

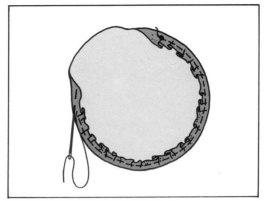

1 Technique Cut a circle of fabric double the desired size of the Yo-Yo. Fold the edges 6mm/¼in to the WS. Knot a length of sturdy thread and work short, even running stitches all around the circle, securing the folded edges.

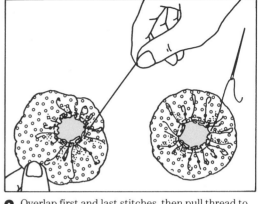

2 Overlap first and last stitches, then pull thread to gather the fabric tightly. Secure end of thread with several backstitches or a knot; clip away excess thread.

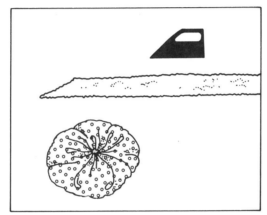

3 Flatten fabric circle so that gathered edges are centred on one side. Steam-press gently beneath a damp towel. Sort Yo-Yos by colour; store in marked bags until use.

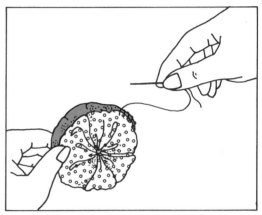

1 Joining Place 2 Yo-Yos together with smooth sides facing. Work 4-5 whipstitches to join, catching only the folds of each piece. Secure end of thread with several backstitches or a knot; clip away excess thread.

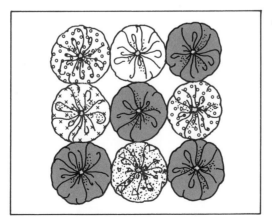

2 Join Yo-Yos in rows to create desired size project. For extra warmth and strength, appliqué the Yo-Yos to a backing such as a large blanket or sheet in a harmonizing colour.

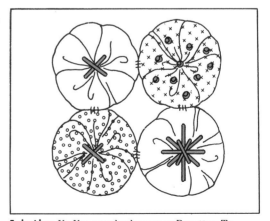

Embroidery Yo-Yos are also known as Rosettes. To create a "flowery" appearance, embroider cross stitches, French knots or star stitches over the gathered middle on the RS of each Yo-Yo. Use bright contrasting embroidery thread.

SPECIAL EFFECTS WITH FABRIC

After you have mastered the traditional forms of patchwork covered in this chapter, you may wish to experiment with what you have learned. One way is to modify conventional piecing methods by the manipulation of fabrics. This section will introduce you to some easy ways to add texture and 3-dimensionality to your patchwork.

The ideas on these two pages are meant to spark off creativity and introduce you to a different approach to patchwork than you may have originally intended when you started learning this craft. Be open to experimentation. If another method occurs to you, try it – that's how all these procedures came into being in the first place. The instructions that follow are very general and are intended more to suggest ideas than to give precise step-by-step instructions. Though many of the techniques are easy, basic knowledge of sewing and quilting is required.

As your interest in patchwork grows, you'll find yourself becoming a collector of fabrics. It's inevitable and healthy, so don't fight it; just make space for your new additions! When you find a fabric that you can't live without, buy half to one metre/yard of the material. If you buy too much you'll get bored with the fabric because it will appear in too many of your projects. If you buy too little, you may find that you don't have enough for some special commission. Buying in small quantities gives you the ability to be freer in your use of colours and textures because you'll have so many more fabrics to choose from when you are designing. Do not limit your choices to cottons – look through the rest of the fabric shop and select pieces that appeal to you because of either their colour or composition.

Try each procedure with assorted weights and textures of material; the same technique will look quite different if made in cotton or satin, wool or silk. When you are experimenting with special effects, the chances are that you will be combining dissimilar fibres. This is fine as long as you don't intend to machine-wash the piece. Hand-washing or dry cleaning is recommended.

Just because you are experimenting doesn't mean that your standard of work should suffer. Take as much care with measuring, cutting, stitching and pressing as you would if you were piecing a complicated block.

Try all the techniques here and make up some of your own, then combine your experiments to make an unusual wall hanging or quilt; you can later refer back to this piece for guidance and inspiration. To best accomplish this, make each of your test blocks 20.3cm/8in square so that they can be joined easily when you've finished. For tucks, gathers and waffles, each individual piece of fabric should be larger than the desired finished size. To judge how much material you will need make a test piece: measure a small square of fabric and try the technique; measure the fabric again to see how much has been taken up in the pleating or gathering.

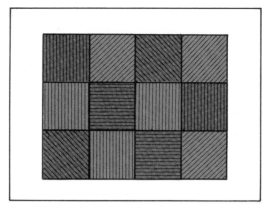

Nap Fabrics such as corduroy, velour and velvet have nap – a raised surface finish that lies in one direction. Turn napped fabrics in different directions to create a series of light and dark effects. This will also work with fabrics that have an obvious grain.

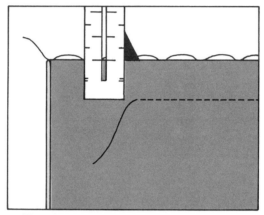

2 To make wide tucks, work line of basting on straight grain. Fold fabric WS facing so that basting lies on fold. Measure desired width of tuck with adjustable marker; indicate line with chalk, then stitch through both layers on line. Remove basting.

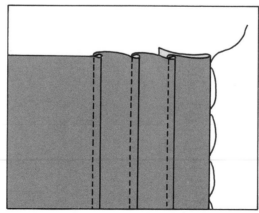

4 To make pin tucks, mark the centre of the first tuck as in step 2. Fold fabric WS facing so that your basting stitches lie on the fold. Press. Stitch 3-6mm/⅛-¼in from fold; remove basting. Make subsequent pin tucks as directed in step 3.

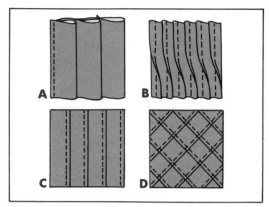

1 **Tucks** For texture, stitch parallel folds into your fabric before using it in patchwork. Wide tucks can be pressed in same direction (A) or twisted (B). Pin tucks can be stitched diagonally or vertically (C) or sewn in 2 directions for a checkerboard effect (D).

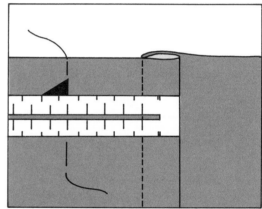

3 Press tuck to one side. Use marker to indicate centre of next tuck at desired distance from first one; tucks may overlap or lie some distance from one another. Baste line; fold on basting and stitch as for first tuck. Repeat for subsequent tucks.

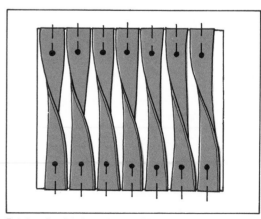

Twisting Cut fabric strips 5.1-7.6cm/2-3in wide and same length as base; stitch long edges together. Turn to RS; press with seam at one edge. Pin top of first strip to base 6mm/¼in from side edge. Twist strip; pin bottom edge to base. Repeat until base is covered.

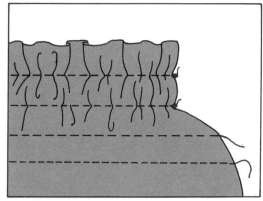

1 Gathers Mark parallel lines on fabric about 13-19mm/½-¾in apart. Baste along each line with matching thread. Gently pull basting threads to gather fabric to desired degree; knot thread ends. Baste gathered fabric to a fabric base for stability.

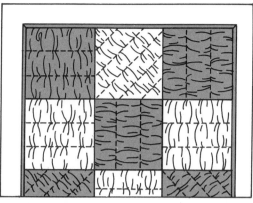

2 Sew gathered fabric squares together, turning the squares in different directions for a textured effect. Gathers can also be worked diagonally across a square as shown.

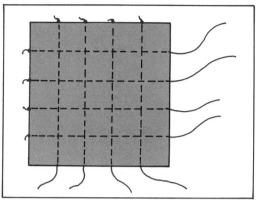

1 Waffles Mark parallel horizontal and vertical lines on fabric approximately 13-19mm/½-¾in apart. Baste along each line with matching thread. For each row of stitching, knot thread at one edge and leave long thread-end at the opposite edge.

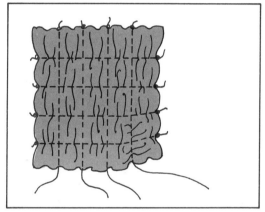

2 Gently pull basting threads sewn in one direction to gather fabric evenly; knot thread-ends to secure. Pull threads sewn in the other direction, balancing gathers evenly across the fabric. Baste waffled fabric to a fabric base for added stability.

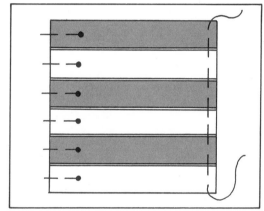

1 Weaving Cut fabric strips on straight grain about 5-7.6cm/2-3in wide and length of base. With WS facing, stitch long edges together. Turn to RS press with seam centred on one side. Pin and baste strips to base with seam facing base; alternate colours.

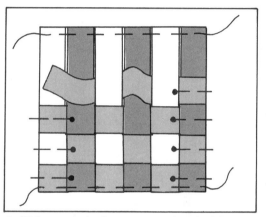

2 With seam facing base, weave strips of a different colour over and under strips on base as shown. Pin, then baste edges of new strips to base. Use woven block in same way as a standard patchwork block.

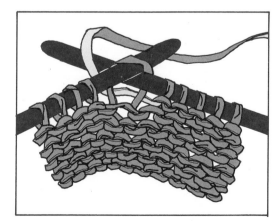

1 Knitting Cut many fabric strips 6mm/¼in wide from selvage to selvage: knot strip ends together to make long length of "yarn". Knit fabric "yarn" as for normal knitting, keeping all knots on WS. Test needle sizes to find one you are most comfortable using.

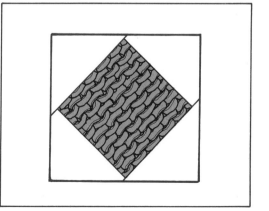

2 With RS facing, stitch plain fabric in matching or contrasting colour to edges of knitted piece to form a square block; steam-press gently. Use as standard patchwork block. Fabrics can also be crocheted, then used as insertions in blocks.

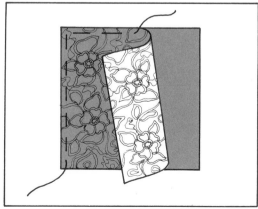

Lace Add dimension and texture to a plain or sheer fabric by sewing lace on top, then using the piece as a standard patchwork block. Cut lace to same size as foundation; baste lace smoothly on foundation base close to the edges.

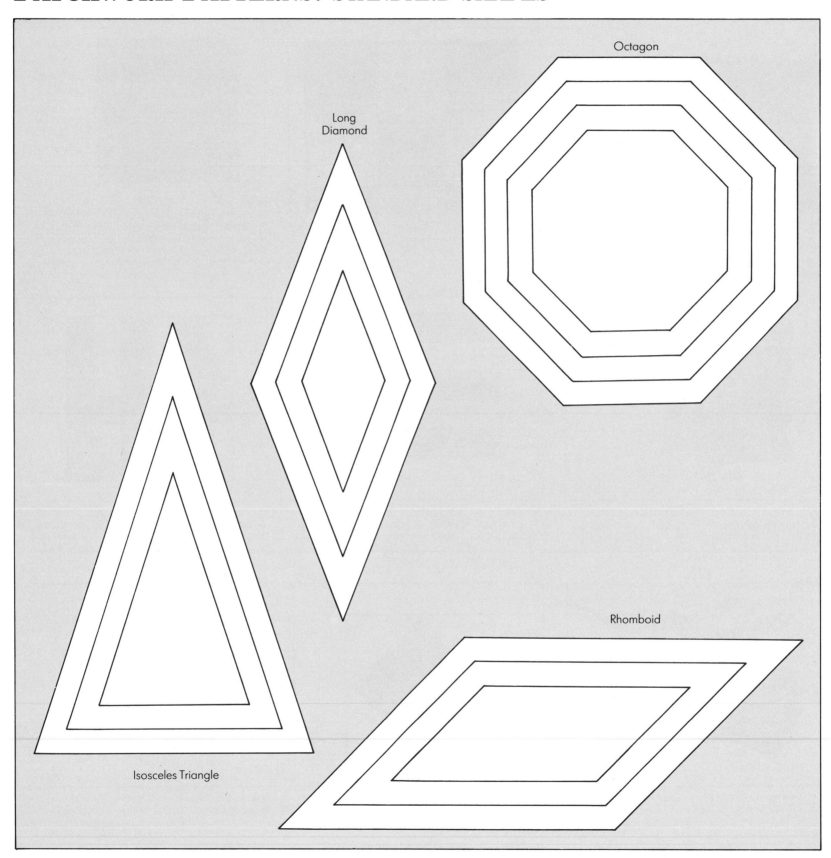

Octagon

Long Diamond

Rhomboid

Isosceles Triangle

STANDARD SHAPES

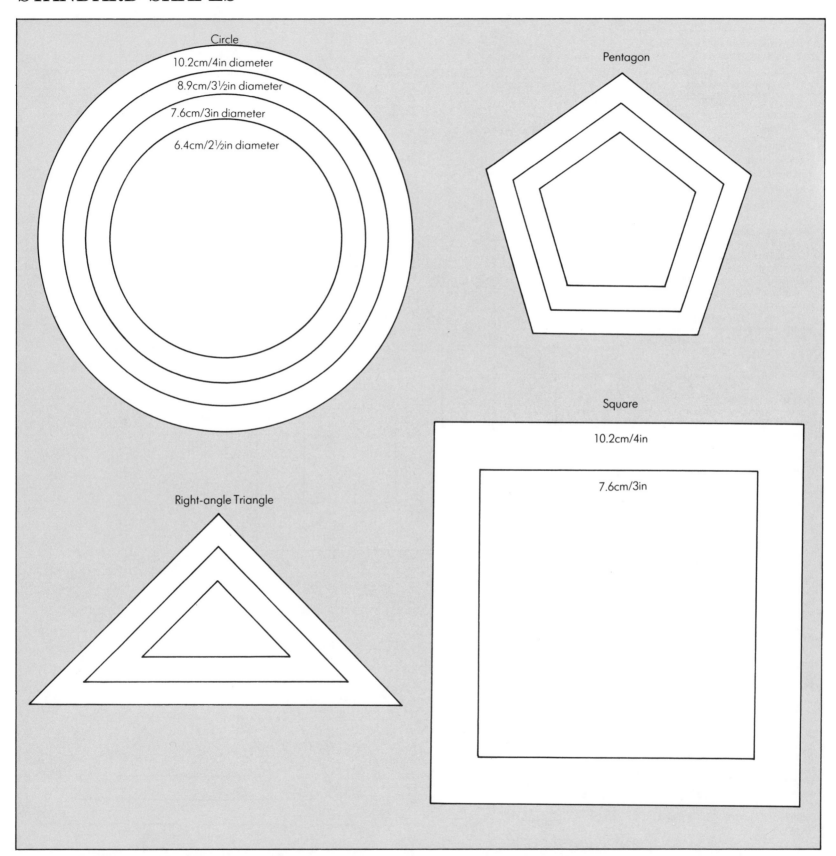

Circle

10.2cm/4in diameter

8.9cm/3½in diameter

7.6cm/3in diameter

6.4cm/2½in diameter

Pentagon

Square

10.2cm/4in

7.6cm/3in

Right-angle Triangle

LOG CABIN

All measurements include 6mm/¼in seam allowances

Base Sizes for Standard Log Cabin

Centre square	Base (square)
3.8cm/1½in	24.2cm/9½in
6.4cm/2½in	26.7cm/10½in
8.9cm/3½in	29.2cm/11½in
11.4cm/4½in	31.8cm/12½in

Cut all strips 3.8cm/1½in wide

Off-Centre Log Cabin
Centre: 3.8cm/1½in square
Base: 22.9cm/9in square
Dark strips: 2.5cm/1in wide
Light strips: 3.8cm/1½in wide
   Measure 7cm/2¾in in from lower left corner of base and mark dot. Draw diagonal line across base as shown. Place lower left corner of centre square on dot, aligning upper right corner on diagonal line. Add dark strips to lower edges of centre square and light strips to upper edges.

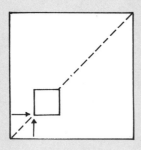

Hung Centre Log Cabin
Centre: 6.4cm/2½in square
Base: 24.2cm/9½in square
Strips: 3.8cm/1½in wide
   Draw horizontal and vertical lines on base to indicate centre. Place centre square on base, aligning corners with drawn lines. Add strips to each edge until base is covered. Trim away excess strips extending beyond edge of base.

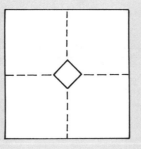

Triangle Log Cabin
Centre: equilateral triangle
Base: 21.6-26.7cm/8½-10½in square
Strips: 3.8cm/1½in wide
   Draw diagonal lines on base to indicate centre. Place equilateral triangle on base, matching dot on triangle to centre of base. Add strips to each edge until triangle is desired size. Trim base to match edge of pieced triangle.

Diamond Log Cabin
Centre: short or long diamond (*see page 92*)
Base: 24.2-29.2cm/9-11in square
Strips: 3.8cm/1in wide
   Draw diagonal lines on base to indicate centre. Place diamond on base, matching dot on diamond to centre of base and corners to diagonal lines. Add strips to each edge until diamond is desired size. Trim base to match edge of pieced diamond.

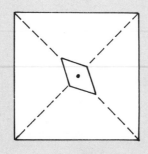

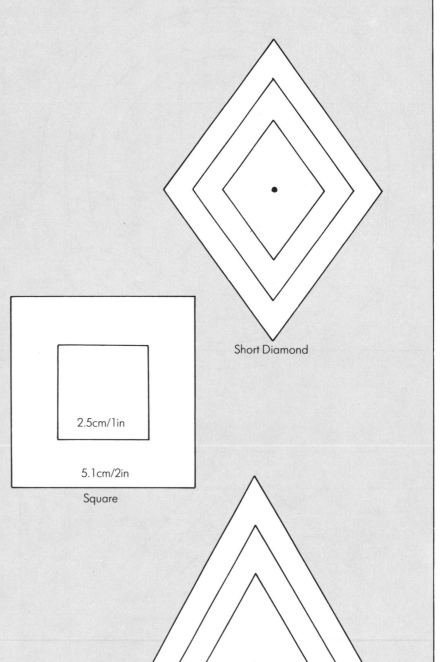

Short Diamond

2.5cm/1in

5.1cm/2in

Square

Equilateral Triangle

PINEAPPLE

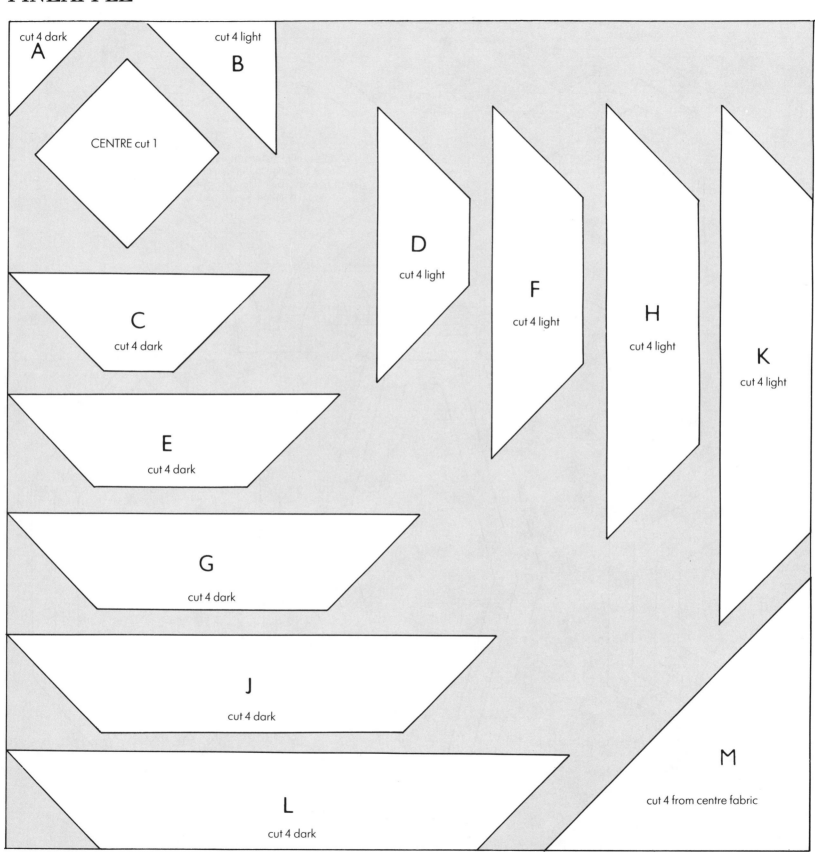

cut 4 dark

A

cut 4 light

B

CENTRE cut 1

C
cut 4 dark

E
cut 4 dark

G
cut 4 dark

J
cut 4 dark

L
cut 4 dark

D
cut 4 light

F
cut 4 light

H
cut 4 light

K
cut 4 light

M
cut 4 from centre fabric

SHELL AND HEXAGON SHAPES

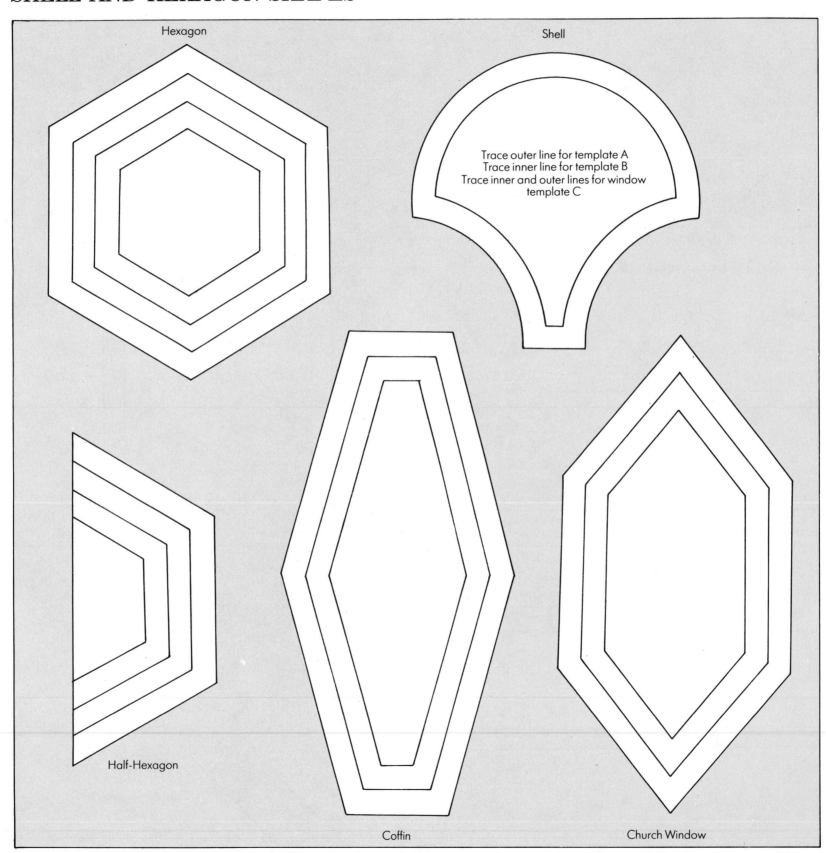

Hexagon

Shell

Trace outer line for template A
Trace inner line for template B
Trace inner and outer lines for window
template C

Half-Hexagon

Coffin

Church Window

DOUBLE WEDDING RING

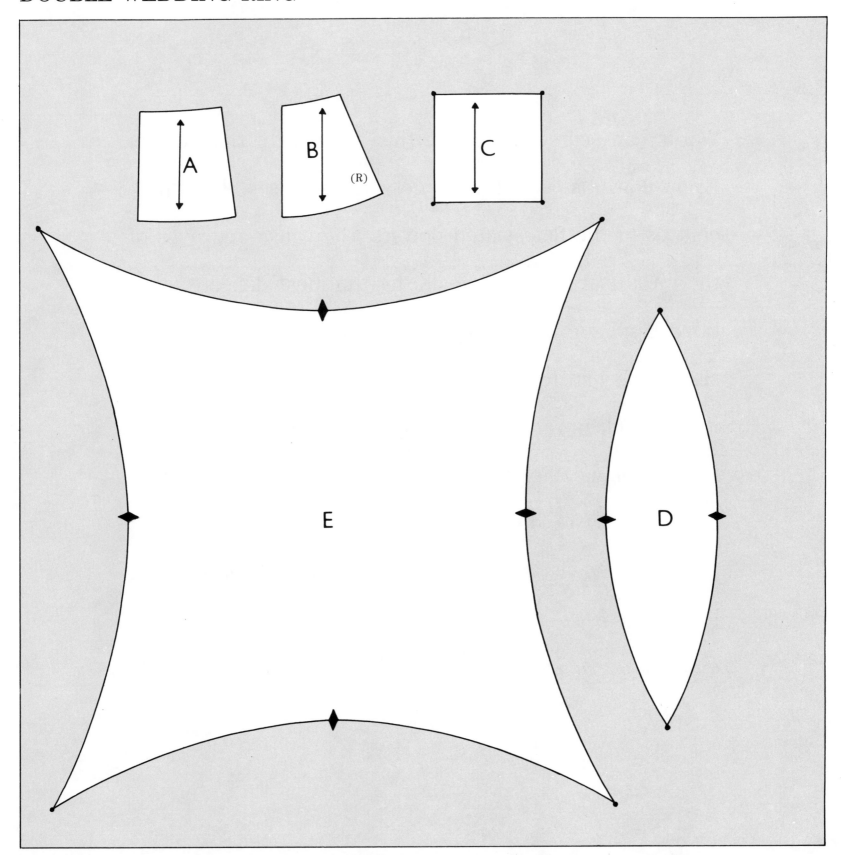

Words can scarcely describe this triumph of the needle. Every flower is perfect... The detail of the roses, the double centres of the flat-pleated flowers, the wings and eyes of the birds... are all produced... by the most delicate additional appliqué. The stems of the bell-like flowers are as slender as a string. The whole is so accurate and true that it looks... like a very complicated but successful stencil. It is the sort of accomplishment one does not visualize short of beholding... Not one woman in a thousand, could have accomplished, let alone conceived, anything approaching its beauty. *Ruth E Finley's description of an appliqué quilt made in 1857 by Arsinoe Kelsey Bowen.*

3

THE ART OF APPLIQUÉ

THE ART OF APPLIQUÉ

Appliqué is the method of securing one piece of fabric on top of another, either for functional or decorative purposes. In decorative appliqué, the components of a design are cut from a variety of fabrics, then the fabric edges are turned under and sewn to a background with invisible slipstitches or visible embroidery stitches. Appliqué has served many different purposes: from repairing worn clothing to decorating banners for use in battles. It has been practised for centuries by people from all over the world who have generated many distinctive forms. The diversity of appliqué is obvious when one compares intricate Persian examples covered with delicate bird and flower motifs to the bold and charming folk art quilts found in America. Appliqué from different parts of the world can also be startlingly similar, as evidenced by the Reverse Appliqué work of the Hmong in Indochina and the Kuna Indians in Panama.

Although appliqué work can be utilitarian, it has evolved into the method quilters use to flaunt their expertise with a needle. Yet depending upon the design, anyone can appliqué—from a young child sewing a flower onto a piece of fabric to an experienced needlewoman embellishing a wall hanging with delicate Inlay Appliqué. The basic methods are the same. What makes each appliqué project special is the flair, creativity and choice of techniques and materials used to create it.

HISTORY

Applied work is one of the oldest forms of needle art. Thousands of years ago it was being done in Eygpt to decorate funeral tents. The Boulak Museum in Cairo has what is probably the earliest surviving example: a ceremonial appliqué canopy from *c.*980 BC worked on gazelle hide.[10] During medieval times, appliqué flourished throughout Europe on household furnishings, banners, and military and ecclesiastical clothing.

Hanging tapestries decorated with appliqué played a significant part in the ornamentation of palaces, castles and houses during the Tudor period in Britain. They were hung on walls both for decoration and warmth, and in archways as screens between rooms. Appliqué hangings were also draped around beds to keep out the dank night air.[11] Some early British appliqué work was done in the 16th century by Elizabeth, Dowager Countess of Shrewsberry, known as Bess of Hardwick. The panelled hangings can be seen today in Hardwick Hall in Derbyshire. Mary Queen of Scots worked on several appliqué hangings and cushions while a prisoner in Hardwick Hall.

APPLIQUÉ IN AMERICA

It wasn't until after 1750 that appliqué began to be used on quilts in America. However, after that it became more and more popular, peaking in the mid-19th century.[12] Applied work became popular as the developing country became more established and women had more time to lavish on their quilts.

A popular manifestation of appliqué work in America was the album quilt. The blocks comprising each quilt were different and often carried the signature of the maker. Friendship, presentation and freedom quilts are the most well known, but mourning quilts, patriotic and political quilts as well as Bible quilts were also being made. However, it is undoubtedly the remarkable Baltimore album quilts that display appliqué work at its finest. Wreaths, garlands, birds, baskets and bouquets of flowers and fruit, and even public buildings and monuments were expertly rendered by the women living in the Baltimore area in the mid-19th century. Many of the patterns found on these quilts are now regarded as the quintessential appliqué designs; some are featured on the following pages.

An appliqué bedspread was often considered a "best quilt". It was not uncommon for someone to be working on two quilts at the same time—an easily executed one for everyday use which could be worked on even in poor light, and one masterpiece which could only be done in leisure moments when the light was good.[13] A great many antique appliqué quilts can be seen in museums and private collections. That so many examples have survived is not surprising. A woman who spent years designing and stitching a work of art was not likely to allow her achievement to be used as an everyday quilt. Consequently these quilts were reserved for display, for special occasions or for guests.[14] Because these quilts were only taken out from time to time to be stroked, loved and admired, they have been well preserved. These appliqué masterpieces are the work of truely talented artists who would probably have achieved great fame had they been able to turn their hands to more accepted art forms than quilts. Well-known quilt author Carter Houck expresses the concept of quilts as art:

> It is interesting to consider a quilt as an object of art, viewing the materials, the techniques, and the driving force behind the artist. A quilt is not something that one dreams up on a Saturday morning and completes by Sunday night, as one might a small painting or a simple piece of pottery. In terms of hours expended it is more on the order of creating a marble statue or painting a fresco.[15]

APPLIQUÉ MOTIFS

Flowers are by far the most common appliqué shapes, both in Britain and America. The rose is a frequently used flower, with the Rose of Sharon design repeatedly appliquéd on bride's quilts. Leaves are also popular. Pictorial designs from apples to zebras have been rendered in appliqué. The eagle has always been a great favourite in America, particularly during war times and periods of great patriotism such as the American Centennial. Human figures such as the Sunbonnet Children became popular during the early part of the 20th century. Today, the designs on appliqué quilts run the gamut from copies of traditional patterns to breathtaking abstract innovations.

Patchwork and appliqué have always been successfully combined in quiltmaking. Early appliqué medallion quilts consisted of a central printed motif surrounded by borders of patchwork. It was common for designs such as stars or fans to be pieced and then applied to a background fabric. There are also combination patterns constructed from both needle arts, although they are usually classified as patchwork. Pieced Basket and Maple Leaf on *page 50* are two examples.

Appliqué quilts are less rigid than patchwork, both in design and execution.[16] Patterns can be drawn freehand or shapes can be cut using templates. Unlike patchwork, appliqué does not require that scraps be fitted together jigsaw-fashion, which means that there is much greater freedom in the design stage and while a piece is being made.

PATTERNS AND FABRICS

Appliqué patterns can be found everywhere, in books and magazines as well as in nature. Carry your camera with you to record flowers, animals and scenes that can be recreated in fabric. Children's colouring books are an excellent source of simple appliqué patterns. Also, study printed fabrics for ideas for the *Broderie Perse* style of appliqué.

Beginners should select a design with straight lines or gradual curves and a relatively small number of large or medium-sized pieces. As you become adept at turning the edges under smoothly and sewing them invisibly to a background, you can graduate to more complex shapes and designs. It is important that you meticulously preserve the shape of appliqué pieces. Clip curves and points where necessary so as to turn the edges under smoothly and maintain crisp corners.

For hand appliqué, choose your fabrics carefully. Beginners should use 100% cotton fabrics which hold a crisp edge and are not inclined to fray. Select light to medium-weight fabrics. You can choose just about any type of fabric for machine appliqué, but avoid material that frays too much as this will make your work look messy. Felt is a wonderful fabric for appliqué. Because it is non-woven it will not ravel so you never need to turn under the edges. Do not limit yourself to fabrics when creating appliqué designs. Incorporate other textures by using feathers, leather, stones or shells, lace and various types of yarns and threads.

APPLIQUÉ DESIGNS: WREATHS, FEATHERS AND FRUIT

Wreath of Roses

Wreath of Pansies

Presidential Wreath

Floral Wreath

Princess Feather

Feather Crown with Ragged Robin Interior

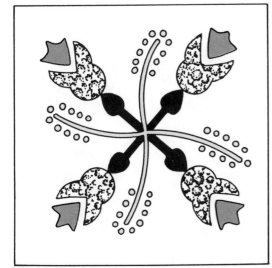

Currants and Coxcomb

Flower and Grapes

Pomegranate

FLOWERS

Flowers

Lotus Bud

Peony

Meadow Daisy

Water Lily

Bouquet of Garden Flowers

Carnations

Windblown Tulips

Tulips and Ribbons

ROSES

Original Rose

Whig Rose

Conventional Wild Rose

English Rose

Indiana Rose

Rose Tree

Rose of Sharon

Rose of Sharon

Rose of Sharon

LEAVES

Leaves

Bay Leaf

Foliage Wreath

Mountain Laurel

Heart of Leaves

Pride of the Forest

Hickory Leaf

Oak Leaf and Cherries

Oak Leaf and Reel

REPRESENTATIONAL DESIGNS

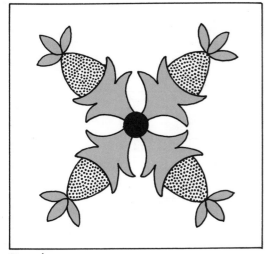

Pineapple

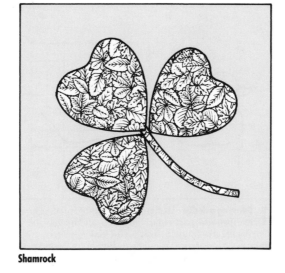

Shamrock

Sunbonnet Sue

The Lobster

Dresden Plate

Hearts

Birds and Flowers

Turkey Tracks

Eagle

PREPARATION FOR BASIC APPLIQUÉ

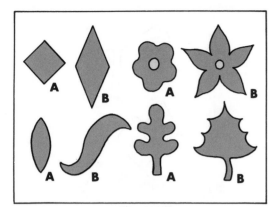

Designs Before selecting an appliqué design, study it carefully. Straight edges, wide corners and gentle curves are easy to appliqué (A). Appliqués with sharp points, deep curves, pointed "valleys" (between flower petals) and intricate edges are difficult. (B).

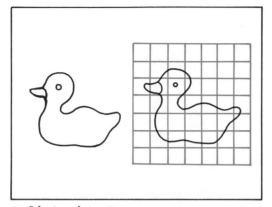

1 **Enlarging a design** Designs for appliqué can be found everywhere, particularly in books and magazines. Once you have found a design, you may need to enlarge or reduce it. Trace the design, then draw a grid of squares over it in another colour.

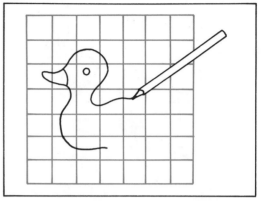

2 On a separate sheet of paper, accurately mark same number of squares to desired size enlargement or reduction. Hold original drawing next to new grid and draw lines of design to correspond with larger or smaller size squares.

1 **Appliqué quilts** Appliqué quilts can be made in a variety of styles. To make a block-style quilt, appliqué a design to a block of any size or shape, then repeat the block across a quilt. Divide blocks with sashing. Add a border which echoes one of appliqués.

2 Medallion-style appliqué quilts are very impressive. Select a bold design for the centre, then surround it with one or more borders to create a balanced arrangement that relates well to the central area.

3 A more spontaneous style of appliqué quilt is an off-centre arrangement. It is best to design this type of quilt using the actual shapes and fabrics, adding or removing pieces until the composition is satisfactory.

Appliquéd clothing Appliqués have many functions, from embellishing a woman's jacket to repairing a torn area on a child's trousers. Cut appliqués from fabrics compatible in fibre content with clothing to which they will be applied.

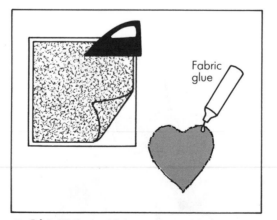

1 **Fabric** While any fabrics can be used for appliqué, a light- to medium-weight 100% cotton is the easiest to work with. Stabilize flimsy or stretchy fabrics with lightweight iron-on interfacing. Add a tiny drop of fabric glue to prevent edges from ravelling.

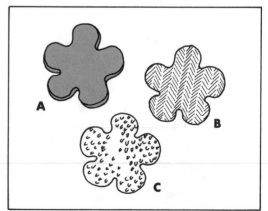

2 Felt (A), closely-woven wool (B), or leather (C) will add interesting textures to appliqué work and will not ravel. Whenever luxury fabrics or unusual fibre combinations are used, it is best to dry-clean the finished item.

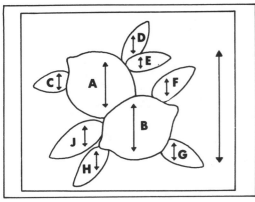

1 **Basic procedure** Decide on a design, enlarge or reduce it to the correct size and draw a full-size pattern. Label pattern pieces by letter; indicate correct direction of grain on each shape so that the grain matches on base and appliqué.

2 Where shapes overlap, allow extra fabric so that foreground pieces can be lapped over background pieces. Draw these areas on your pattern with dotted lines. Make template by tracing complete shape; *see pages 34-35*. Do not include seam allowance.

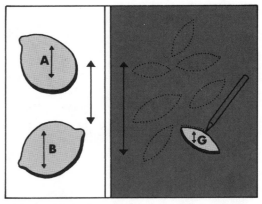

3 Select fabrics for appliqué pieces. Use templates to mark outlines on RS of fabric, adding 6mm/¼ in seam allowances for hand appliqué, none for machine appliqué. Align grain of templates with grain of base so pieces will lie flat without puckering.

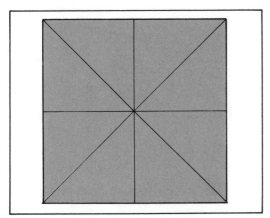

4 Cut fabric for the base 2.5cm/1in larger than desired size to allow for the take-up that will occur when appliqués are sewn in place. Press the base diagonally, horizontally and vertically to indicate the centre and make placement of the pieces easier.

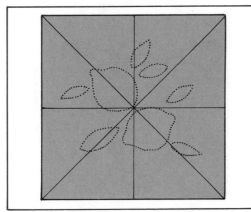

5 If desired, draw placement lines for appliqués on RS of base. Do not mark exact outline of pieces, as these marks may show up around the edges of your appliqués. Rather, mark about 10mm/⅜in within outline so that lines are mere indications of placement.

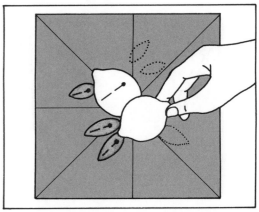

6 Arrange appliqués on base following your pattern or marked placement lines. Position background pieces first, with foreground pieces on top, and fabrics overlapping where necessary. Pin, baste or attach pieces to base with a glue stick.

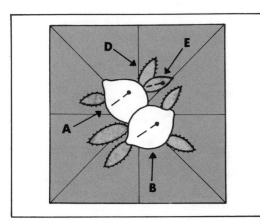

7 Sew appliqués to base with the foreground pieces lapped over the background pieces. In this design for example, sew the leaves in place before the lemons, with leaf D sewn first, overlapped by leaf E. Sew lemon A first, overlapped by lemon B.

8 If you wish to quilt the finished design, to eliminate puckers or to reduce bulk from the many layers of fabric, turn the completed appliqué design to the WS and carefully cut away the base fabric, leaving a 6mm/¼in seam allowance as shown.

9 To add stuffing to an appliqué, stitch shape to the base leaving a small opening. Insert stuffing into opening using a crochet hook or tip of a knitting needle; gently work stuffing into the corners. Stitch opening closed. Do not cut away base.

Hand Appliqué

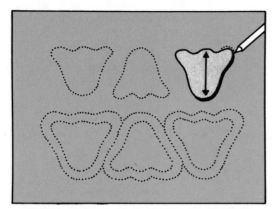

1 Technique Position templates on RS of fabric and mark outlines, leaving at least 13mm/½in between pieces. If desired, mark 6mm/¼in seam allowances around each piece, or cut out appliqués adding a 6mm/¼in seam allowance around all edges.

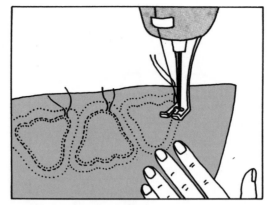

2 Do this optional step before appliqués have been cut out. Stay-stitch each appliqué by hand or machine by working small stitches just outside marked outline. These strengthen edge of fabric and allow it to roll under more easily, for a smooth edge.

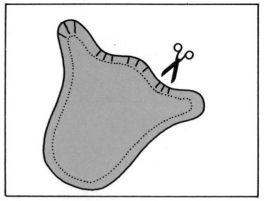

3 Clip the curved edges of each appliqué perpendicular to the marked outline or stay-stitching line. Clip just to the line, not beyond it. Straight edges do not need to be clipped. Make extra clips along deep curves for ease in turning.

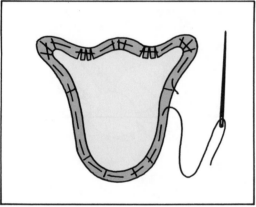

4a There are 2 different appliqué methods. The pre-basted method of appliqué is used for designs where exact placement of pieces is required. Turn raw edges 6mm/¼in to WS and hand-baste in place. Steam-press just the folded edges carefully.

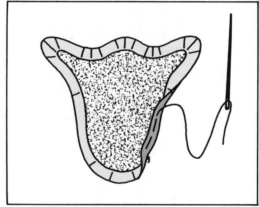

4b If you are pre-basting and wish to have crisp edges or add stability to flimsy fabrics, cut iron-on interfacing to size of appliqué without seam allowances. Centre on WS of appliqué and press. Fold seam allowances over interfacing and baste.

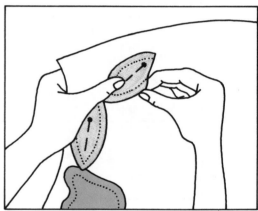

5a To appliqué by the second, quicker method pin appliqué in position on RS of base and turn edges under as you are sewing fabric in place. Use your fingertips to roll seam allowance under, just hiding your pencilled outline or stay-stitching lines.

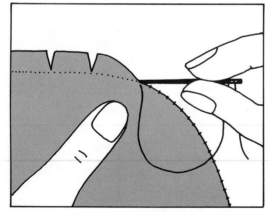

5b For curved or difficult areas where your fingers may obstruct your view of the work, stroke the seam allowances underneath the appliqué using the tip of your needle. Use the needle tip in all your work to ensure that the edges of your appliqués are smooth.

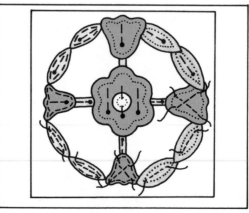

6 Illustration shows appliqués secured to a base by pinning (top) and basting (bottom). On the left are the pre-basted appliqués, arranged in exact position. On the right are the unbasted appliqués, which overlap each other because of the seam allowances.

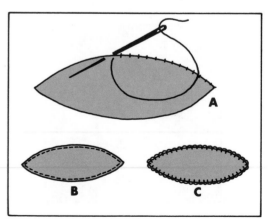

7 Using thread to match appliqué, sew to base with closely worked slipstitches (A). Catch just a few threads on fold of appliqué; pull stitches firmly but not so tightly that they show. Appliqués can also be secured with running (B) or buttonhole stitches (C).

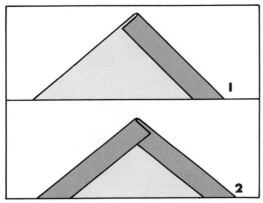

1 **Corners** For wide corners, fold one edge of appliqué 6mm/¼in to WS (1), then fold second edge to WS overlapping first (2). To appliqué corner you may need to "stroke" seam allowances beneath appliqué with tip of needle; step 5b on facing page.

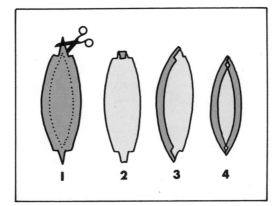

2 If corner is narrow, clip into seam allowance 6mm/¼in below corner and trim to 3mm/⅛in; trim off point just above marked turning line (1). Fold down to WS (2). Fold one edge of appliqué 6mm/¼in to WS (3); fold second edge to WS, overlapping first (4).

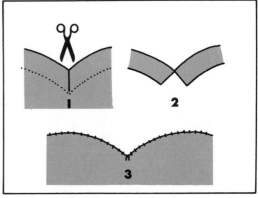

Valleys A sharp dip in an appliqué is called a valley. Clip into seam allowance to outline or stay-stitching line (1). Fold raw edges to WS (2); note that seam allowances separate, leaving virtually no fabric at dip. Work close stitches at dip to secure raw edges (3).

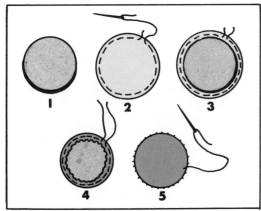

Circles Use thin cardboard for template (1). Work a round of basting stitches close to raw edges of circle appliqué (2); place template on WS (3). Pull basting stitches, gathering edges tightly around template (4). Press gently, then pop out template. Sew in place (5).

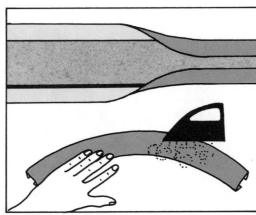

1a **Stems** Cut fabrics for stems on the bias; add 6mm/¼in allowance to each edge. Cut thin cardboard template to required width; centre on WS of bias strip. Press raw edges over cardboard; remove cardboard. Shape stem on base, using fingers and steam.

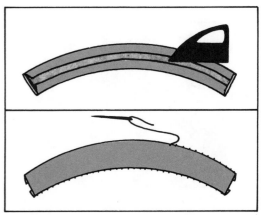

1b Alternatively, you can cut a template to exact shape of stem. Centre template on WS of bias strip and steam-press edges gently over template. Remove template without distorting stem; stitch to base. Always stitch concave curves first.

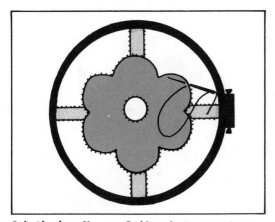

Embroidery hoop You may find it easier to prevent your appliqués from puckering if the work is held taut in an embroidery hoop. Do not position the hoop over the piece you are sewing as it may distort the shape; rather centre the appliqué within the hoop.

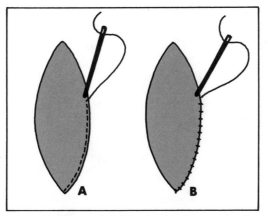

Non-fraying fabrics such as felt, closely woven wool and leather do not need seam allowances. Sew these pieces to the base with stab stitches, worked about 3mm/⅛in away from the raw edge in a line (A) or worked just over the raw edge (B).

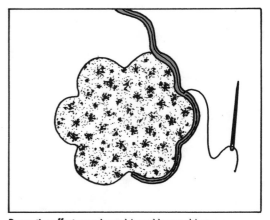

Decorative effects can be achieved by working embroidery stitches on the appliqués, or by adding a variety of trims such as lace or Russian braid, shown here. Place braid exactly on edge of appliqué; secure with running stitches in matching thread.

MACHINE APPLIQUÉ

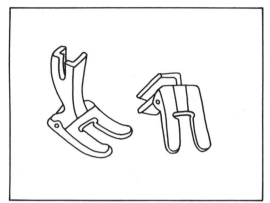

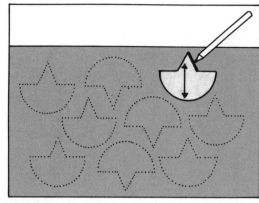

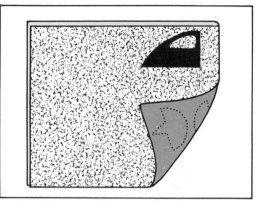

Preparation Clean and oil machine; insert a new needle. Use 100% cotton thread in colour to match appliqué. If you have one, attach appliqué foot which has a wide space between prongs and a groove on underside; otherwise use a zigzag foot.

1 Technique Position templates on RS of fabric and mark outlines. Because seam allowances are not required for machine appliqué, mark appliqués close to one another to conserve fabric. Cut out appliqués along marked outlines.

2 This step is optional and can be used to add stability to flimsy fabrics; it will also prevent puckering of light- and medium-weight fabrics. Fuse featherweight iron-on interfacing to WS of marked fabric, then cut out appliqués on outlines.

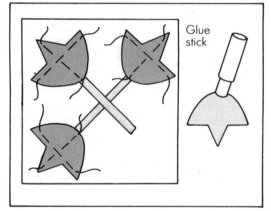

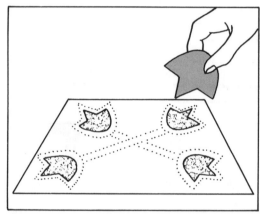

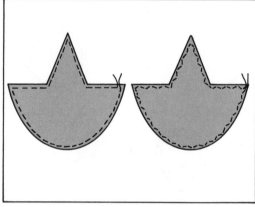

3a Arrange appliqués in correct position on base and attach securely using basting stitches or a glue stick. Be sure to test glue stick on a scrap of fabric to ensure that it will not permanently mark the appliqué.

3b Alternatively, you can secure appliqués to base with adhesive/fusible web. Cut appliqué shape from adhesive web about 3mm/⅛in smaller than fabric appliqué; position correctly on base. Place appliqué over adhesive web; press to attach appliqué to base.

4 Using matching thread, stitch close to the edges of each appliqué using a medium-length straight stitch or an open zigzag stitch. Sew slowly and carefully to prevent appliqué from puckering. Appliqués should lie flat and smooth against the base.

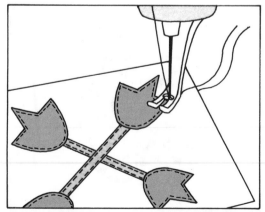

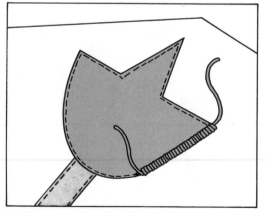

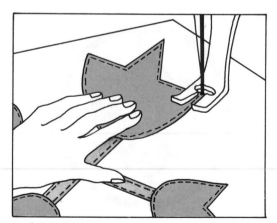

5 Set your sewing machine for a close zigzag satin stitch; practise on a scrap of similar fabric before beginning. Tension should be even and should not pull or pucker fabric edges in any way. Leaving a long thread end, begin stitching along edge of appliqué.

6 Cover raw edges of appliqué with zigzag stitch. Stitch width depends upon fabrics being used: fine fabrics require narrow stitch; heavy fabrics may need a wide one. Standard stitch width is 3mm/⅛in. Loosen top tension of machine if bobbin thread shows on RS.

7 Gently guide fabric around curves so that the machine sews smoothly without stopping or piling stitches on top of one another. Work slowly so that you have complete control over your stitching.

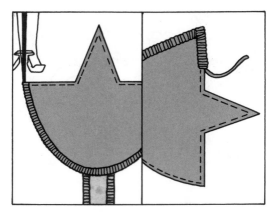

8 Approach corners slowly. Zigzag up to corner, leaving needle in fabric at outside edge of appliqué. Raise presser foot and swing fabric in new direction. Lower presser foot and begin sewing so that first stitches overlap previous line of stitching.

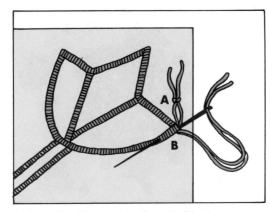

9 Leave long thread ends when stitching is completed. Pull threads from beginning and end of stitching to WS and tie into a knot. Insert thread ends into a sewing needle and weave into the back of the zigzag stitches to secure. Clip off excess thread.

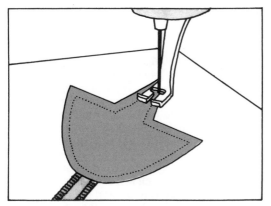

1 **Alternative method** Use this method if you have difficulty sewing close to raw edges. Cut out appliqués, adding 6mm/¼in seams; secure in correct position on base. Sew on marked outline of appliqué with short straight stitch and matching thread.

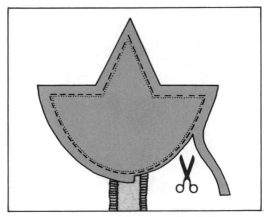

2 Using sharp embroidery scissors, trim off excess seam allowance of appliqué beyond stitching line. Set machine for close zigzag satin stitch and zigzag over line of stitches, covering raw edges.

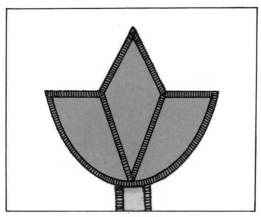

1 **Decorative effects** Use zigzag satin stitch to delineate flower petals as shown, to add veins to leaves and create a variety of other embellishments. Also use satin stitch to add details that are too small to execute in fabric, such as facial expressions.

2 Use a highly contrasting thread for special effects on machine appliqués. Black or dark grey will create a stained glass appearance. Add embroidery details such as the antennae on this butterfly with tiny satin stitches.

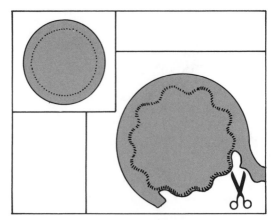

3 Some sewing machines are capable of making decorative embroidery stitches. If yours does, use machine embroidery around a plain appliqué to create a fancy edge. Machine-embroider on marked outline, then cut away excess fabric close to stitching.

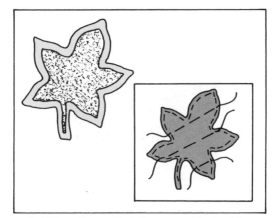

1 **Invisible machine appliqué** Cut out appliqués adding 6mm/¼in seam; attach iron-on interfacing to WS. Clip, fold and baste raw edges to WS as for hand appliqué; baste appliqué on base. Use clear thread in needle and thread to match base in bobbin.

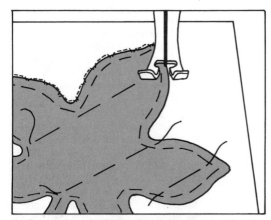

2 Set machine for 20 blind hem stitches per 2.5cm/ 1in. Sew with inner right edge of presser foot on folded edge of appliqué. Straight stitches are sewn on base. Jump stitches catch fold of appliqué every 6mm/¼in and secure points and intersections.

BRODERIE PERSE

The technique of cutting out motifs from printed fabrics and appliquéing them onto a plain fabric grew out of the necessity to conserve material and out of a passion for the brilliantly coloured yet durable fabrics manufactured in India during the 18th century. Known as Broderie Perse, because it was thought to resemble Persian embroidery, this craft became extremely popular during the 18th century in England and the 19th century in America.

As early as the 17th century, England imported cotton fabrics from India. These chintz fabrics (or *chinces*) were prized because the colours were bright and fast owing to the use of mordant dyes that were painted onto the cloth by hand or printed with blocks. By contrast, fabrics printed in England seemed drab and inferior. Chintz fabrics featured human figures, birds, animals, trees, flowers and vines with an Oriental flavour. However, traders felt that sales could be increased if the fabrics were printed to satisfy English tastes, so many English embroideries of the time were sent to India to be copied.[17] This proved to be enormously successful and the import of fabrics from the East India Trading Company, as it was called, grew to staggering proportions. As the volume of trade increased, so did the discontent of fabric manufacturers in Britain and France, until in 1700 the British passed measures to outlaw the shipping of Indian chintzes into the country. This had little effect on trade, so in 1721 another law was passed, banning the use of the fabric on any clothing, furniture or bedcoverings.[18] This new law, more effective than the 1700 embargo, encouraged the popularity of Broderie Perse. Those who managed to acquire small amounts of chintz cut them apart and appliquéd them to a larger piece of cloth to make them "stretch" further. Those who had complete bedcoverings and draperies of chintz were naturally reluctant to dispose of them when they began to show signs of wear: instead, they cut out the salvageable bits and reused them as appliqués.

This method was so fashionable in America during the 19th century that chintz fabrics were specially designed for cutting out and displaying in the centres and corners of appliqué quilts.[19] The backs of the cutouts were often coated with a paste to add stability. When the paste dried, the appliqués were positioned on the background and sewn in place; the paste rinsed away when the bedcovering was washed.[20]

Chintz bedcoverings of the 19th-century were relatively large, as they were generally made for the grand four-poster beds typically used in the South. Three favourite styles of Broderie Perse emerged. By far the most popular was the Tree of Life. Another style featured an informal array of chintz cut-outs which covered the background in an all-over pattern. In the third type, the pieces were organized within a framed central medallion.

1 Techniques Wash chintz fabrics before you start, to prevent shrinkage. Study design carefully to decide which pieces should be cut and used as appliqués. Do not cut intricate pieces such as fine stems or thorns – these can be embroidered later.

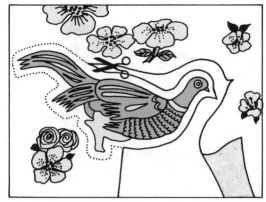

2 Cut out the pieces you wish to appliqué, adding a 6mm/¼in seam allowance around all edges. The edge of a motif may not always be well defined – you must decide where the line will fall. Cut intricate areas (eg feathers) in one piece for ease in sewing.

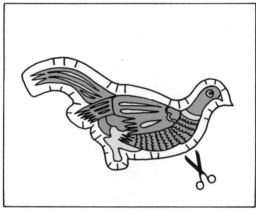

3 To aid in turning seam allowances to the WS, clip curved edges of fabric cutout just to the main par of the design. If desired, fold and baste raw edges to WS and press gently; otherwise, pieces can be finished while on the background as in step (5).

4 Arrange your chintz cutouts on the background fabric, moving the pieces around until you have created the best composition. Secure the pieces to the background using pins, basting stitches or a glue sitck.

5 Fold raw edges of each cutout 6mm/¼in to WS, easing around curves as necessary. Slipstitch each appliqué securely in place using matching thread. Pieces can also be machine-appliquéd if desired. Add any fine details in embroidery; *see page 64*.

Variation Any fabric with printed motifs can be used for Broderie Perse. Children's designs are particularly suitable for this type of work. Simply follow the instructions above to cut out the motifs and sew them on a compatible background fabric.

CUT-AND-SEW APPLIQUÉ

This quick and easy technique involves cutting appliqués from a single piece of fabric as you are sewing them to a background. You'll save time in your work because you won't have to mark and cut out individual appliqués. This method is suitable for single image designs consisting of one piece of fabric or intricate designs that have many pieces cut out of the same fabric. Cut-and-sew appliqué can give more consistent results than basic appliqué methods because the pieces do not require as much handling; only minor basting is necessary. The need to mark the design on the base is eliminated, and it is impossible for appliqué pieces to shift into the wrong position as you work.

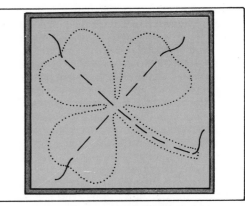

1 Technique Using a sharp pencil or fabric marker, draw the entire design on the RS of the fabric you have chosen for the appliqué.

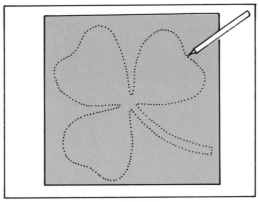

2 Position WS of marked fabric on RS of background fabric so that the grain of both fabrics runs in the same direction. Baste the marked fabric to the background within the lines of the design; do not baste closer than 6mm/¼in of any marked line.

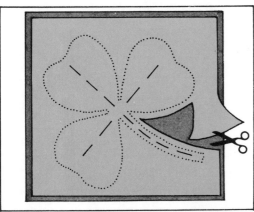

3 Begin cutting away the fabric around the marked design, leaving a 6mm/¼in seam allowance; do not cut more than a few centimetres/inches at a time. Trim off the excess fabric so that you don't have pieces dangling and getting in your way as you sew.

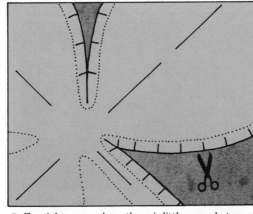

4 For tight areas where there is little space between the lines of the design, simply clip between the marked lines. For sharp points, make 3 clips to the marked line as shown. Also, clip any curved edges to the line to make turning easier.

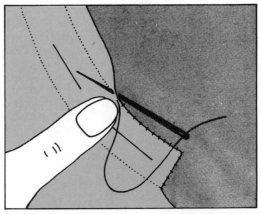

5 Slipstitch the appliqué to the base with matching thread, using the point of your needle to turn the seam allowance under as you work. Make sure that your marked line is just beneath the turning so that it doesn't show.

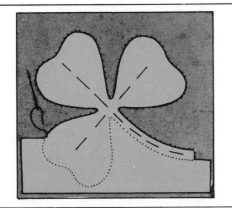

6 Continue working your way around the appliqué design, cutting and slipstitching the edges in place as you go along. Remove the basting stitches after the sewing is finished.

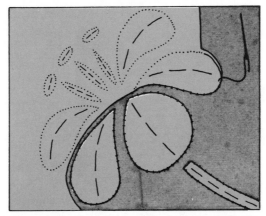

Separate pieces You can use this technique to appliqué a design consisting of several different shapes onto a base. Simply work around the design, cutting and sewing the pieces to the background in the most convenient order.

Inner spaces This method is effective for complicated designs, especially those with inner spaces that must be removed. First cut-and-sew all the outer edges in place. Then using small sharp scissors, cut and sew the inner edges, a small amount at a time.

HAWAIIAN APPLIQUÉ

On April 3 1820 seven missionary ladies and four Hawaiian women took part in the first sewing circle ever organized in the Hawaiian region. They were on board a ship, the *Thaddeus*, drifting along the Kona coast, and the native women were learning how to do patchwork.[21] They were having some problems: the Hawaiians lacked the scrap bags that other American women had, and it went against the grain to cut apart whole fabrics in order to create a pieced design. But somehow the two groups of women came to a compromise, sowing the seeds of the unique Hawaiian Appliqué style.

A Hawaiian Appliqué quilt has three basic characteristics. First, the large central design is cut from folded paper, in much the same way that children cut out snowflakes; this one-piece pattern covers most of the background and is known as a *kapa lau*. Second, Hawaiian quilts are made in two solid colours, most often red, green, orange or blue on white. Third, Hawaiian Appliqué is always quilted in multiple rows that echo the edges of the central *kapa lau*. This is called contour or wave quilting because the quilting lines resemble the contour lines on a map or the pattern of waves lapping on a shore. In Hawaiian, the quilting is known as *luma-lau*. It is always done in a thread to match the fabric.

There is a theory that the first true Hawaiian quilt was designed by a young Hawaiian woman who left a sheet of white fabric on the grass to bleach in the sun. Upon her return she noticed that a nearby tree was casting an interesting shadow on the sheet. She drew the design that she saw and cut it out of a contrasting fabric which she then applied to the sheet.[22]

Traditional patterns are quite intricate and time-consuming to complete, which is why Hawaiian quilts are often prize winners at quilt shows. However, you can make your Hawaiian Appliqué as uncomplicated as you wish. In fact, it is best to make up your own designs in keeping with the Hawaiian tradition of not copying another's pattern; plagiarism was a serious matter and women who stole another's design were often denounced at public gatherings! Try designing your own pattern based on the same natural objects that the Hawaiian women use, for example flowers, fruit, leaves, waterfalls and comets. Birds, animals or people in designs are deemed unlucky. Also, it is forbidden to sit on an unfinished Hawaiian quilt unless you are making it yourself.

Borders or *leis* are made in the same way as the central design, by the cut paper method. These are entirely optional, but can often add a spectacular finishing touch. A *lei* must be compatible in design with the *kapa lau*.

After you have made your Hawaiian Appliqué quilt, be sure to put your signature and the date (or the name of the recipient) in the middle or in one corner. Bind the edges of the quilt with the same fabric that you have used for the appliqué.

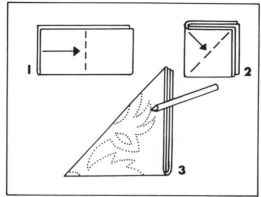

1 Making templates Decide on the size of your central appliqué, then cut a sheet of paper to same size. Fold in half (1), then fold in half again (2). Fold one corner down to the opposite corner (3). Holding paper as shown, draw a design in pencil.

2 Cut out shape on marked lines, then unfold paper to see what design looks like. If it is not intricate enough, refold and make more cuts. When you are satisfied with design, cut out one folded segment (one-eighth of the design) for your template.

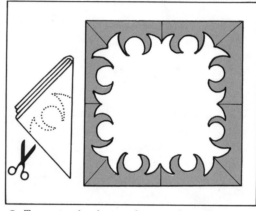

3 To create a border template, cut sheet of paper to size of entire quilt; fold following step 1. Draw a design that is compatible with your central design along outer edges of paper; cut along marked lines and unfold. If satisfied, make a template following step 2.

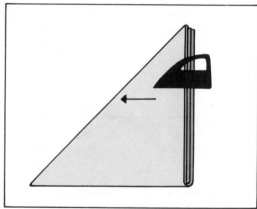

1 Technique Cut a piece of fabric slightly larger than your central appliqué. Fold the fabric as you folded the paper in step 1; press the fabric each time you make a fold. Place the folded fabric on a flat surface as shown in the illustration.

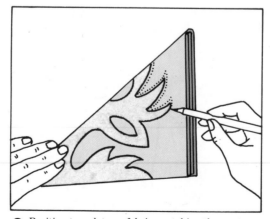

2 Position template on fabric, matching the centre, straight and bias edges. Holding the template firmly on the fabric with your hand, draw around the shape to transfer lines of design to fabric.

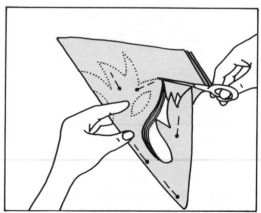

3 Remove the template and carefully pin the fabric layers together within the lines of the design. Make sure that your pins secure all layers firmly to prevent shifting. Using very sharp scissors, carefully cut the fabric along the marked lines.

4 Cut background fabric to full size of quilt, piecing if necessary; fold and press same as for appliqué fabric. Unfold and place on flat surface. Unfold appliqué; position on background matching press lines and straight and bias edges. Pin from centre outward.

5 Carefully baste appliqué to base fabric, keeping your basting at least 6mm/¼in away from raw edges of appliqué. Baste thoroughly so that the appliqué is firmly secured to the base.

6 Make small clips no deeper than 3mm/⅛in into the edges of the appliqué at all deep curves and corners to facilitate easy turning of fabric to WS.

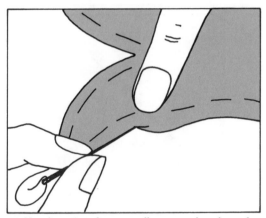

7 Use the point of your needle to turn the edges of the appliqué 3mm/⅛in to the WS

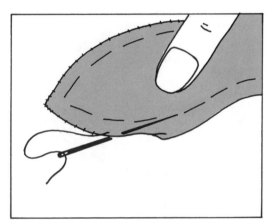

8 Secure appliqué to base with slipstitches; use a thread colour to match the appliqué rather than the base.

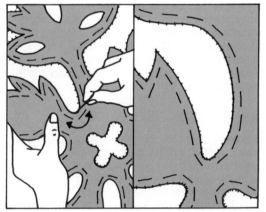

9 When sewing around curves, carefully run the tip of the needle back and forth at the sharpest dip of the curve so that fabric edges are firmly tucked beneath fold of fabric. Then sew the edges down with very close slipstitches.

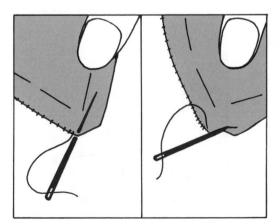

10 When sewing pointed edges, work right up to the point, sewing close slipstitches as you get within 6mm/¼in of the tip. Use your needle to push adjacent seam allowance beneath the fabric, then This is called contour or echo quilting.

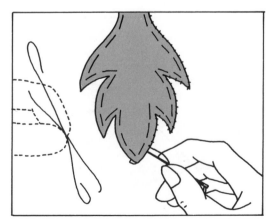

11 When working with a large design, it will be impossible to hold the fabric between your thumb and forefinger as you sew. Instead, keep your "holding" hand beneath the work to keep it taut, if necessary pinching the fabric for grip as shown.

Quilting Use quilting thread to match the fabric you are quilting. Work first row of quilting stitches close to edge of appliqué; work subsequent rows 6-16mm/ ¼-⅝in apart, depending on the size of the project. This is called contour or echo quilting.

INLAY APPLIQUÉ

Inlay Appliqué is a variation of the basic technique, and is similar to Reverse Appliqué; *see pages 118-120*. The finished appearance can range from simple to complex, depending upon the method that you choose.

SIMPLE INLAY

This is the easiest method, and is particularly useful when making quick bold projects such as banners or wall hangings meant for large spaces. The basic procedure is to fit a design shape into a "frame" or background fabric from which an identical shape has been cut; both pieces are then secured to a base. You must be accurate when cutting out the frame and the design shape so that the pieces fit together perfectly.

This technique is best accomplished using non-fraying fabrics such as felt, leather or closely woven wool. The base fabric can be any material, since it will not be seen. For a sturdy hanging, use medium- to heavy-weight fabric; for a soft, supple result, use a lightweight fabric or interfacing. Several different hand-embroidery stitches are suggested, but there are many more that are suitable. If you want to make a project quickly, use machine-embroidery or the machine satin-stitch illustrated. For a super-quick result, simply glue the frame and shape to the base fabric.

MACHINE INLAY

Also known as Découpé, this is a simple and quick method of inlaying an appliqué by machine. Stitch two contrasting fabrics together along the lines of the design, then trim the top fabric away to reveal the fabric underneath. Finish the raw edges with machine satin stitch; then cut the excess base fabric away, leaving a smooth, neat result.

APPLIED INLAY

Add depth and dimension to appliqué designs by trying this procedure. It is extra work, but the finished result will look far more complex than the simple steps required might suggest. You simply apply contrasting fabric shapes over basic or Reverse Appliqués, then slipstitch the new fabrics in place to create thin channels of colour.

REVERSE INLAY

This is a quick way to make two similar but contrasting designs and is useful when constructing a pair of matching cushions, or the front and back of a tote bag. Cut two appliqués out along the marked design lines, creating two uncut "frames" of fabric at the same time. Sew each frame to a base, then switch the appliqués and sew each one within its contrasting frame. Accuracy in cutting is important. You must make sure that your first cut is exactly on the marked line, as you will be using both the frame and the appliqués in your project.

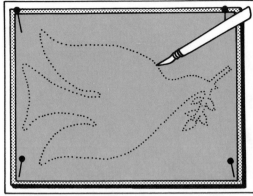

1 **Simple inlay** Select 2 non-fraying fabrics; draw the lines of your design on RS of each piece. Pin each fabric in turn to a cutting mat or cardboard. Run the blade of a utility knife along marked lines to cut out the shapes. Cut slowly, carefully and accurately.

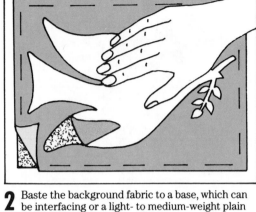

2 Baste the background fabric to a base, which can be interfacing or a light- to medium-weight plain fabric. Insert the cutout shape into the frame, easing gently to fit; pin or baste in place.

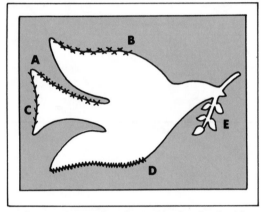

3 Secure pieces to base by working hand embroidery over cut edges; cross-stitches (A), herringbone (B) and feather stitch (C) would be appropriate. Pieces can be joined by machine satin-stitch (D), or for a quick result, simply glue both fabrics to base (E).

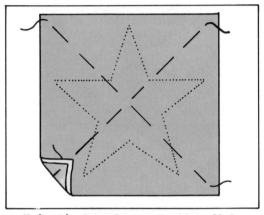

1 **Machine inlay** Select 2 contrasting fabrics. Mark your design on RS of one fabric for top layer. Baste WS of top layer to RS of bottom layer; bottom layer does not have to be same size as top, but should be slightly larger than the marked design.

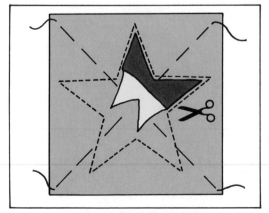

2 Machine-stitch along marked design lines on RS of top layer. Using very sharp scissors, trim away top layer within stitching lines, about 3mm/⅛in away from machine stitching. Remove any basting stitches that may be in your way.

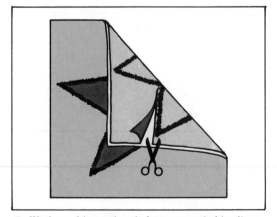

3 Work machine satin-stitch to cover stitching lines and raw edge of top layer. Turn piece to WS and trim away excess fabric of bottom layer, close to machine satin-stitch.

1 **Applied inlay** Work a design in basic hand appliqué as directed on *pages 106-109*, or in Reverse Appliqué as directed on *pages 118-120*

2 With the same templates used in step 1, mark the same number of shapes on contrasting fabrics for the inlays. Do not add seam allowances, but cut out directly on the marked lines. Make 6mm/¼in clips into edges of inlays as necessary for ease in turning.

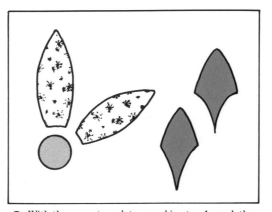

3 Place each inlay exactly over its matching appliqué shape and baste in position.

4 Slipstitch each inlay to its matching appliqué shape, turning edges of inlay 6mm/¼in under with tip of needle as you go along. Turn all raw edges of inlays to WS; do not under or overlap pieces as you may have done on original appliqué.

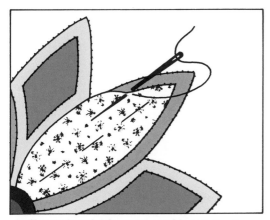

5 Continue stitching all inlays to the original appliqués until design is complete. As you sew, try to keep the same width between the edges of the new shapes and the edges of the original pieces so that the channels formed are even.

1 **Reverse inlay** Select 2 contrasting fabrics for frames and inlays; cut to same size. Mark design line on RS of one fabric. Pin the fabrics together and cut out carefully and accurately exactly on marked lines.

2 From a third contrasting fabric, cut 2 pieces for base same size as frames. Baste WS of frame to RS of base; slipstitch inner edges of frame to base, turning edges under 6mm/¼in with tip of your needle as you go along. Clip edges of frame for ease in turning.

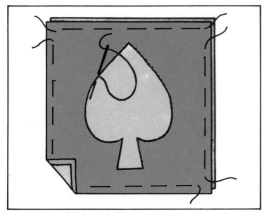

3 Place fabric inlay that contrasts with frame over base, centred within frame; baste in position. Make 6mm/¼in clips into edges of inlay as necessary for ease in turning.

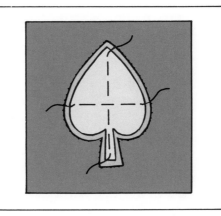

4 Slip-stitch edges of inlay to base using thread to match inlay. As you sew, try to keep the same width between the edges of the inlay and the edges of the frame so that the channels formed are even. Repeat in same manner for the second design.

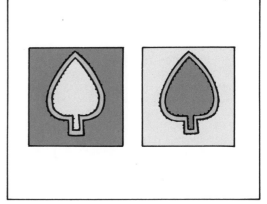

REVERSE APPLIQUÉ

Anyone who enjoys appliqué work will relish the pleasure to be got from Reverse Appliqué. The exact opposite of basic appliqué where shapes are added to a base fabric, this technique involves *removing* layers of fabric to reveal the design. The end-product has a rich, almost incised surface. You can do Reverse Appliqué with one or several layers; when you use more layers, the outcome will be heavier and textured. Keep a master pattern handy for reference.

MOLAS

The Kuna Indian women living on Panama's isolated San Blas Islands have elevated Reverse Appliqué to a high art. Their maze-like designs, sense of colour and intricate workmanship have become world renowned. A mola is a short-sleeved blouse with a Reverse Appliqué panel worked on the front and back. The designs were originally quite simple but the panels became more complex in the 19th century when traders brought brightly coloured fabrics to the Indians, who then translated their body paintings into needlework. The asymmetrical patterns represent people, plants, animals, demons from Indian lore and contemporary events. A deeply layered effect is aimed at, the designs often being worked on two to four layers of cloth, with the bottom layer pieced from several different fabrics. Fabric inserts, basic and embroidery stitches are used to add yet more layers and colours. A mola is easy to recognize because of the narrow channels, dots and sawtooth lines that fill every available space.

PA NDAU APPLIQUÉ

At the same time that the Kuna Indians were working their magic with needle and thread in Panama, the Hmong people were doing similar work in Laos, Vietnam and Thailand. *Pa ndau* refers to the entire needlework tradition of the Hmong culture, which includes intricate embroidery as well as appliqué work. The Hmong use their needlework to decorate hats, belts, baby carriers and aprons, as well as coverings for their beds and tables. Hmong designs are quite distinctive and completely different from those of the Kuna Indians. The symmetrical patterns are worked on three or four layers only, with the bottom layer serving as a base which doesn't show. The geometric shapes, inspired by natural themes such as snails, elephants, stars, worm tracks and spider webs, have deep symbolic meaning.[23] A design is not actually drawn onto fabric, rather, the fabric is folded and cut to provide guidelines for stitching; and the stitching is then worked from one cut to another. Embroidery is often used to highlight the designs. This is not a technique for beginners: *Pa ndau* appliqué is so complex that a book has been written specifically on the subject. If you are interested in exploring *Pa ndau*, this book is invaluable.[24]

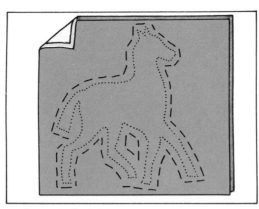

1 **Reverse appliqué** Cut 2 pieces of fabric in desired size. Draw full-size design on RS of one fabric for top layer. Pin RS of second layer to WS of top layer; baste together about 10-13mm/⅜-½in outside marked line.

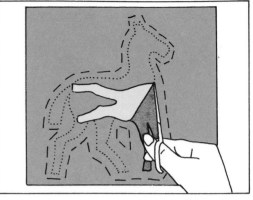

2 Using a small pair of sharp, pointed scissors, carefully trim away top fabric 6mm/¼in within marked line, being careful not to cut through the second layer. Clip all curves and corners to line of marked design.

3 Thread needle with colour to match top layer. Using point of needle, turn raw edges of top fabric to WS along line of marked design; slipstitch to second layer. Continue until top layer is completely sewn to second layer and all raw edges are hidden.

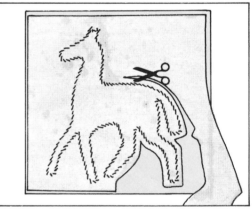

4 Turn to WS. Trim away excess fabric of second layer 6mm/¼in away from stitching lines. To add stability, do not trim away second layer; stitch fabrics together at outer edges. Gently steam-press design RS down on a thick towel.

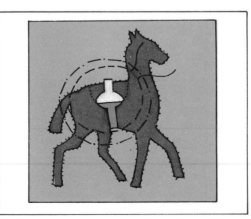

5 To add another piece, draw outline of shape on RS of appliquéd fabric; cut new fabric slightly larger than shape. Baste RS of new fabric centred beneath drawn shape; dot/dash line indicates edge of new fabric. Cut and stitch following steps 2-4.

Variation Use a pieced fabric for the second layer. This layer can be randomly pieced with strings, strips or crazy pieces, or worked in a traditional patchwork pattern. Baste RS of pieced fabric to WS of top fabric, then work Reverse Appliqué as described above.

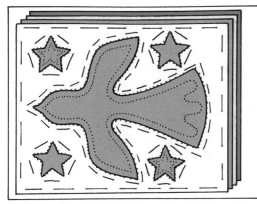

1 Multiple layers Cut fabric layers 5cm/2in larger than desired size as piece will pull in a bit. Draw shapes to be cut from top layer on top fabric; work in Reverse Appliqué; *see facing page.* Replace pattern; draw shapes to be cut from second layer.

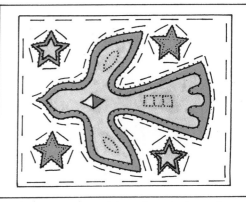

2 Insert point of scissors through second layer of fabric only and cut away newly drawn shapes, leaving 6mm/¼in seam allowances. Work new shapes in Reverse Appliqué, sewing through all layers so that fabrics are held together securely.

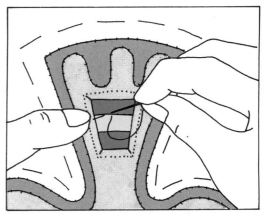

3 Replace pattern and draw shapes to be cut from third layer. Work as described in step 2. Continue working in same manner until all layers are exposed. Bottom layer must remain intact to hold all other layers together.

4 If you mistakenly cut through an extra layer of fabric, cut piece of matching fabric slightly larger than cut-out area. Using tip of needle, insert new piece into opening. Smooth in place, then sew design making sure that stitches go through the insert.

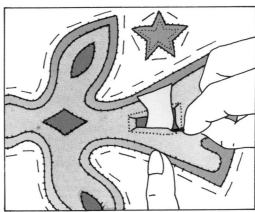

5a To add an extra fabric between layers, cut the new shape 6mm/¼in larger than desired size all around. Using the tip of your needle, insert the fabric in the correct position, slipping raw edges beneath the upper layer where required.

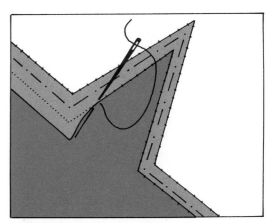

5b Fold the exposed raw edges of the insert to the WS and slipstitch in place using matching thread.

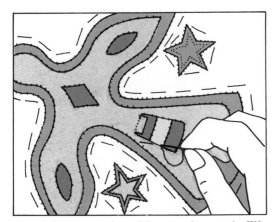

5c Fold the raw edges of the upper layer to the WS and slipstitch in place, covering the raw edges of the insert.

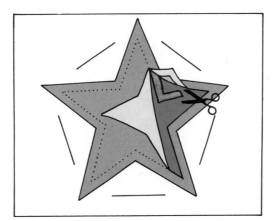

6a You can cut through several layers of fabric at one time to expose an underlying layer. Do not hem each layer separately, as the top layer will cover all raw edges. Trim back the edges of the underlying layers slightly to eliminate bulk.

6b Fold seam allowance of upper layer over raw edges of middle layers. Slipstitch to lower layer using matching thread. Dot/dash line indicates trimmed edges of middle layers.

REVERSE APPLIQUÉ

1 **Molas** Mola panels are featured on short-sleeved blouses worn by the Kuna Indians. *Note:* When making molas, baste fabric layers together, starting in centre and working out to edges. Cut basting as you work, leaving enough to remain effective.

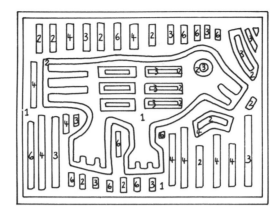

2 Draw master pattern on tracing paper. If design is complex, number the shapes to correspond with the number of layers. Additional colours may be added by piecing the bottom layer or by inserting scraps of fabric; *see previous pages.*

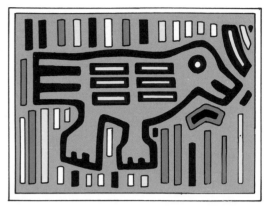

3 Transfer design to fabric and work layer by layer in Reverse Appliqué as described on the previous pages. Embellish with embroidery and additional appliqués if desired. Remove all basting when design is finished.

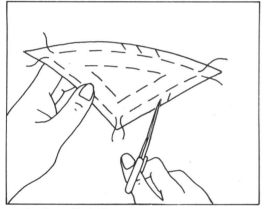

1 **Pa ndau appliqué** This intricate and complex method of Reverse Appliqué requires careful folding, basting and clipping of the fabric to indicate the lines of the design.

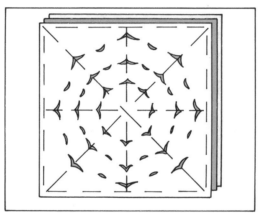

2 Unfold the clipped fabric and position RS up on RS of middle layer. Position 2 top layers on a base, which will not show. Baste the 3 layers together horizontally, vertically, diagonally and around the edges.

3 Following the clips you made in step 1, fold fabric edges under and sew in place using matching thread. Clip through uncut areas as you come to them. Work from the middle outward to the edges. Embellish with embroidery if desired.

4 Hmong textile artists memorize the hundreds of basic designs unique to *Pa ndau* appliqué. Here is a simple Star pattern. Often the centres and corners of *Pa ndau* are adorned with basic appliqués. Note the embroidered seed designs that cover the surface.

5 Many traditional *Pa ndau* patterns are combinations of other designs. Elephant's foot, shown here, uses the common Snail motif repeated 4 times and then surrounded by borders.

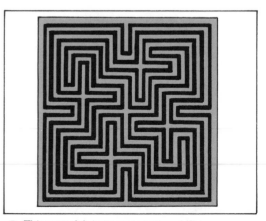

6 This very elaborate maze pattern is known as Crooked Road or Froglegs and is considered one of the most difficult designs to attempt.

SHADOW APPLIQUÉ

This appliqué procedure is deceptively simple. Cutout shapes are applied to a base and then covered with a transparent fabric such as voile or organdy. The layers are held together with small running stitches which also serve to hold the appliqués in position. It is best to use solid fabrics for this technique; white is traditionally used for the base and the sheer top fabric, although a Shadow Appliqué project would look very dramatic if made with a dark base and a top in a matching pale colour. Use very bright fabrics for the appliqués because the colours are toned down considerably by the transparent top. The delicate muted effects you can achieve with Shadow Appliqué lend themselves beautifully to making clothes, cushions and extra-special quilts and wall hangings.

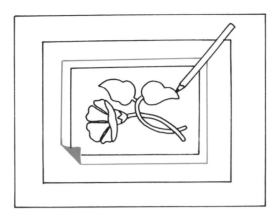

1 Technique Use a medium-weight cotton fabric such as broadcloth for base; position base RS up on a flat surface. Using dressmaker's carbon and a hard lead pencil (or a pen that has run out of ink), transfer design lines base, centred between sides.

2 Use the same pattern to mark the individual appliqué pieces on brightly coloured cotton or cotton/blend fabrics; do not add any seam allowances. Cut out with very sharp scissors; handle the pieces as little as possible to prevent appliqués from fraying.

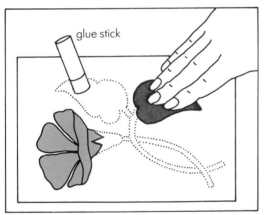

3 Rub a fabric glue stick very lightly on the base within the marked lines of the design. Position each appliqué on the base in its correct position within the marked lines; gently rub the centre of each appliqué to secure it to the glued area.

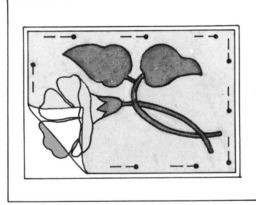

4 For the top, use a pale sheer fabric such as voile, organdy, organza, fine batiste or chiffon. Carefully lay the sheer fabric over the design. Smooth the fabric gently in place and pin the layers together temporarily through the outer edges only.

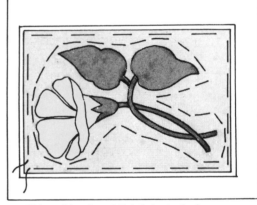

5 Using white thread, lightly baste the layers together all around the design without disturbing the appliqués. Also baste the outer edges together and remove the pins.

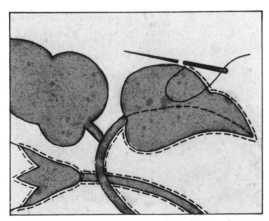

6 Using a good-quality sewing thread or pearl cotton, work running stitches all around each of the appliqués. Your stitches should either lie directly on the edge of the appliqué or exactly next to it. Add any details such as leaf veins in running stitch.

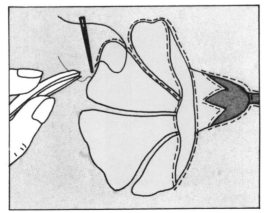

7 If the edge of an appliqué frays while you work, carefully probe through the sheer top layer of fabric with the tip of your needle to coax the thread out. Using tweezers, gently pull out the thread, holding the appliqué firmly in position.

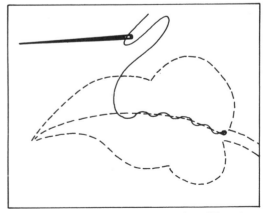

8 At the end of last stitch, pull needle to WS; make a small knot, then weave needle through several stitches on back of work and pull thread through. Clip off excess thread close to fabric. Remove basting. If desired, gently soak and rinse project to remove glue.

STAINED-GLASS APPLIQUÉ

Stained-glass windows have enthralled through the centuries with their bold patterns and brilliant colours. The methods of developing a good design, selecting compatible colours and neatly arranging the pieces are similar in both glass and textile art, so it seems only natural that fabric artists should try to imitate the appearance of stained-glass in their work. However, whereas real stained-glass methods require years of training, and hours of preparation and hard work, Stained-Glass Appliqué can be quickly accomplished by anyone who can cut and sew fabrics together.

There are two ways to achieve a Stained-Glass Appliqué effect: the Bias method and the Overlay method. The Bias method makes use of bias strips of fabric to resemble the came – the narrow channels of lead used to join the pieces of glass. Keep your designs bold and simple. Avoid using small pieces as it would be difficult to curve the bias strips around them. While it may seem easier to buy double-fold bias tape in a package, don't be tempted to do so: this tape is never of the same high quality as the fabrics you will be using, and the colour is unlikely to match other fabrics in your project. *See page 167* for instructions on cutting bias strips.

The Overlay method is actually a form of Reverse Appliqué (*see pages 118-119*). A dark top fabric is cut down and sewn to coloured fabrics beneath to create the design. Try both methods to determine which you prefer.

When designing a Stained-Glass Appliqué project, you should follow the same design principles that a stained-glass artist would apply. Study books of stained-glass patterns to get an idea of how to design your own compositions. For example, stained-glass windows never have floating shapes – each piece has what is called an exit line, where the line of the piece is continued to the edge. Make sure that your appliqué shapes also have exit lines.

FABRIC CHOICES

If you study stained-glass windows, you will see that no two pieces of glass are exactly the same. Glass can range from transparent with tiny bubbles to opaque streaked with a pale colour or with white. Within one window there will be several different shades of the same colour, depending on the thickness of the glass and which part of the sheet it has been cut from.

It is desirable to try to imitate the look of genuine stained glass as closely as possible in your appliqué work. Only use solid-colour fabrics, employing several different shades of the same colour in one project. Look for fabrics that change colour gradually across the yardage; if you cut shapes for one project from different parts of the fabric it may look as though you have used several different fabrics. Use bright primary colours whenever you can.

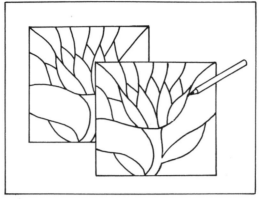

Making a pattern Draw a full-size pattern (cartoon) for your Stained-Glass Appliqué project, making sure that the pieces aren't too tiny and that each shape has an exit line. Indicate colours or fabrics on cartoon. Trace cartoon for your working pattern.

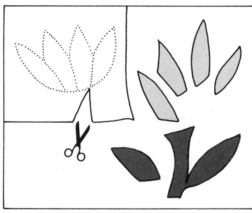

2 Cut the working pattern apart and use to mark the appliqué pieces on RS of your chosen fabrics. Where appliqués touch one another, as with the foreground petals on the flower, cut shape in one piece for easier handling. Do not add seam allowances.

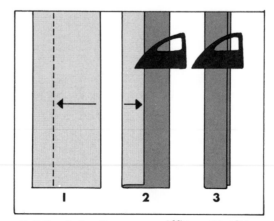

4 Follow instructions on *page 167* for cutting ¾in-wide bias strips of fabric. Use black for a genuine stained glass effect; pink is used here for clarity. Fold one long edge over 6mm/¼in and press (1-2). Fold remaining edge over 6mm/¼in and press (3).

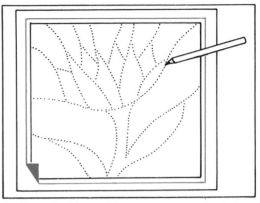

1 **Bias method** Use working pattern to transfer design to RS of background fabric using dressmaker's carbon and a hard lead pencil. If background is going to be several different colours, transfer design to lightweight base or interfacing.

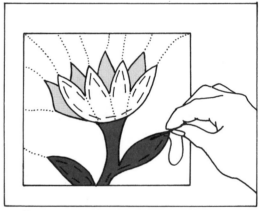

3 Position the appliqué shapes on the base or background and pin in position. Edges of the pieces should be flush; if not, trim away excess fabric where pieces overlap. Baste each appliqué in place.

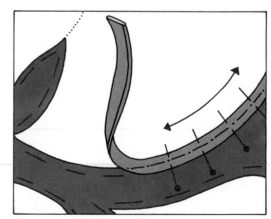

5 With folded side face down, position bias over raw edge of each appliqué shape. Pin each inner curved edge first; inner edges will pucker if they are compressed, so always pin and sew those edges first. The outer edges of a bias strip will stretch easily to fit.

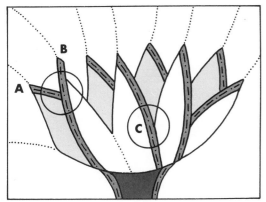

6a Use one length of bias for each area; do not piece. Ends of strips are overlapped, so study design to determine which strips should be sewn first; for example, sew strip A before strip B. Leave unsewn areas where other strips will be inserted (C).

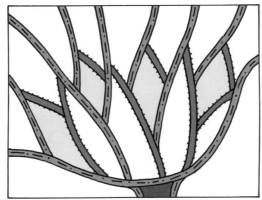

6b Continue to position strips until all pencil lines and raw edges of appliqués have been covered; overlap raw edges of previously sewn bias strips (shown here in dark pink). Pin and stitch strips to base, being sure to sew inner curved edges first.

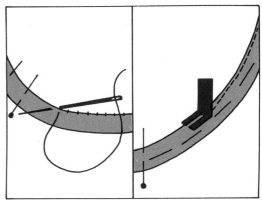

7 Using thread to match bias, sew in place by hand or machine. By hand, use slipstitch. By machine, stitch very close to edge of strip. Because you must be certain about exactly where pieces will overlap when machine sewing, baste all bias strips in place first.

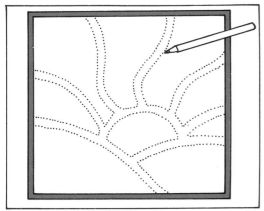

1 **Overlay method** Make a cartoon and working pattern; *see facing page.* Adapt pattern for this method by drawing a double line on each side of pencil lines, making 6mm/¼in-wide channels. Transfer all lines to RS of dark fabric.

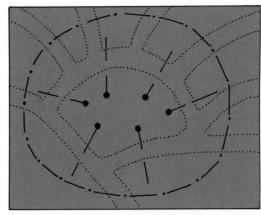

2 Cut a scrap of fabric slightly larger than the design area; edges of scrap are indicated by dot/dash lines. Pin scrap to WS of marked fabric, making sure that entire design area is covered; baste in place and remove pins.

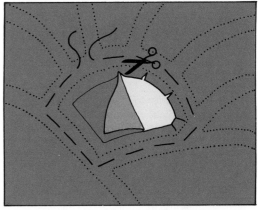

3 Mark cutting line (indicated by fine line) 6mm/¼in within design area. Using sharp pointed scissors, trim away dark fabric along marked cutting line. Clip into seam allowance to marked line at all curves and corners.

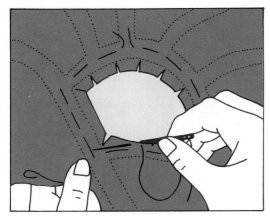

4 Using the tip of your needle, fold the raw edges of the dark fabric under along marked design line, then slipstitch to the scrap of fabric using thread to match dark fabric.

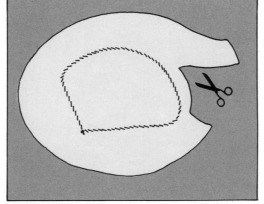

5 When all edges have been sewn in place, turn fabric over to WS. Carefully trim away excess scrap fabric, about 6mm/¼in away from stitching lines. Continue adding scraps and sewing them in place in same manner until entire design is complete.

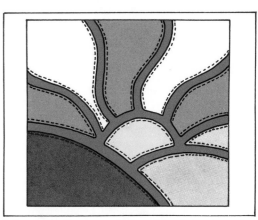

Quilting Quilt close to each edge of the dark strips using thread to match the "lead came".

SPECIAL EFFECTS WITH APPLIQUÉ

Appliqué lends itself well to representational designs. It is easy to depict natural and man-made forms because appliqués can be manipulated into many different shapes. Also, unlike patchwork, appliqué can combine fabrics of substantially different weights and textures to create special effects.

Substituting unusual fabrics, trims and even yarn will add another facet to your work; a design worked in a variety of unusual fabrics will look quite unlike the same design worked entirely in cottons. Fake fur, for example, can be used to represent animals and hair; the three-dimensional result adds interest and novelty to what otherwise might be a rather staid composition. Lace can embody a wide variety of design concepts: place white lace over a plain white fabric to simulate snow on the ground; cut small lace motifs and use them as flowers or snowflakes; or use ruffled lace trim in much the same way as it is used on clothing – standing out from the background, it will add dimension to a project. Shiny fabrics can simulate the sun, stars and planets, wet surfaces or smooth man-made forms such as buildings. Use rickrack to add texture and dimension to flower designs.

Because appliqué is representational, you will want to use fabrics that provide a sense of realism, particularly when depicting clothing on human figures. When using prints, plaids or napped fabrics, make sure that they are in scale with the design: use tiny prints, miniature plaids and very fine corduroy. Utilize lush fabrics such as velvet, satin, moiré taffeta and silk when you are portraying women's evening clothes. Try denim for jeans, jersey knits for sweaters and trousers, and vinyl for shoes and raincoats.

There are two opposite approaches to design, both of which are equally valid. One is to let the fabric inspire you and create your design around it. The other is to have a specific design in mind, then search through your scrap bag until you have found suitable materials. Be imaginative. If you're worried about whether or not a certain fabric will "work", do as much of the appliqué as you can, then place the doubtful fabric in position to see whether it will strengthen or detract from the design.

Appliqué work can sometimes be enhanced by adding a raised effect to a design. For example, flower petals and leaves, can be attached at one edge only so that the tips stand out from the background. Petals and leaves can be stuffed for extra dimension.

Directions for stuffing basic appliqué pieces are given on *page 107.* However, the amount of stuffing you can insert is limited: add too much and the background fabric will be pulled out of shape. If you wish to have a very raised shape, such as the centre of a flower, make a high-relief appliqué as directed on the facing page. This will add height without adversely affecting the surrounding fabric.

1 Fabric Study your appliqué design to determine the fabrics that will create interesting effects. In this design, for example, use fake fur or velvet for the cat, a shiny satin for the sun, sheer net or lace for the curtains and ribbons for the tie-backs.

2 Use fabrics in the correct scale for a realistic effect – for example, a small plaid for the scarecrow's shirt and a fine corduroy for his trousers. Use yarn to add dimension to a design; baste the ends to the background, then sew an appliqué securely over them.

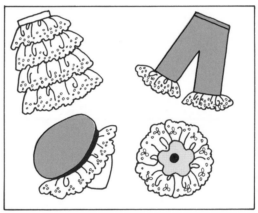

3 Use ruffled lace trim to embellish a skirt, underclothes, hats and even flowers. Stitch only the bound edge to the background fabric to add a 3-dimensional effect to your design.

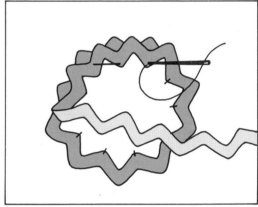

4a Use rickrack to add texture to flowers. Draw desired size circle on RS of background fabric using a compass. Position 6mm/¼in-wide rickrack within circle, working from outer edge to centre and sewing only the inner edges in place.

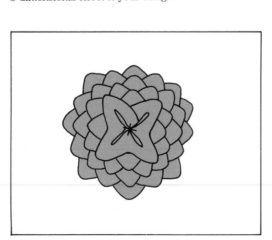

4b Continue adding rickrack within the marked circle, stitching rickrack in place as you go along and overlapping previous row by 3mm/⅛in. At centre, arrange rickrack so that 4 points meet exactly in middle; stitch points together.

1 Gathering Will create a 3-dimensional effect. Use basic appliqué template to mark shape on fabric, adding at least 2.5cm/1in to top edge for gathering. Bottom and side edges are same size. Add 6mm/¼in seam allowances to all edges.

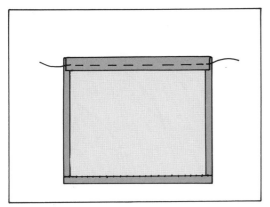

2 Fold all edges 6mm/¼in to WS and press. Hem the bottom edge. Baste across the top edge; pull basting to gather fabric to fit the appliqué shape marked on your fabric.

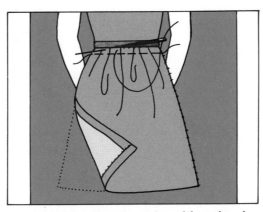

3 Slipstitch the side and top edges of the gathered appliqué to the background in the marked position, securing the gathered edge firmly in place. Leave the bottom edge free. Remove the basting stitches.

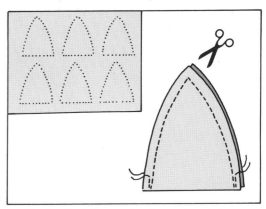

1 Raised appliqué Draw twice the number of shapes required on WS of fabric; cut out, adding 6mm/¼in seam allowances. Pin 2 pieces together with RS facing and raw edges even; stitch, leaving bottom edge open. Clip corners and turn to RS.

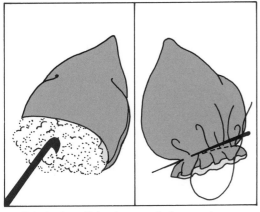

2 If desired, stuff the shape until plump, using a crochet hook or knitting needle. Baste bottom edge closed; pull basting to gather edge to desired width.

3 Arrange pieces on background fabric and slipstitch in place securely over the basting stitches, so bottom edge only is attached to background. Do not sew finished edges of appliqués to the background.

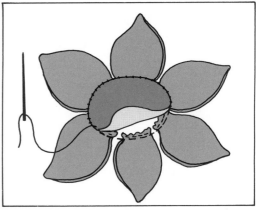

4 Place an appliqué over the raw edges and slip-stitch in place securely so as to cover the basting and the raw edges. Be sure to sew through the background as well as the raised appliqués.

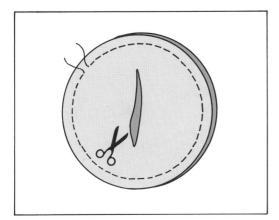

1 High-relief appliqué Use basic template to cut 2 appliqué pieces, adding 6mm/¼in seam allowance. Stitch together with RS facing and raw edges even. Using sharp scissors, clip into one fabric only (the facing) to make opening for turning.

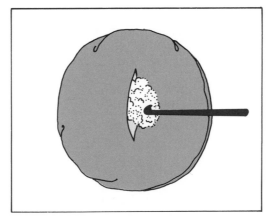

2 Turn to RS through the opening. Use a crochet hook or knitting needle to smooth seam from inside, pushing out any corners or points. Press so that seam does not show on RS. Stuff to desired degree of plumpness, pushing stuffing evenly into all parts.

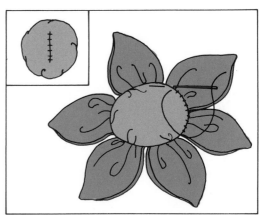

3 Lap cut edges of opening over one another and whipstitch together. Place stuffed appliqué on background in correct position, with the facing side down. Slipstitch in place securely.

MISCELLANEOUS

LEAVES

Thus the day was spent in friendly gossip as they quilted and rolled and talked and laughed... Unrestrained gayeties followed... Serious matrons commentated on the cake, and told each other high and particular secrets in the culinary art... One might have learned in that instructive assembly how best to keep moths out of blankets; how to make fritters of Indian corn undistinguishable from oysters; how to bring up babies by hand; how to mend a cracked teapot; how to take grease from a brocade;... how to make five yards of cloth answer the purpose of six; and how to put down the Democratic party. *Description of a quilting from "The Minister's Wooing" written in 1859 by Harriet Beecher Stowe.*

4

QUALITY
QUILTING

QUALITY QUILTING

There is something immensely satisfying about quilting. Perhaps it is the rhythmic simplicity of the stitching, or the sensation of the needle gliding smoothly through the layers of fabric and padding. Possibly it is because quilting provides a quiet time to remember joys, contemplate sorrows or dream about the next project. Maybe it is the fact that a project is just about done: the quilter has one last chance to survey, analyse and caress her work as she adds the stitches that will hold the layers together and bring the design to life. Whatever the reason, quilting is addictive, as every quiltmaker will attest.

HISTORY OF QUILTING

A quilt is composed of three layers: the top, which can be plain, pieced or appliquéd; the padding, which can be cotton, wool, silk or a synthetic material; and the back which is usually in a fabric to match the top. The process of securing these three layers together is called quilting. The fact that such an essentially simple process has evolved into so many variations attests to its great antiquity. Although it is impossible to pinpoint an exact date of origin, quilting can be traced back to *c.* 3400 BC where it was being done by the Egyptians, presumably more for decoration than warmth. A carved ivory statue in the collection of the British Museum can be seen wearing what looks like a quilted robe stitched in a traditional diamond pattern. What is probably the oldest surviving example of quilting is a carpet found on the floor of a tomb in Mongolia. Dated between the first century BC and the second century AD, the floor covering is quilted in spirals and bordered by a diamond filling pattern.[25]

Because of the frailty of fabric and its susceptibility to disintegration, there is very little other evidence of quilting until the 11th century, although it was undoubtedly done throughout the intervening years. In the 11th century, quilting was used both for body armour and as a source of warmth and comfort beneath the Crusaders' heavy metal armour. During the 13th and 14th centuries, Europe suffered through climatic changes that brought extremely cold temperatures during the winter seasons. Warm quilts and quilted clothing thus became essential for survival. Near the end of the 14th century, quilting lost its purely utilitarian function as it evolved into a means of decorating the clothing and household furnishings of the wealthy; *see Corded Quilting on page 146 and Trapunto on page 150*. From the 15th to the 18th centuries, quilted clothing and bedcoverings are mentioned in household inventories. Although records of this type were mostly kept by the wealthy, it is safe to assume that there must have been an incalculable number of quilts made by the poorer classes that have not survived either in written registers or in reality.

QUILTING IN THE 19th CENTURY

By the 19th century, quilting had evolved into a cottage industry in England and Wales. Mavis Fitzrandolph defines three types of men and women who quilted professionally at that time. *Village Quilters* prepared quilts with fabrics and padding supplied by their customers; they usually worked alone or with an apprentice. A village quilter could also be a stamper—a person who marked a quilt top with a design for quilting.[26] The most well known stampers were Joe the Quilter of Northumberland, George Gardiner of Allendale, and his apprentice Elizabeth Sanderson, who developed a reputation in her own right; *see page 9* for a quilt that is thought to have been stamped by Elizabeth Sanderson. *Itinerant quilters* travelled from one farm to the next, usually with a quilting frame, and lived on the farm while they augmented that family's supply of quilts. *Quilt Clubs* were established by women who wanted to quilt for extra money or for a living, but who didn't have the capital to pay for the materials out of their own pockets. They were therefore paid on an installment plan, usually on a weekly basis, until a quilt was finished.

The art of quilting was taken very seriously. While neighbours would sometimes work together on a quilt, this was not viewed approvingly by the professionals. One Mrs. Thomas of Aberdare said, "The making of a quilt was regarded as a craft. The craftswoman would start and finish the job herself; it was something in which any casual caller was not allowed to interfere."[27]

What a different attitude from the communal gatherings that were quilting bees in America! These events were eagerly anticipated, and to be excluded from a quilting bee was considered a terrible slight.[28] In the early days, particularly when homes were little more than huddles of logs in a clearing and the nearest neighbour was many miles away, a quilting bee was one of the only forms of social interaction. It served a fruitful purpose, the completion of a quilt, but more importantly, it allowed men and women to meet and interact, exchange gossip and recipes and generally give them something to anticipate and enjoy. It was not unusual to finish a quilt in one day because the participating women would often refuse to go home until the work was complete. Everyone got into the act, even the children who were paid a penny to keep the needles threaded.

QUILT CUSTOMS AND SUPERSTITIONS

At your quilting, maids don't dally,
Quilt quick if you would marry,
A maid who is quiltless at twenty-one
Never shall greet her bridal sun!
This well-known poem may seem ludicrous today, but when it was written, it was extremely important for a girl to have at least a dozen quilts in her dowry. This is not surprising when one considers that there was no central heating, and manufactured blankets were as costly as the sizable looms on which they were woven. Quilts provided warmth and comfort, as bedcoverings and as mattresses. They were also used to screen broken windows and even given as payment during years when crops failed.[29]

A quilt was never really regarded as finished until it had been quilted, no matter how much time and effort had been lavished on the patchwork or appliqué top. But because of the expense involved in completing a quilt, ie. paying for the padding and the fabric for the back, the quilts in a girl's bottom drawer or hope chest were never finished until she actually became engaged. The invitation to "quilt a girl's tops" was tantamount to an engagement announcement.

It was considered foolish to stitch heart motifs on a quilt before a girl became engaged; otherwise she would never marry. One quilting superstition advised that a broken border on a marriage quilt was a certain omen of trouble—there could be no broken ends or twisted lines of stitching. One lovely idea found on an old quilt can easily be reproduced by someone making a family heirloom today. The maker of a quilt had drawn the outline of each of her children's hands and worked the outlines in quilting; the owner's name was embroidered on each palm.[30]

While there are a number of different ways to mark a design on a quilt top, *see pages 138-139*, there is an old-fashioned method of marking straight lines that is no longer being used much, although it is probably very interesting to watch. A firm cord is drawn repeatedly across a piece of chalk or through cornstarch until it is well coated. Then the cord is stretched tightly near the appropriate spot on the quilt and pulled up with a snap, thus marking a straight white line.[31]

STITCHING

The aspect of quilting that most people worry about is stitch length. While it is true that some antique examples were quilted with 18 stitches per inch, it must be remembered that the padding was much thinner then and that those women had been sewing since they could hold a needle. Today's quilters should, of course, strive to make small stitches, but more importantly, make stitches that are even in length with the same appearance on the top and bottom. For some quilters, the stitches on the bottom of a quilt may look slightly smaller than the ones on the top. This result depends upon the way that you are holding the needle as you stitch. If this is the case, don't feel that you have to rip out your stitches to get them right. As long as the work looks attractive on both sides and you have used enough stitches to hold the three layers together securely, you can feel proud of your efforts.

QUILTING PATTERNS: MEDALLIONS

True Lover's Knot

Feather Medallion

Tudor Rose Medallion

Feathered Heart

Hearts and Flowers

CORNERS

BORDERS

Quilted pattern for Double Wedding Ring *see page 19*

AMISH

PREPARATION FOR QUILTING

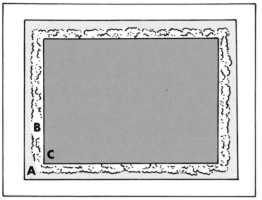

Quilt sandwich A quilt is made up of 3 layers joined together like a sandwich: the back (A), the padding (B), and the top (C). (Note: Padding may be termed "wadding" in Great Britain, and "batting" in the United States.)

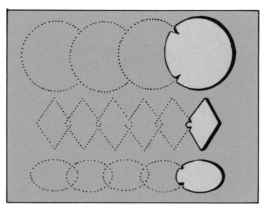

1 Templates Because quilting templates are used repeatedly, make them in a sturdy cardboard, plastic or metal. To mark evenly spaced designs, notch the repeating template; place notches in same position when drawing each design unit.

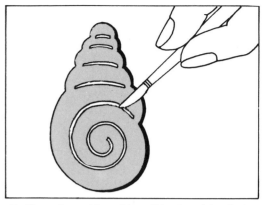

2 Channels must be cut in quilting templates that have interior design lines. Cut channels wide enough to accommodate a sharpened pencil point. For complicated interior lines, cut channels only for major design lines; mark rest of design freehand.

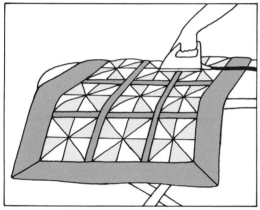

1 Marking the designs First prepare the quilt top on which the quilting designs will be marked. If top is patchwork or appliqué, cut off loose threads and trim raw edges neatly on WS. Press top thoroughly because you will not be able to press it again.

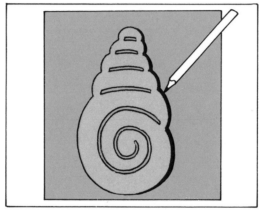

2 The quickest way to mark a design is to place quilting template on RS of fabric and trace around edge with a pencil or fabric marker. Lead pencil marks sometimes remain after quilting, so try using coloured pencils that are slightly darker than quilt top fabric.

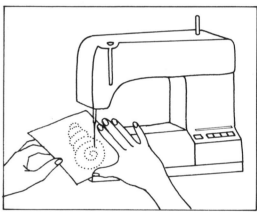

3a To transfer design by pouncing, insert large needle in machine, remove presser foot. Place paper pattern beneath unthreaded needle; stitch while guiding pattern so needle pierces paper on design lines. Rub WS with sandpaper to open up holes.

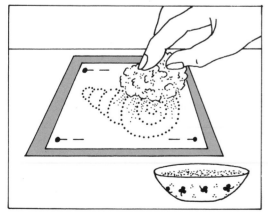

3b Pin perforated pattern to fabric in correct position. Rub powder through holes with a cotton ball or soft cloth to transfer design to fabric. Use French chalk or cornstarch for dark fabrics; cocoa or cinnamon for light fabrics.

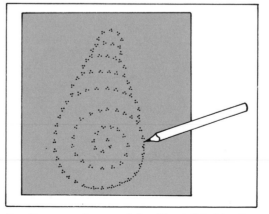

3c Remove pattern carefully without disturbing the powder and go over design lines with a pencil or fabric marker to make the lines permanent. Shake or brush the powder away. Pouncing is an excellent way to mark very intricate designs on fabric.

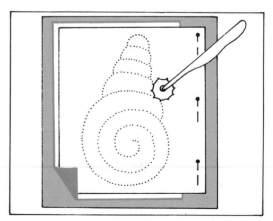

4 Designs can also be transferred using dressmaker's carbon (test to see if it will wash out) and a tracing wheel. Pin pattern to fabric along one edge and slip dressmaker's carbon, face down, in between pattern and fabric. Go over all lines to transfer.

5 You can use a light box to transfer designs. Place a light bulb beneath a sheet of clear glass; a glass coffee table makes an excellent light box. Tape pattern to glass above light source; place fabric RS up over pattern. Trace pattern.

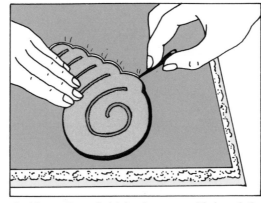

6 After quilt sandwich has been assembled, mark the top with a large blunt yarn needle; this is known as needlemarking. Position template on quilt top and trace around edge with the needle, creasing fabric. Hold needle at sharp angle and press firmly.

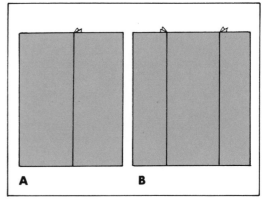

1 **Assembling a quilt** Cut the quilt back 5–10cm/2–4in larger all around than top to allow for take-up in quilting. Usually only one central seam is necessary to achieve correct width (A); if extra width is required, make 2 seams, centred evenly (B).

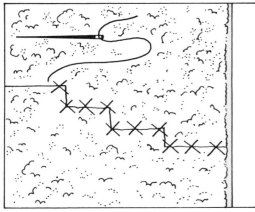

2 Cut padding slightly smaller all around than quilt back. If piecing is necessary, stagger the join so that it is not noticeable when quilt is assembled. Cut pieces as shown or tear them, then fit together smoothly. Join with large cross stitches.

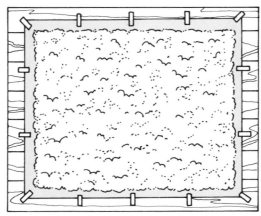

3 Tape back to a large flat surface such as the floor; make sure all corners are true and fabric is smooth. Centre padding on back, patting it into place smoothly. If using cotton or wool padding, make sure that it is spread evenly without lumps or thin spots.

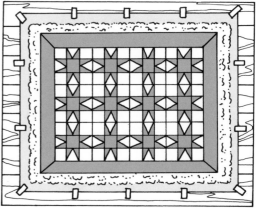

4 Centre quilt top on padding so that all edges are parallel with edges of back. Adjust as necessary so that corners are true. If quilt top ripples slightly, pat the wavy area until it lies flat.

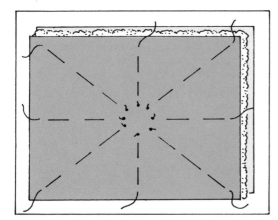

5a Knot a long length of thread for basting; use a light contrasting colour for easy removal. If quilting the project in a frame, baste the 3 layers together horizontally, vertically and diagonally, starting in centre and working outward to the edges.

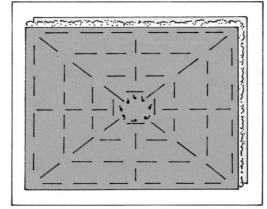

5b If quilting the project in a hoop or by machine, add extra basting lines to hold the 3 layers together securely.

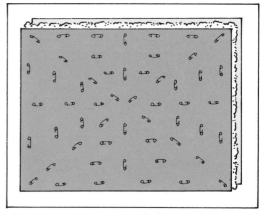

5c Alternatively, you can pin-baste the 3 layers together with size 2 safety pins. Be sure to use enough pins to hold the 3 layers together very securely; about 500 pins are needed to pin-baste a double-size quilt.

QUILTING DESIGNS

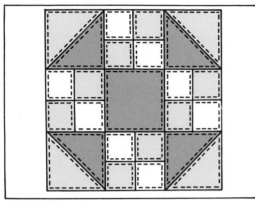

Outline quilting An easy way to quilt patchwork and appliqué projects is to outline each part of the design, as on this pattern called Prairie Queen. Work your quilting lines about 6mm/¼in away from the seams so that you are not quilting through seam allowances.

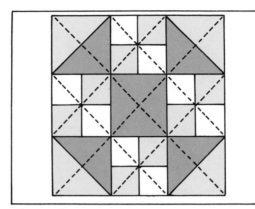

Selective quilting Emphasize certain portions of a patchwork or appliqué pattern by working selective lines of quilting on the design. Highlight some pieces by quilting on these only, or quilt across seamlines to create secondary designs.

Echo quilting Create complex quilting patterns by echoing the shapes of the patchwork or appliqué pieces with 2 or more parallel lines of quilting stitches. Work quilting lines about 6–13mm/¼–½in apart using thread to match the fabric you are quilting.

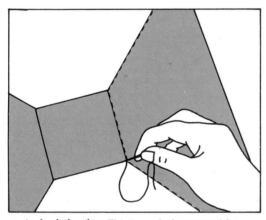

1 In-the-ditch quilting This is used when you wish to add puffiness to a quilt but do not want the quilting lines to intrude upon your design. By hand, work running stitches exactly in centre of seam allowance using an unobtrusive thread colour.

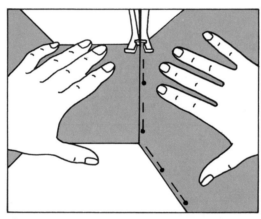

2 By machine, pin the 3 layers together close to seamline. Place project under presser foot. With your hands placed on each side of seam, spread seam open so that needle penetrates easily. Stitch slowly to keep stitches exactly in the "ditch".

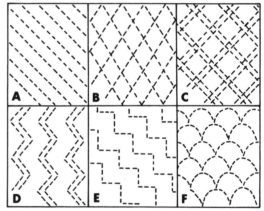

Filling patterns can be used to quilt an entire project ignoring the seams, or as a background filler on a wholecloth quilt; *see page 160*. Filling patterns can be as simple or complex as you wish; simple designs (A–E) are particularly suited to machine quilting.

Medallions are single quilting motifs. These self-contained design units can be simple or elaborate, large or small. Use medallions to quilt plain fabric blocks on a patchwork or appliqué quilt, or make one medallion the central focal point of a wholecloth quilt.

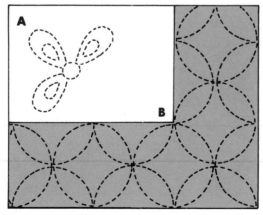

Corners can be difficult to execute because designs don't always begin and end where you want them to. For a successful corner, either place one complete pattern in the corner (A) or begin design in the corner and work inward from there (B).

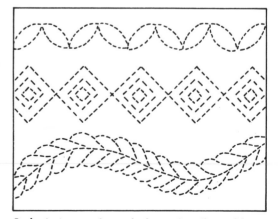

Border designs can be worked on strip quilts, sashing and around the perimeter of a quilt. Select a border to complement entire design. For contrast, use a curving border on a geometric quilt, or an angular border on an appliqué quilt. Feather borders enhance any design.

HAND QUILTING

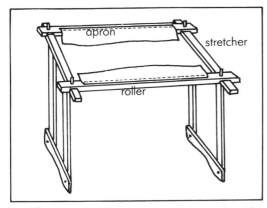

1 **A frame** maintains a consistent tension on the quilt layers, enabling you to work even quilting stitches. A roller frame has 2 wooden bars (rollers) the width of the quilt, and 2 cross pieces (stretchers) that hold rollers in place to keep quilt taut.

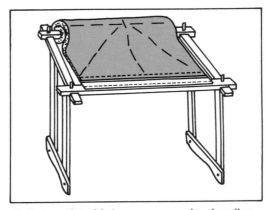

2 Baste quilt to fabric aprons secured to the rollers; roll quilt around one roller until exposed area is taut. When you have fully quilted exposed area, roll quilted portion out of the way, displaying a fresh area. Continue in this manner until the quilt top is finished.

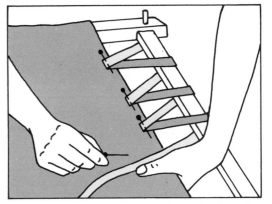

3 To maintain an even tension along side edges of the quilt, use bias tape or fabric strips about 2.5cm/1in wide. Wind and pin tape or strips to sides of quilt and to stretchers, pulling gently until quilt is taut. Remove tape and reattach as necessary when rolling.

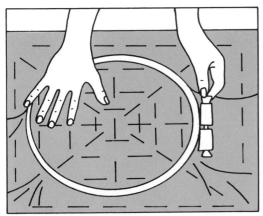

1 **A hoop** is an excellent alternative to a roller frame if you don't have a lot of room to spare. Place inner hoop on a flat surface. Centre a portion of the well-basted quilt over it. Place outer hoop over quilt and screw the wing nut tightly to hold the quilt taut.

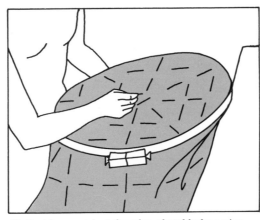

2 Rest hoop against the edge of a table for easier quilting. Sit comfortably in a well-lit area with your sewing hand on top of the quilt and the other hand below—ready to guide the needle in its up-and-down motion.

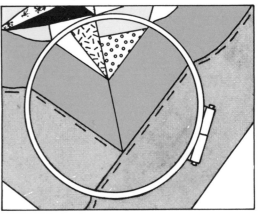

3 To quilt the outer edges of a project when you are working with a hoop, baste wide strips of plain fabric to the edges of the project. Insert project into hoop as shown, so that the plain fabric holds the edges taut.

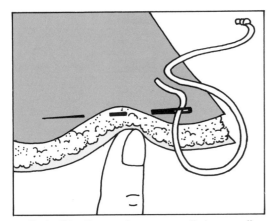

1 **Hand quilting** Choose a between needle in as small a size as is comfortable for you; size 8 is average. Use one strand of quilting thread in your needle. Make a small knot at the end of the thread. Insert needle through the top and padding of your project.

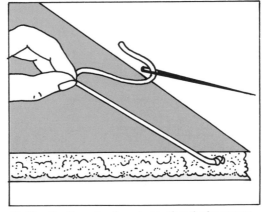

2 Give the thread a sharp tug so that the knot pops below the surface of the quilt top and buries itself in the padding.

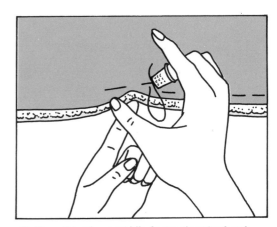

3 Use a thimble on middle finger of sewing hand. Rest eye of needle against thimble. Guide needle at an angle into quilt top so point makes contact with finger below quilt. Exert pressure from below to form a ridge, to help you aim the point.

HAND QUILTING

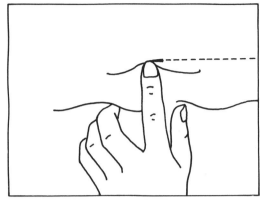

4 As point of needle touches finger below quilt, direct it back to the surface and pull needle and thread through. To prevent finger beneath quilt from getting sore, use a thimble (try leather), tape the fingertip, or allow a callous to form.

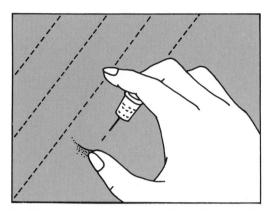

5 Work evenly spaced running stitches through all 3 layers of the quilt sandwich, weaving needle in and out of the fabric in a smooth motion. As you become proficient, "load" the needle with several stitches at one time before pulling it through.

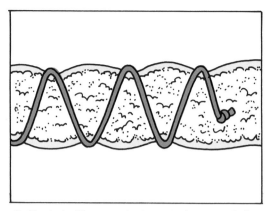

6 To start with, concentrate on sewing even stitches; later strive to make small stitches. Stitches may appear smaller on back of quilt. Tugging thread gently, stitch to cause indentations in padding.

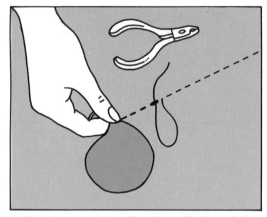

7 If you have trouble pulling the needle through the layers of fabric after you have made a series of quilting stitches, use a deflated balloon or pliers to grip the tip of the needle and pull it through.

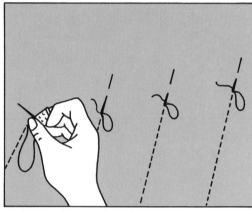

8 Some quilters prefer to have several threaded needles going at once, especially when quilting a border or filling pattern. If you are using several needles at the same time, the work can advance evenly across the quilt.

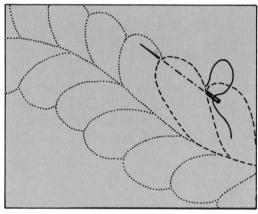

9a To skip from one part of a quilting design to another, run the needle through the top and padding at the end of your last stitch. Bring the point up where the new line of stitches will start.

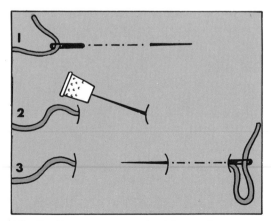

9b To skip across an area that is longer than your needle, insert needle through padding as far as possible (1). Pull needle through to the eye without letting eye come out of fabric; use a thimble to push point forward (2). Pull eye of needle out of fabric (3).

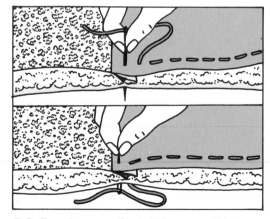

10 To make even quilting stitches across thick areas such as seamlines, work 2 to 4 stab stitches across the bulky area, giving the thread an extra tug with each stitch.

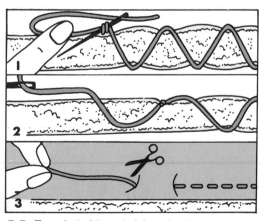

11 To end stitching, wind thread twice around needle; insert through quilt top and padding only (1). Run needle 2.5cm/1in away from line of stitching (2). Tug thread to pop knot beneath surface; hold thread taut and clip close to quilt top (3).

MACHINE QUILTING

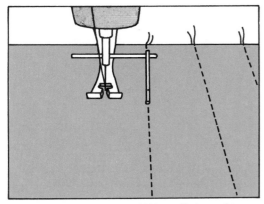

1 Equipment Insert a size 14 (90) needle in machine, loosen tension slightly and set stitch length for 12 stitches per 2.5cm/1in. Use a zigzag foot or attach a quilting foot if you have one. Attach a spacer to quilt parallel lines without having to mark them.

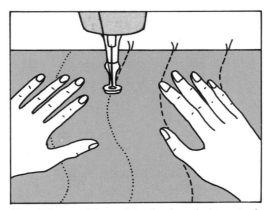

2a When machine-quilting freeform designs, attach a darning foot and drop the feed dogs. Spread layers under machine foot with your hands to imitate the tension of a frame. Stitch slowly; because feed dogs are down, you must control stitch length yourself.

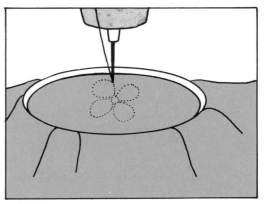

2b You can insert quilt into an inverted hoop to keep layers under tension. Drop feed dogs, remove presser foot and place hoop beneath needle. Lower presser foot bar to engage top thread tension. Guide hoop to control stitch length.

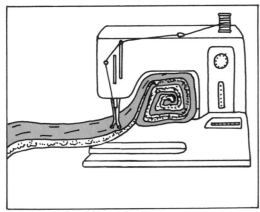

1 Technique Thoroughly baste the quilt; *see page 139.* To begin quilting in the centre, roll the well-basted quilt as tightly yet evenly as possible so as to fit it beneath the head of the sewing machine. Insert the rolled portion beneath the machine as shown.

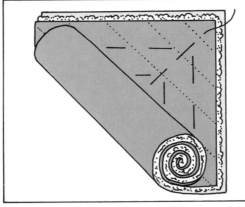

2 To machine-quilt diagonal lines, roll the quilt diagonally from one corner. Quilt from the centre outward to the edges so as to get the most hard-to-manoeuvre part of the work done first and to prevent puckering and uneven shifting of the layers.

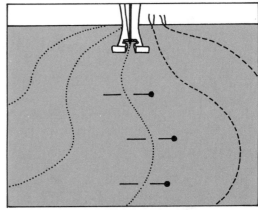

3 Always machine-quilt in the same direction across project to prevent layers from shifting. To stop top layer from easing ahead of needle when sewing a long line, pin the 3 layers together directly over each marked line; remove pins as you come to them.

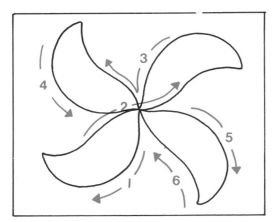

4 Each time you begin and end a line of stitching, the thread ends must be finished off, which can be very time consuming. For speedier machine quilting, adapt your designs so as to quilt in a continuous line, thus avoiding breaking the threads too many times.

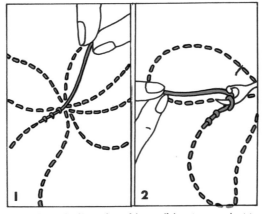

5a To end a line of machine quilting, turn project to WS and pull thread end gently, drawing up thread from RS (1). Use an unpicker/seam ripper or a needle to coax the thread to the WS (2); pull through gently.

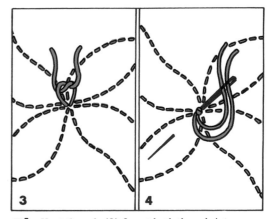

5b Knot threads (3). Insert both threads into a needle and run them through the back and padding, bringing needle out at least 2.5cm/1in away (4). Pull threads gently and clip away excess close to fabric; ends will pop back into padding out of sight.

QUILT-AS-YOU-GO

The Quilt-as-you-go technique enables you to quilt a project in sections by hand or machine. There are two different ways to accomplish this. You can assemble and quilt each block individually and then join the pre-quilted sections to complete a project. Or you can piece and quilt a block at the same time by sewing the pieces over padding and a back.

Make or buy a Quilt-as-you-go frame. It is easy to make a frame yourself following the directions in step 1 of *Technique*. The strips of wood should be 10–15cm/4–6in longer than the largest size block you will make. The wing nuts will allow you to adjust the size of the opening to accommodate the block you are quilting. Alternatively, you can quilt each block using a quilting hoop; sew strips of fabric to the edges of the block so it can be held firmly in the hoop; *see page 141*.

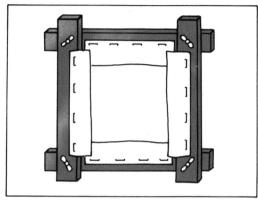

1 **Technique** Make a Quilt-as-you-go frame, which consists of 4 strips of wood (of desired length) held together with wing nuts. Staple narrow fabric aprons to each strip of wood so that the 3 quilt layers can be assembled within the frame.

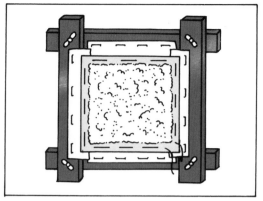

2 Cut backing fabric about 2.5cm/1in larger than block and position WS up within frame; baste to aprons so fabric is taut. Smooth a layer of padding over back, then centre a pieced, appliquéd or plain top fabric over padding, RS up. Baste together.

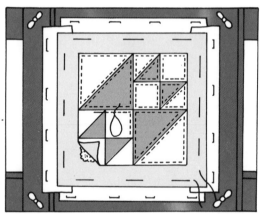

3 Quilt the block by hand; *see pages 140–142*. To join blocks in smooth, non-bulky way, leave 13mm/½in unquilted all around edge of each block. If you wish to quilt close to the outer edges of the block, you must join blocks using strips; *see facing page*.

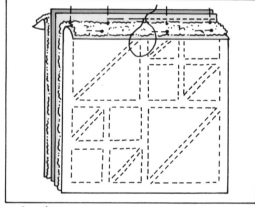

1 **Smooth joining** Hold 2 blocks together with RS of top layers facing and raw edges even; pin top layers together, folding and pinning padding and back out of the way. Stitch together from corner to corner by hand- or machine-making a 6mm/¼in seam.

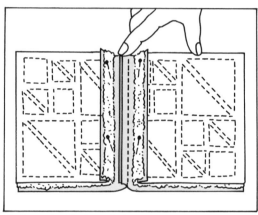

2 Open the blocks and place top side down on a flat surface. Finger-press the seam allowance of the top fabrics to one side; *see page 43*. Remove pins holding the padding and back in place.

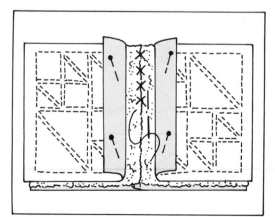

3 Smooth padding over seam allowance of top layers, patting the padding with your fingers so that the edges meet neatly. Trim away excess padding if edges overlap. Sew edges of padding together with large cross stitches using white thread.

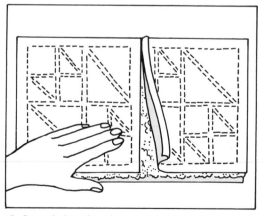

4 Smooth the edge of one backing fabric flat over the padding. Fold and finger-press the edge of the other block 6mm/¼in to WS.

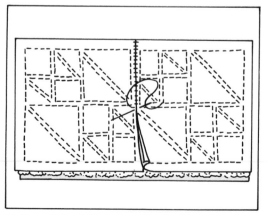

5 Smooth the folded edge of the backing fabric down and pin in place onto the other backing. Slipstitch securely together using matching thread.

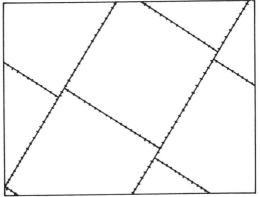

6 Continue joining blocks together to make rows, then join rows of blocks in the same way. To eliminate bulk where the blocks meet, you need to pre-plan: position the seam joins so that they face in opposite directions on alternate rows.

1 Strip joining Use fabric to match backing. Cut strip to length of seam and 3.2cm/1¼in wide; press one long edge 6mm/¼in to WS. Pin blocks together RS facing and edges matching; pin strip along same edge RS to backing. Stitch together.

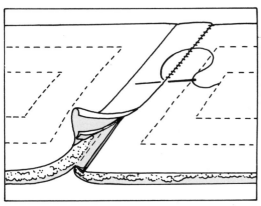

2 Trim seam, then open blocks and place top side down on a flat surface. Fold trimmed seam allowance to one side and smooth strip over it. Slipstitch folded edge of strip to backing, covering trimmed seam allowance.

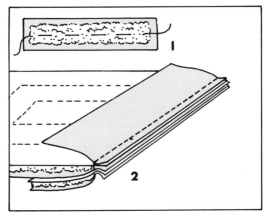

1 Sashing Cut 2 strips to length of seam and desired width; add 6mm/¼in seam allowance. Cut padding 6mm/¼in smaller at each edge; centre and baste on WS of one sashing strip (1). Pin sashing strips to same edge of one block with RS facing; stitch together (2).

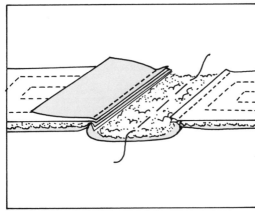

2 Open out padded sashing strip only. Stitch a second block to opposite long edge of padded sashing strip with RS facing.

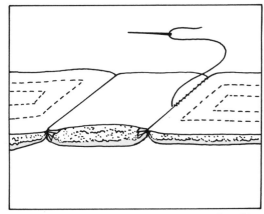

3 Fold raw edge of unpadded sashing strip 6mm/¼in to WS. Smooth over padded sashing strip and pin so that folded edge covers stitching line. Slipstitch in place securely. Continue joining blocks to make rows, then join rows together in same manner.

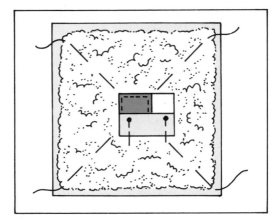

1 Quilt-and-sew Centre and baste padding on WS of backing, then assemble design by the *Press Piecing* method described on *pages 75-76* . In this way, you are sewing and quilting at the same time. Log Cabin designs are very effective when made this way.

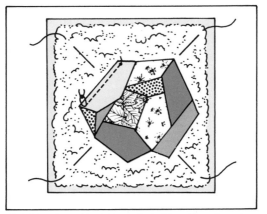

2 To begin and end lines of stitching, draw threads to RS and tie in a knot before adding more pieces. Or, you can backstitch if backing is a busy print that will conceal backstitches. Quilt-and-sew Crazy Patchwork designs to create textured results.

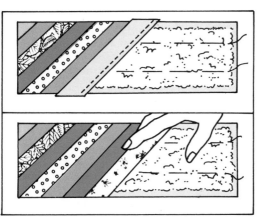

3 Quilt-and-sew is suitable for making blocks of any size or shape. As you sew pieces in place, finger-press each one to RS and pin to backing before attaching next piece. Try making String Patchwork with this technique.

CORDED QUILTING

A purely decorative form of needlework, Corded Quilting can be traced back many centuries. The earliest example, in London's Victoria and Albert Museum, is a German corded quilt which dates back to the 16th century. However, most of the work that has survived was done throughout Europe in the 17th and 18th centuries, when the style was fashionable for embellishing quilts and clothing for men, women and children. Waistcoats, cuffs and caps were made into ornate sculpture by the addition of cord inserted into stitched channels. Corded patterns became particularly elaborate in England: toward the end of the 17th century many English quilts were so densely corded that no space was left for any other type of quilting.[32] Because Corded projects are not padded, they do not provide much warmth, which is probably why this technique matured in sunny Italy. Corded quilting is commonly known as Italian quilting.

A Corded quilting design is a composition of double parallel lines. Two layers of fabric are joined along these lines with running or backstitches. A strand of cord or yarn is inserted from the wrong side in between the layers of fabric and the cord is pulled through the channels to create a raised shape. Corded designs can be solid, with one channel adjacent to the next, or flat spaces can be left between the cords. When cording is separated by flat areas, the design must be well balanced so that the cording does not pull the fabric out of shape.

Use cotton piping cord or candlewick that has been pre-shrunk and dried. Pre-shrinking will ensure washability of the finished piece and will also make the cord more pliable. The cord should fill the channels comfortably, and you should be able to thread it through a blunt yarn or tapestry needle. If you wish to use a very thick cord that cannot be threaded through a needle, stitch the end of the thick cord to the end of a thinner one. Then run the thinner one through the channel, pulling the thick one along behind it. You can use other types of filling for the channels: rug wool, thick knitting wool or several thicknesses of yarn are suitable, although they may flatten if the project is washed repeatedly.

Great accuracy is needed for this type of raised quilting, more so than with any other. The space between the lines of stitching must be the same throughout and must be the correct size for the cord being used. If the channel formed by the stitching lines is too narrow, you will have trouble threading the cord through and the surrounding fabric will pucker when you are finished. If the channel is too wide, the cord will not show up as a raised area.

You can adapt any design to Corded Quilting. First study the pattern and try to eliminate all but the most important design lines. Then draw the simplified design full size on a sheet of paper. Draw a second line about 6mm/¼in away from the first, depending on the size cord you will use.

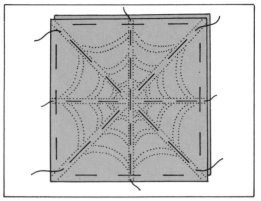

1 Technique Use a fine cotton or linen for the top and a loosely woven fabric for the back. Cut back and top to same size. Transfer design to RS of top by one of the methods covered on *pages 138-139*. Pin back and top together with WS facing; baste to secure.

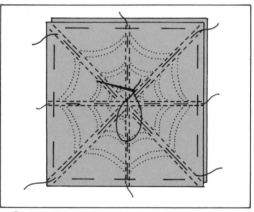

2b Sew along main outlines of design first, then fill in details. When channels cross, do not allow stitches to cross or you will not be able to thread cord through. Decide which channel will overlap the other one and stitch the design lines accordingly.

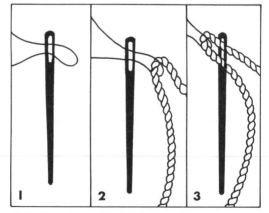

4 To thread a needle with thick cord, loop a short length of thread and insert loop through eye of needle (1). Insert end of cord through loop (2), then pull thread loop through eye of needle (3), drawing the end of the cord through the eye as well.

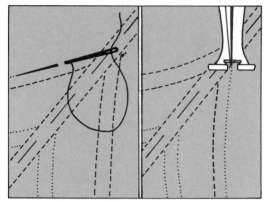

2a Stitch along marked design lines by hand or machine to create evenly spaced channels. If sewing by hand, work small even running stitches; for a bold effect, work line in backstitch or chain stitch; *see page 64*. By machine, sew with medium stitch.

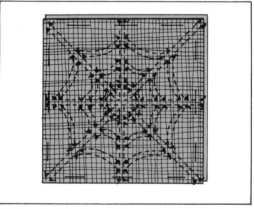

3 If sewing the design by hand, begin all stitching with a knot on WS. If sewing by machine, pull all threads to WS and tie off; clip thread ends close to the knots. Remove basting.

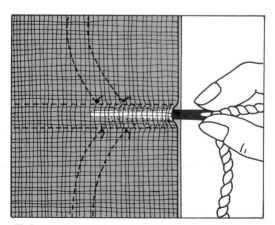

5 Insert the cord from the back of the work. To begin, insert point of needle at the beginning of a channel between the 2 layers of fabric. Be careful not to penetrate through to the RS of the work.

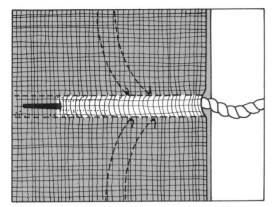

6 Push the needle through the channel, making each stitch as long as is comfortable according to the length of the needle you are using. Pull the needle and cord gently through the channel, leaving a 13mm/½in tail at the beginning.

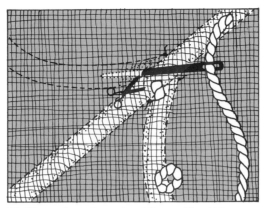

7 Where channels cross, cut the cord leaving a 13mm/½in tail. Insert needle through fabric on other side of channel and continue. Do not carry cord over another line of cord, or it will make the work too bulky at that point.

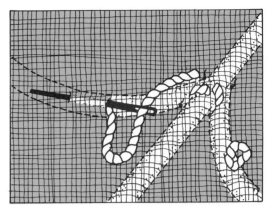

8 To work curves, bring needle out at the point where you would be bending the fabric. Reinsert needle into same hole and continue guiding needle through channel. Pull cord gently through, but do not pull cord taut; leave a loop at each exit point.

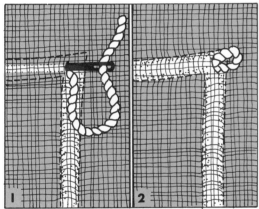

9 To turn a corner, bring the needle out at the corner point and reinsert it again in the same hole (1). Continue guiding the needle through the channel in the new direction. Do not pull the cord taut, but leave a loop at the exit point (2).

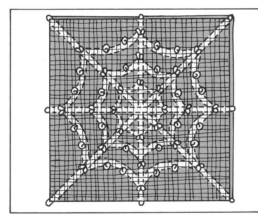

10 Back of work should look like this. The loops remain in the work because they will allow for stretch and shrinkage as the piece is handled. Note how the cord is cut where it crosses another channel.

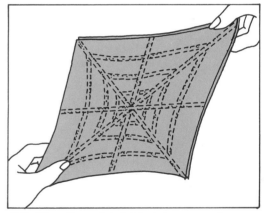

11 When the work is finished, grasp opposite corners firmly and pull on the bias to allow the cord to settle into the channels and to remove any puckers that may have formed.

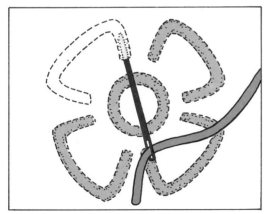

Variation To create a Shadow Cording design, choose a sheer fabric for the top layer. Stitch to a backing fabric as described, then insert a brightly coloured cord through the channel. You can use colourful thick yarn or dyed cotton cord.

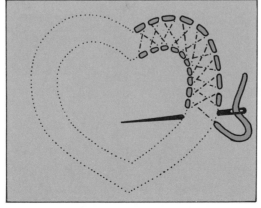

1 **One-layer cording** Mark design on RS of fabric, insert RS up in a frame. Holding cord beneath marked design lines with your fingers, work backstitches alternately on each of the marked lines, running the thread over the cord on the back with each stitch.

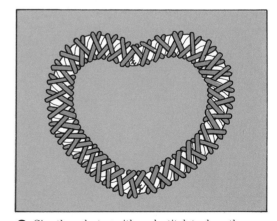

2 Give thread a tug with each stitch to draw the fabric slightly over the cord and raise the design. Work backstitches over entire design in this manner. Design will look like this on WS. Use this method to eliminate bulk, such as when decorating clothing.

SASHIKO

In the early 18th century, Japanese wives made heavy jackets for their husbands, who wore them while working on farms, in forests and on fishing boats. The women constructed the garments by sewing together two layers of indigo-dyed cloth with running stitches; it was believed that the closer the stitches, the more durable the garment.[33] The geometric stitches were purely functional at first; they later became a type of decorative embroidery.

Even though Sashiko is basically a form of embroidery, it is eminently suitable as a quilting medium. Very little adaptation is needed other than adding the other layers of the quilt sandwich—the padding and back. Use sturdy white thread such as no. 3 pearl cotton on dark blue cotton fabric for a traditional appearance. However, you can work Sashiko in any colour thread on any solid colour fabric.

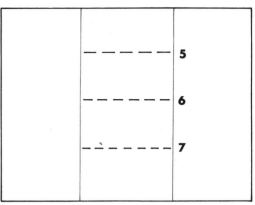

1 **Technique** Select a design on this page or from a book on Sashiko; *see Bibliography*. Enlarge design to desired size; *see page 106*. Transfer design to solid fabric and assemble the quilt layers; *see pages 138-139*. Work design in running stitch.

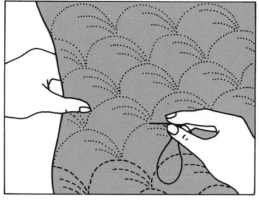

2 Sew either 5, 6, or 7 stitches per 2.5cm/1in. Test your stitches on a scrap of fabric to find the length that is most comfortable for you. Do not attempt to make very tiny stitches; longer stitches are traditional in Sashiko quilting.

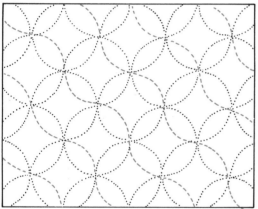

3 Work continuous lines of stitching. Study the design to determine the best way to stitch in order to avoid breaking the thread too often. This pattern is called *Shippo Tsunagi* (Seven Treasures of Buddha).

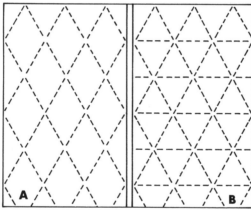

4 Work the same number of stitches in each section of a Sashiko design. For example, in the designs above, work the same number of stitches between each intersection as shown. Pattern A is called *Yarai* (Bamboo Fence); B is *Uroko Tsunagi* (Fish Scales).

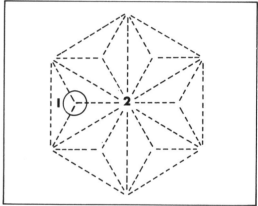

5 When working corners, do not bring all stitches to same point; leave space where stitches would intersect (1). Where many lines intersect at one point, as in this one called *Asanoha* (Hemp Leaf), leave unstitched area in centre (2).

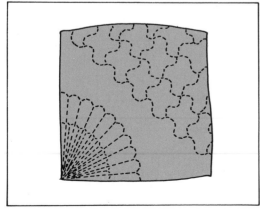

1 **Projects** Work 2 different Sashiko designs on one fabric and make it into a cushion; *see page 171*. Try to combine designs that work well together; leave some space between them as shown here.

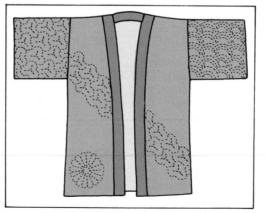

2 A Sashiko kimono is an ambitious project, but one that will show off many different patterns. Use one of the many kimono patterns available from the major pattern companies. Carry a design from one area of the kimono to another for continuity.

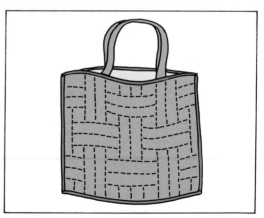

3 Try making a tote bag in Sashiko. Work a different Sashiko pattern on each side of the bag, or combine several patterns to create a sampler effect. Use dark blue fabric and white thread for a traditional appearance.

TIED QUILTING

Tying is an excellent way to finish a quilt quickly. A Tied or Tufted quilt will not have the same flat appearance as one that has been quilted in running stitch: rather, it will be soft and billowy. A Tied quilt can be much thicker than a hand-quilted one because you don't have to worry about making even stitches through many layers; the fill can be several layers thick for a warm puffy result. Tied quilts are fun to make— a beginner, even a child, can successfully construct one. You can tie a quilt in different ways: the knots can be on the front or back of the quilt, you can make fluffy tufts using extra yarn, or use buttons or bows to enhance the work. Because it will not be closely quilted, you should select a bonded or needlepunch polyester padding for the fill; or you can use a blanket.

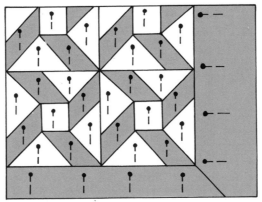

1 **Technique** Assemble the quilt layers as directed on *pages 138-139*. Pin-baste the layers together at each spot that will be tied. If quilt is wider than 7.6cm/3in, you must tie the border too. Make sure pins go through all 3 layers to prevent shifting.

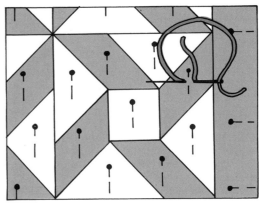

2 Thread needle with long unknotted strand of sturdy thread, crochet or pearl cotton, or yarn. Make a backstitch over each pin through all 3 layers; leave 5–7.6cm/2–3in tail. Make another backstitch over same spot; trim excess thread, leaving same length tail.

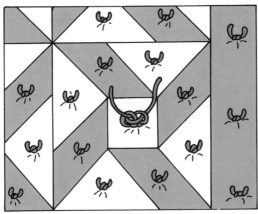

3 Tie tails into a square knot, first right over left, then left over right. Pull knot tightly, then trim tails evenly. Make one tie every 15cm/6in, or every 7.6cm/3in if the quilt will withstand much washing.

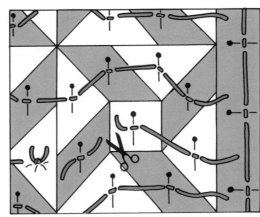

Quick method Work 2 backstitches over first pin. Continue on to next pin without cutting thread; leave thread slack between pins. Make 2 backstitches at next pin; continue until you run out of thread. Clip thread between pins; tie square knots. Trim tails.

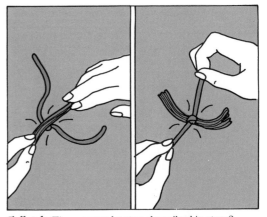

Fluffy tufts Tie a square knot as described in step 3, leaving 12.7cm/5in tails. Cut 3 strands of yarn, each about 5cm/2in long; centre over square knot. Tie another square knot over the yarn, securing the strands. Cut all tails evenly.

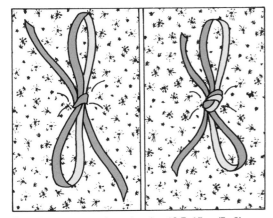

Bows Make a square knot, leaving 12.7–15cm/5–6in tails. Tie the tails into a bow (1), then tie a square knot over the centre of the bow to secure it (2). Try using a narrow flexible ribbon instead of thread or yarn.

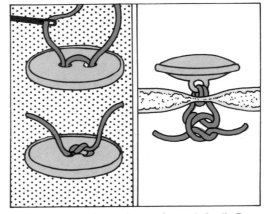

Buttons will add a decorative touch to a tied quilt. Pass needle through 2-hole button to WS of quilt leaving 5cm/2in tail; bring up through other hole and stitch once more, then tie ends into a square knot on RS. For shank buttons, stitch securely, then knot on WS.

Special effects If you are making a pictorial quilt, use tufts as a design element. Red thread or yarn can simulate flowers or apples on a tree. Try white thread to portray snowflakes or stars, blue or yellow to resemble birds or flowers.

TRAPUNTO

Trapunto is one of the most admired forms of quilting. The technique, while not difficult, is nevertheless painstaking and time-consuming. Even to the casual observer, Trapunto quilts are impressive both visually and because of the obvious amount of labour involved in their production. Also known as stuffed quilting, Trapunto is worked by sewing two layers of plain fabric together, creating a design which is then stuffed from the wrong side. The design stands out in high relief. This form of raised quilting is often enhanced by closely-worked filling stitches which flatten the background, causing the stuffed areas to stand out.

Trapunto is a very old style of quilting. The earliest existing example is the famous Sicilian quilt made at the end of the 14th century, which details scenes from the Legend of Tristram.[34] Prominent parts of the design were stuffed with cotton to make them stand out in much the same way as bas-relief sculptures of the day. During the 17th and 18th centuries, Trapunto work reached a peak of popularity throughout Europe, mainly as a means of decorating the clothing and furnishings of the wealthy. Men wore cloaks, jackets and waistcoats decorated with intricate Trapunto designs, while women and children wore Trapunto petticoats, caps, coats and dresses.

By the end of the 18th century, with a falling economy and the advent of thinner fabrics, Trapunto gradually declined in popularity in Europe. However, stuffed quilting had been brought to America with its founders, and as life became more stable, Trapunto became more common. Intricate patterns were wrought on quilts of linsey-woolsey, and then of cotton. By the early 19th century, the all-white Trapunto quilts made by wealthy ladies living in the northeast and southern parts of the United States reached a high level of splendour.

There are two different ways to work Trapunto. With the Hidden opening method, you must use a loosely-woven backing fabric so that the threads can be separated without breaking. The filling is inserted through the opening, then the threads are pushed back into their original position. The Visible opening method is undoubtedly easier though slightly messier. The backing fabric is slit and the filling inserted through the opening; the slit is sewn together to hold the filling in place. A project made by this method must be lined.

If you are making a quilt or wall hanging in Trapunto, vary the amount of stuffing throughout the piece to emphasize certain parts; use a glazed fabric so that the stuffed areas reflect light. Add decorative embroidery stitches to your work using matching thread. French knots or stem stitch are normally used to enhance Trapunto; *see page 64*. Combine Trapunto with Corded Quilting for a traditional effect; *see pages 146-147*.

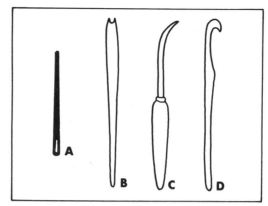

Equipment You must have a tool that will enable you to stuff the filling into very tiny spaces. Any of the following will do: a thick blunt needle such as a yarn needle (A), a wooden stick notched at one edge (B), a nut picker (C) or a small crochet hook (D).

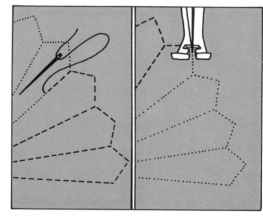

2 Sew the 2 layers together by hand or machine along marked design lines. If sewing by hand, work small even running stitches, backstitch or chain stitch; *see page 64*. If sewing by machine, set stitch length for medium straight stitch.

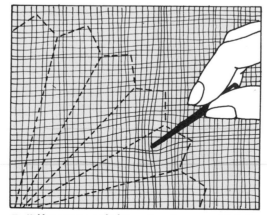

1 **Hidden opening method** Use a loosely-woven fabric for the backing. Holding your chosen tool at an angle, gently insert the point in between the woven threads at centre of area to be stuffed. Wriggle point to enlarge hole without breaking the threads.

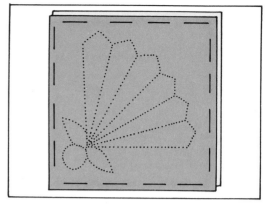

1 **Preparation** Use a fine cotton or linen for top; for backing, see instructions for method you have chosen. Cut backing and top to same size. Transfer design to RS of top; *pages 138-139*. Baste backing and top together with WS facing.

3 Alternatively, you can use a printed fabric for the top. Cut backing to same size as printed top; pin and baste layers together with WS facing. Work stitches along lines of printed design, outlining areas you wish to emphasize through stuffing.

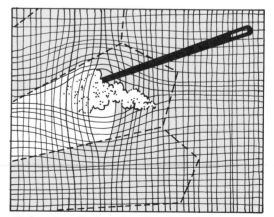

2 Insert small wisps of stuffing through the opening, a little at a time, until the area is stuffed to desired degree of plumpness. Use the point of your tool to gently push the bits of stuffing into tiny spaces.

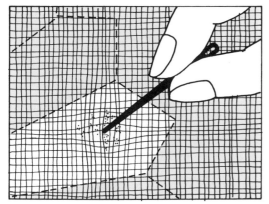

3 After the area has been stuffed, use the point of your tool to gently coax the threads around the opening back into their original position.

1 **Visible opening method** Choose a medium-weave fabric for the backing. Using a small pair of sharp pointed scissors, make a slit in centre of area to be stuffed, being careful not to cut through to top fabric. Make opening large enough to stuff area comfortably.

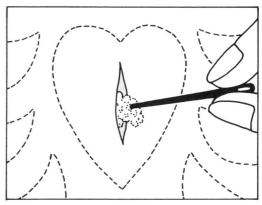

2 Insert the filling through the opening using your tool to push it evenly into all parts of the area being stuffed.

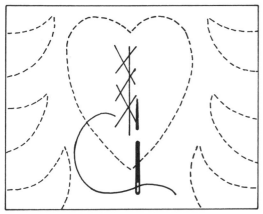

3 After the area has been stuffed, hold cut edges together without overlapping them. Join cut edges with large cross stitches; allow stitches to sink into the filling for added security. Do not pull fabric edges together or this will cause puckering.

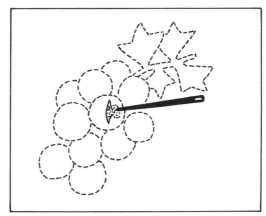

1 **Hints** When you are making a large design, begin stuffing from the centre and work outwards. Do not jump from one part of the design to another, but work outwards in a circular manner.

2 Use very small wisps of filling so as to stuff each area without forming lumps (A). Do not overstuff (B) or the filling may swell in the wash and break your quilting threads. An overstuffed area may also feel hard and rigid to the touch, which is undesirable.

3 If you need to stuff a large area, cut a piece of padding slightly smaller than the exact size of the area to be stuffed. Insert padding into the opening, smoothing it in place. You must use the *Visible opening method* in order to do this.

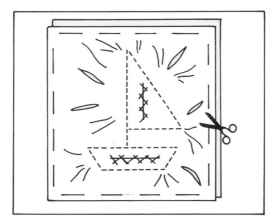

4 To prevent the stuffed piece from buckling, pull the work firmly on the diagonal alternately from each corner, stretching the work on the bias. If that doesn't help, try making slits in the backing fabric only at the buckled areas as shown.

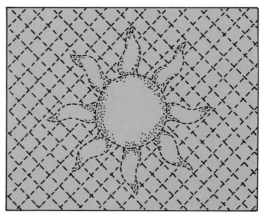

5 To make stuffed areas stand out in high relief, quilt filling stitches across entire background of the piece around the stuffed areas. *See page 140* for a selection of filling stitches.

SPECIAL EFFECTS

For some people, quilting is the most enjoyable aspect of quiltmaking. It is rewarding and relaxing to establish a smooth rhythm of stitching and watch your quilt develop into a tactile, three-dimensional work of art. On this page are some alternative methods of quilting that you may wish to try. The techniques are a bit more time-consuming than working traditional straight running stitches, but the results will add a special quality to your work, setting it apart from the rest.

If you find that you don't really like hand-quilting, there are some alternative methods of making unusual yet warm quilts. The methods on the facing page are very quick and easy to do—you may decide to try them to make quick quilts for people who may not appreciate the time put into a hand-quilted project, but who nevertheless value a handmade gift.

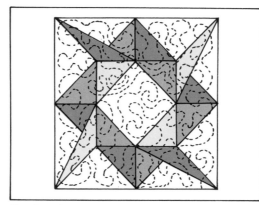

Meander quilting Work short, even running stitches in a random curvilinear fashion all over your quilt top, or only in certain areas to highlight a design. Meander quilting will soften the appearance of a stark geometric pattern.

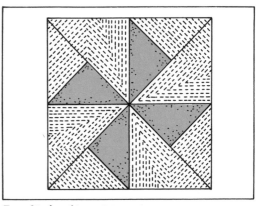

1a Stipple quilting will flatten your quilt sandwich, raising other parts of the design. Use thread to match area you are quilting so that stitches blend into background. Work parallel lines very close to one another: 1–3mm/$\frac{1}{16}$–$\frac{1}{8}$in apart.

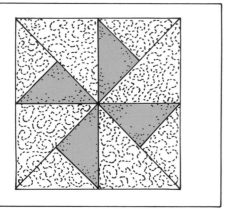

1b Alternatively, you can sew close meandering stitches all over area to be flattened; do not allow them to touch one another. Work with a frame or hoop, pulling stitches tightly to make them sink into the fabric. Use a solid glazed fabric for best results.

2 To stipple-quilt by machine, program machine to sew zigzag or embroidery stitch. Drop feed dogs, remove presser foot and place area to be quilted beneath needle. Allow machine to embroider randomly, moving quilt manually to spread stitches evenly.

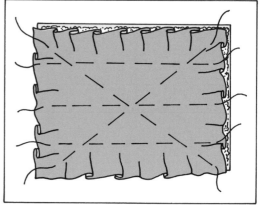

1 Wrinkle quilting Cut fabric for top 5–7.6cm/2–3in larger all around than base. Assemble layers for quilting, *see pages 138-139*. Pleat or gather edges of top to fit base, then pin edges together. Arrange excess fabric evenly across top; baste to secure.

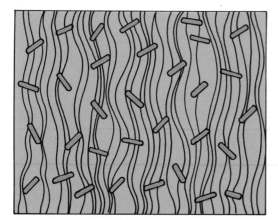

2 Work meandering medium-sized running stitches across quilt top, folding fabric as you sew. Smooth the wrinkles that form either horizontally or vertically. Quilt very closely to exaggerate the folds, or make widely-spaced stitches for a puffier background.

3 After the quilting is finished, appliqué a design on top, padding the appliqués slightly for extra dimension; *see page 107*. Or you can leave the top as it is for a simple textured quilt.

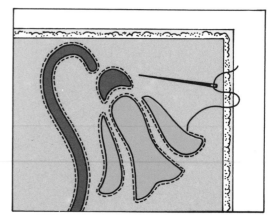

Shadow quilting Review Shadow Appliqué on *page 121*. Prepare top fabrics as directed, then assemble over padding and a back; baste layers together. Work running stitches through all layers so that you are quilting and securing appliqués at the same time.

1 **Prequilted fabric** To make a quilt very quickly, use prequilted fabric for the top and back. Cut fabrics 2.5cm/1in larger all around than desired size; pin together around edges with RS facing. Sew 13mm/½in seam, leaving large opening for turning. Trim corners.

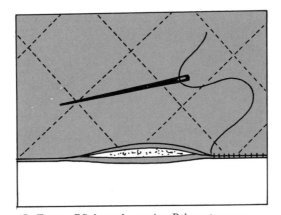

2 Turn to RS through opening. Poke out corners with a knitting needle so that they are square. Fold raw edges at opening 13mm/½in inside; slipstitch opening closed. Secure layers to prevent shifting by tying the quilt at regular intervals; *see page 149.*

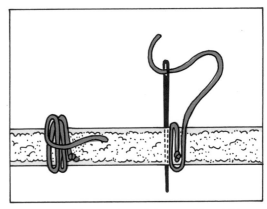

3 For invisible security, tack layers with matching thread. Knot thread end and pop through back, burying it in padding. Make stitches over one another. Run thread through padding some distance from tacking; trim.

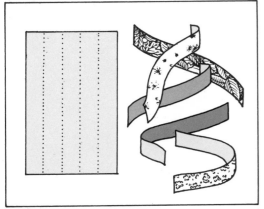

1 **Tubular quilting** Cut backing to desired finished size of quilt; mark parallel lines on WS, each about 10cm/4in apart. Cut strips of fabric for top same length as backing and about 2.5–5cm/1–2in wider than marked channels. Strips can be pieced if desired.

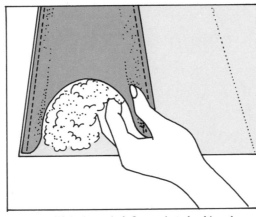

2 With WS facing, stitch first strip to backing along one long edge, 6mm/¼in from edges. Place stuffing or rolled padding on WS of back within marked lines of first channel. Fold fabric strip over padding. Baste so edge of strip aligns with marked line on backing.

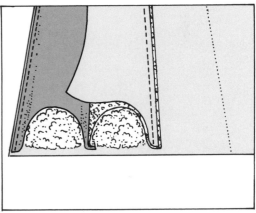

3 Pin second strip to first and backing with RS facing and raw edges even. Stitch in place, making a 6mm/¼in seam. Add padding as for first channel, fold strip of fabric over padding and baste edge in place. Add third strip.

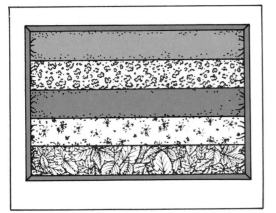

4 Continue to add strips of fabric and padding to WS of back, making one tube at a time until quilt is finished. Bind quilt with a narrow binding, pleating excess fabric at ends of tubes to fit; *see pages 166–167* for binding instructions.

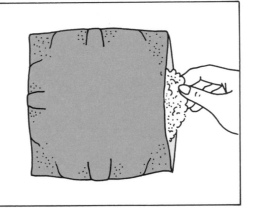

1 **Cushion quilting** Cut fabric squares to desired size; sew together with RS facing leaving an opening for turning. Trim corners; turn to RS, poking out corners so that they are square. Stuff cushion until plump; fold raw edges at opening inside and slipstitch closed.

2 Use a different fabric for the front and back of each cushion so quilt is different on each side. Assemble cushions in a pleasing arrangement; butt edges together, then loosely whipstitch them to hold. Zigzag-stitch edges together by machine.

There was a ring of passionate eagerness in the old voice, and she fell to putting away her tresures as if the suggestion of losing them had made her fearful of their sefety. I looked again at the heap of quilts. An hour ago they had been patchwork, and nothing more. But now! The old woman's words had wrought a transformation in the homely mass of calico and silk and worsted. Patchwork? Ah no! It was memory, imagination, history, biography, joy, sorrow, philosophy, religion, romance, realism, life, love, and death; and over all, like a halo, the love of the artist for his work and the soul's longing for earthy immortality. *From "Aunt Jane of Kentucky" written in 1898 by Eliza Calvert Hall.*

5

Quilts & Other Projects

QUILTS AND OTHER PROJECTS

Why do people make quilts? If you say it is because quilting is an enjoyable, exciting pastime you would be correct, but if you think that the current ardent fascination with quilting is a product of today's environment, you would be mistaken. The following was written by Marie D Webster in 1915:

There are many things to induce women to piece quilts. The desire for a handsome bed furnishing, or the wish to make a gift of one to a dear friend, have inspired some women to make quilts. With others, quilt making is a recreation, a diversion, a means of occupying restless fingers. However, the real inducement is love of the work; because the desire to make a quilt exceeds all other desires. In such a case it is worked on persistently, laid aside reluctantly, and taken up each time with renewed interest and pleasure. It is this intense interest in the work which produces the most beautiful quilts. On quilts that are made because of the genuine interest in the work, the most painstaking efforts are put forth; the passing of time is not considered . . .[35]

These sentiments could just as easily have been written today and they summarize perfectly the way the majority of quilters feel about their work. Marie Webster's point about the painstaking efforts involved in quiltmaking should not be overlooked. In order to make a work that will withstand the test of time and one that you will be proud to bequeath to your heirs, the quilt must be well made.

This chapter will guide you through the final stages of making a quilt—assembling the top, adding a border and a binding, along with some useful suggestions regarding signing, hanging and care. The end of the chapter is devoted to using the techniques described in this book for making projects other than quilts such as cushions, bags and clothing.

QUILT SETS

The following pages illustrate a variety of quilt sets—from quilts comprised of blocks to wholecloth and appliqué quilts. Study the sets carefully to get an idea of the numerous possibilities that are open to you. You can make your quilt exactly like one of the sets illustrated here, or use the designs as a springboard to make up your own creations.

The quilts on the facing page exemplify the four basic quilt sets. The edge-to-edge set is an excellent choice for a dramatic geometric effect. Patchwork or appliqué blocks will take on a whole new life when sewn directly to one another because secondary designs will emerge. Choose this set if your piecing is very accurate and you don't mind making enough blocks to achieve the required quilt size.

If you wish to eliminate a certain amount of work in the piecing or appliqué stage, select a pieced-and-plain set—you'll halve your work since each pieced block is paired with a plain one. Select this set if your blocks are intricate and you wish to isolate them from one another. This set is ideal for those who love fancy quilting because you can work an elaborate design on each of the plain blocks.

In the sashing set, narrow strips of fabric separate the blocks from one another while adding to the size of the quilt. Sashing is an excellent way to link disparate blocks together; select a fabric that harmonizes with all the blocks.

You can achieve exciting results with a diagonal set. A quilt block that may not have looked very inspiring when viewed squarely will take on a whole new appearance when turned on point. A diagonal set can incorporate blocks set edge-to-edge, pieced-and-plain or blocks set with sashing.

The quilt sets on *pages 157-159* are variations of the four basic sets. Remember that a quilt is not just a conglomeration of different ideas; all parts of your creation should work as an integral unit. Sketch your ideas on paper and study them before committing yourself to fabric.

ESTIMATING YARDAGE

If you are buying a large amount of fabric for a quilt, you'll want your yardage calculations to be accurate. The instructions on *page 161* show you how to compute the yardage mathematically.

As you make more quilts, you'll become adept at figuring out how much fabric to buy even when you do not have a specific quilt in mind. Since it is difficult to estimate the exact amount of yardage that you will need to make an unknown quilt, be on the safe side and buy a bit more fabric than you think you'll need. You can always use that fabric in some other project. However, if you do run out of material while you are making a quilt, don't panic and run all over town trying to match it. Some of the best and most spontaneous fabric combinations have come about as a result of a quilter running out of one fabric and having to substitute another.

JOINING QUILT BLOCKS

If you are making a scrap or sampler quilt you must position the blocks so as to show them off to their best advantage. Clear a large flat surface and arrange the blocks in rows, according to the quilt set you have chosen to make. Study your arrangement to see how the designs look next to one another. The range of colours and prints should be evenly balanced throughout the quilt. The corners and middle are key spots in your quilt; try to position your most attractive blocks in these places. Keep moving the blocks around and critically study the effects until you are completely satisfied with your composition. Make a note of the final design arrangement or

pin the blocks together in rows unless you have an excellent memory.

SASHING AND BORDERS

The sashing and border of a quilt will act as a frame and should unify and contain the quilt. The border, particularly, is used to define the outer edges and to hold the design together. Select a harmonizing fabric in a relatively dark value so that you create a definite boundary around the quilt. If you wish to have a light border next to your blocks, then use a narrow inner border to add some spice and vibrancy to the design. One way to unify a quilt design is to make the sashing and borders in the same fabric. Be sure to measure accurately before cutting the sashing and borders so that you will not waste fabric or end up having to piece unnecessarily.

FINISHING

There are a number of different ways to finish off the edges of a quilt, as discussed on *pages 166–168*. Study your quilt top critically to determine the finish that will best enhance your work. A separate binding takes a bit more time to prepare than a self-binding or fold-finishing, but it gives you the freedom to choose any colour or print. Self-binding, while quick and easy to do, is not always recommended for projects when the back is made from the same fabric as the border; in this case a self-binding can make the edges of the project seem to fade away, particularly if the colours in the centre of the quilt are very strong. Piping will add a subtle hint of colour to the edge of a quilt, and may be just right for a refined design. Sawtooth triangles and clamshells are fun finishes and would best suit quilts of a humorous nature.

Your project will have greater personal and historic value if it is signed and dated. The more information you can give about the quilt, the better. We would know much more about the history of quiltmaking today if only more of the makers of antique quilts had signed and dated their work.

MAKING A MASTERPIECE

While you may feel that making a masterpiece quilt is an unthinkable proposition, it isn't as difficult as you suppose and is within the reach of all quilters as long as they don't mind a bit of "painstaking effort". A masterpiece quilt is not a project that is simply well pieced or elaborately quilted, but one that has been effectively designed and executed from the very first moment. Be creative with your quilt design, even if it is a new interpretation of an old pattern. Be meticulous in your construction: seams should match precisely, corners and points should be perfect, curves should be smooth, and pressing should be excellent. The finished quilt should be neat and clean and any markings should be invisible.

BASIC QUILT SETS: BLOCKS

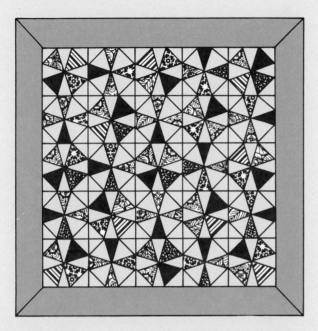

Edge-to-Edge Set: Patchwork or appliqué blocks are sewn directly to one another. The plain border on this quilt has mitred corners. The patchwork design shown on this page is called Kaleidoscope.

Pieced-and-Plain Set: Patchwork or appliqué blocks are sewn to plain blocks. A narrow border separates the blocks from a wide border cut from the same fabric as the plain blocks; the corners are mitred.

Sashing Set: Patchwork or appliqué blocks are separated by narrow strips of fabric, known as sashing. The plain border has squared corners.

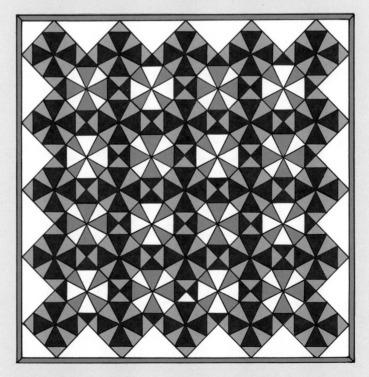

Diagonal Set: Blocks are turned so that the corners are on point. Quarter- and half-squares fill in the edges. The quilt is framed with a simple binding and no border.

BLOCKS

Sashing with Squares: Jacob's Ladder design.

Diagonal Set with Sashing: Tulip appliqué designs.

Patchwork Sashing: Churn Dash sashing; Bay Leaves blocks.

Pieced border: Oak Leaf and Reel designs.

VARIATIONS

Single Block Quilt: Broken Star or Carpenter's Wheel design.

Strip Quilt: Flying Geese design.

Above: **Four Block Quilt:** Spice Pink appliqué design.[36] *Right:* **Medallion Quilt.**

Appliqué Quilt with Scalloped Border

Wholecloth Quilt with Ruffled Border

Wholecloth T-Quilt

Wholecloth Quilt with Round Corners

ESTIMATING YARDAGE

1 Patchwork Make a rough sketch of your entire quilt on graph paper, including sashing and borders. Colour the design with a coloured pencil or crayon to indicate the different fabrics that you will be using.

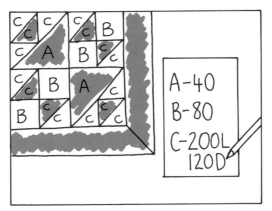

2 Label each of the patchwork pieces. Count up and make a list of the total number of pieces in each colour that will be needed to make the quilt.

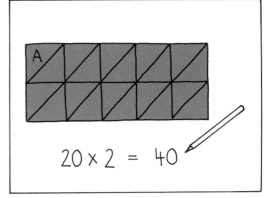

3 Determine fabric width that you need; subtract 5cm/2in from width to allow for selvages and shrinkage. Make a sketch to find number of pieces that can be cut from ¼ metre/yard; multiply by 2 to see how many pieces can be cut from ½ metre/yard.

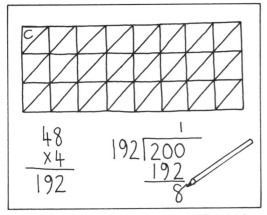

4 If you require more than ½ metre/yard, multiply number of pieces that can be cut from ¼ metre/yard by four to assess how many pieces can be cut from 1 metre/yard. Divide that number into total number to assess how much fabric to buy.

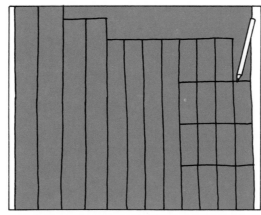

Sashes and borders Cut sashes and borders on lengthwise grain of fabric; add 5cm/2in to length of each border. To assess total yardage needed, draw borders and sashes on paper to see how many pieces will fit across fabric width (subtract 5cm/2in from width).

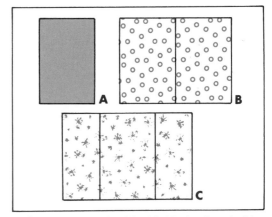

Back Find length and width of finished quilt and add 5cm/2in extra. If back is not wider than fabric, cut from one length (A). If back is longer and wider than fabric, buy 2 lengths and seam (B). If back is wider than B, buy 3 lengths and seam twice (C).

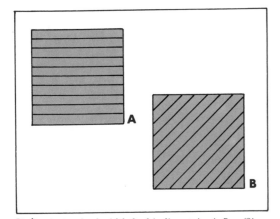

Binding A standard width for binding strips is 5cm/2in. One square metre/yard of fabric (39 × 39cm/36 × 36in) will yield approximately 18 metres/yards of standard width binding cut on straight grain (A) or about 16 metres/yards of binding cut on the bias (B).

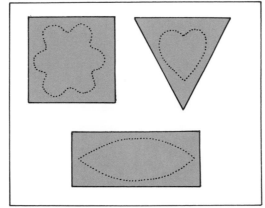

Appliqué Draw the nearest geometric shape around edge of appliqués for easier computation; add a 6mm/¼in seam allowance. Figure number of appliqué pieces required for a project in the same way that you calculate a number required for patchwork.

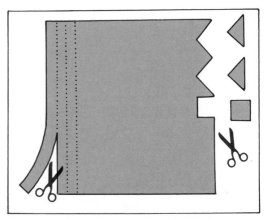

Scraps To make the best possible use of fabric scraps, use one edge for cutting straight strips and the other for cutting irregular shapes. You will have very little wastage and save time by not having to measure and cut a straight edge every time you need one.

JOINING QUILT BLOCKS

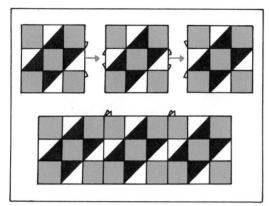

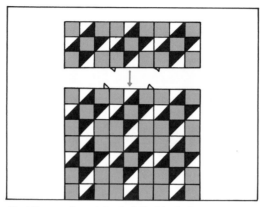

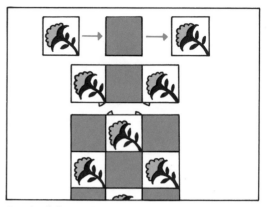

1 **Edge-to edge set** Lay quilt blocks on a flat surface to decide on best arrangement. Join blocks in rows. Sew one to the next with RS facing and raw edges even, making a 6mm/¼in seam. When joining rows, turn seam allowances in different directions.

2 After you have joined all the blocks in rows, press the resulting seam allowances in different directions on adjacent rows. Pin rows together matching seams and easing as necessary to fit. Stitch rows together to complete quilt top.

Pieced and plain set Cut plain fabric to same size as patchwork or appliqué blocks. Stitch together in rows, alternating position of pieced and plain blocks on each row. Press seams away from areas to be quilted. Join rows, matching seams, to complete quilt top.

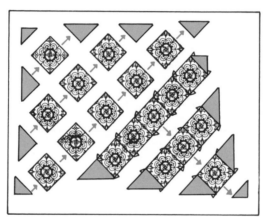

1 **Diagonal set** To make pattern for half- and quarter-squares, draw full-size block. Cut in half diagonally for half-square (A). Cut that in half for quarter-square (B). Add 6mm/¼in to all edges. Cut outer edges of these pieces on straight grain.

2 Join blocks together in rows with a half- or quarter-square at the end of each row. Sew a quarter-square to each unfinished corner as shown. Join rows, matching seams carefully, to complete quilt top.

3 If you sew patchwork or appliqué blocks to plain blocks in a diagonal set, the pieced blocks will appear to float on point. Cut all half- and quarter-squares from plain fabric. If you use diagonal block designs, they will appear straight.

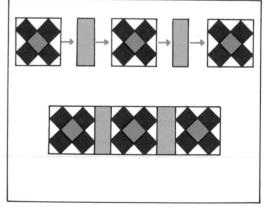

4 For an interesting zigzag effect, sew pieced blocks to plain half- and quarter-squares in offset strips. To offset the blocks on adjacent strips, cut top and bottom blocks in half as shown. Sew strips together to complete the quilt top.

1 **Straight sashing set** Draw quilt design on graph paper to find how long and wide to cut sashing. Cut short sashing to exact length of each block. Cut long sashing and outer frame to length of pieced rows. Add 6mm/¼in seam allowance around all edges.

2 Sew a sash in between each quilt block to make rows. Stitch sash to block with RS facing and raw edges even, making a 6mm/¼in seam. Ease or stretch sides of blocks as you sew in order to match ends of sash with ends of blocks.

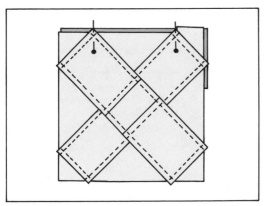

3 Be sure to pin through the 6mm/¼in seam allowance of block at any points that must meet the seam. All edges of all blocks may not be perfectly straight. Use straight edge of sash rather than edge of block as a sewing guide.

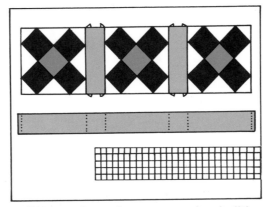

4 To prepare long sashes, measure and mark off the position of all seams to which sash will be attached. Make first mark 6mm/¼in from beginning of sash to accommodate seam allowance of first block; allow same amount at end of sash.

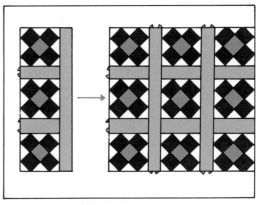

5 Pin and stitch long sash to row of blocks/short sashing, matching markings exactly to seams. Ease to fit; do not trim end of sash to make it come out even. Press seams away from areas to be quilted. Join all rows in same manner.

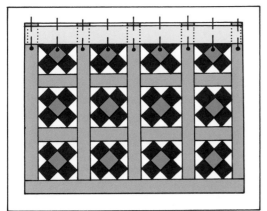

6 If desired, you can frame the outer edges of the quilt top with sashing before adding a border. Measure and mark position of seams on these sashes as described in step **4** above; pin and stitch outer sashing in place as described in step **5**.

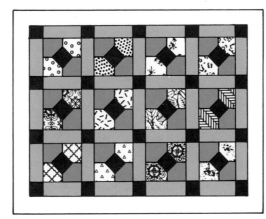

1 **Sashing with squares** Draw quilt design on graph paper to determine how wide to cut the sashing. Cut short strips to exact length of each block. Cut squares to exact width of each sash. Be sure to add 6mm/¼in seam allowances around all edges.

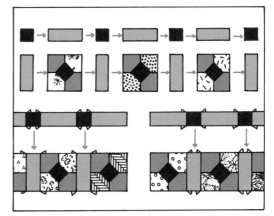

2 Join squares to horizontal sashes in rows; join blocks to vertical sashes in rows. Press seam allowances in opposite directions on sashing rows and block rows. Sew pieced sashing to rows of blocks, matching seams, until complete.

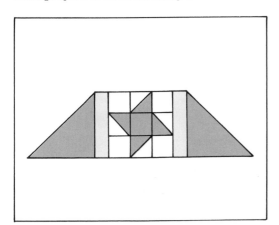

1 **Diagonal set with sashing** Read *Diagonal set* on facing page. Cut short sashing to same length as quilt blocks, adding 6mm/¼in seams. Join quilt blocks in rows with sashing on each side of each block. Sew half- or quarter-square to end of each row.

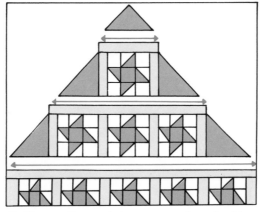

2 Measure distance between outer edges of sashing on each row (see arrows); cut long sashing to that measurement. Prepare, pin and stitch long sashing to each row following steps **4** and **5** above. Stitch rows together to complete quilt top.

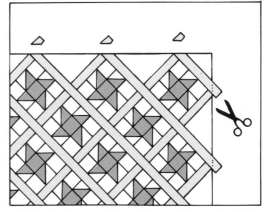

3 Ends of long sashing will extend beyond outside edges of quilt. Trim away excess fabric even with outside edges.

BORDERS

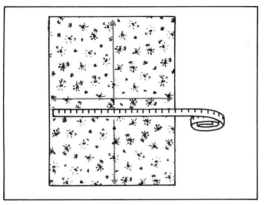

1 **Measuring** To determine the correct size of quilt, measure across the middle. Measurements taken along edges may be inaccurate due to stretching. Cut border strips to desired width plus 6mm/¼in for seams; see individual directions for cutting length.

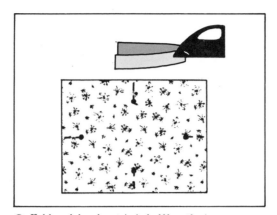

2 Fold each border strip in half lengthwise; crease centre point with an iron. Indicate centre point of each edge of quilt top with a pin. If sewing border directly to pieced blocks, mark edges of border for sashing; *see page 163, step 4.*

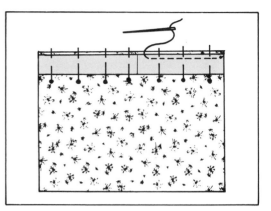

3 With RS facing, pin border to corresponding edge of quilt top, matching pin to crease mark. Some areas may need to be eased; use enough pins to prevent seam from puckering when pieces are sewn together. Baste seam first for added security.

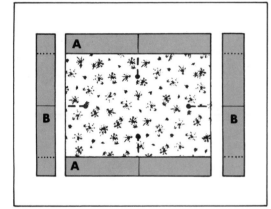

1 **Squared border** Cut border strips to desired width plus 6mm/¼in seam allowances. For length, cut two border strips same length as quilt (A). For width, cut two border strips to width of quilt plus double width of border (B). Add 6mm/¼in for seams.

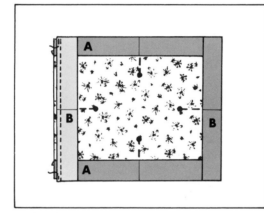

2 Sew the A border strips to quilt top first, matching crease marks on border with pins on quilt top. Ease as necessary to fit. Next sew the B border strips to quilt top. Press seam allowances away from the edge that you plan to quilt.

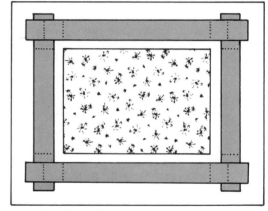

1 **Border with mitred corner** Cut four border strips to desired width plus 6mm/¼in for seams. For length of each border strip, cut 2 strips to length and 2 strips to width of quilt plus twice the width of the border plus an extra 5cm/2in for mitring.

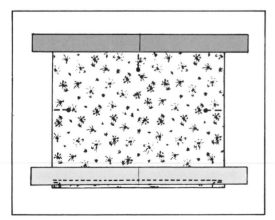

2 Sew border strips to opposite sides of quilt, beginning and ending 6mm/¼in away from corners of quilt top. Excess border fabric will extend beyond each edge of quilt top. Press border strips to RS.

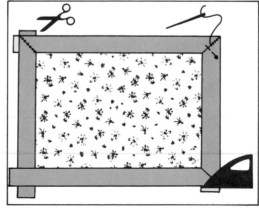

3 Sew remaining border strips to quilt in same manner. To mitre by hand, fold one border strip down at a 45° angle. Press and pin in place. Slipstitch folded edge of border securely in place with matching thread. Trim seam allowances to 13mm/½in.

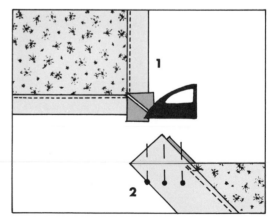

4a To mitre by machine, turn quilt top to WS. At corner, fold border strips back at a 45° angle. The folded edges should touch one another. Press (1). Pick up quilt top and hold it as shown to match the creases. Pin borders together along creases (2).

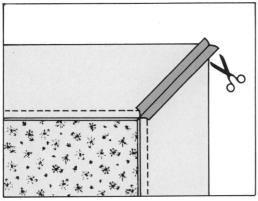

4b Stitch borders together exactly on crease line beginning from outside edge and stitching towards quilt top. Backstitch at beginning and end of seam. Trim seam allowances to 13mm/½in and press seam open. Trim off excess seam allowance.

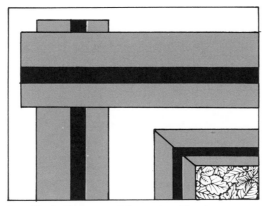

Pieced border If you are adding a pieced border to your quilt, make the border in one complete unit, then sew the border to the quilt. For length, include correct width of entire border plus 5cm/2in for safety. Always mitre corners of pieced or striped borders.

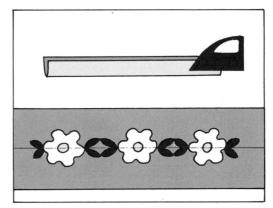

Appliqué border Fold border strip in half lengthwise and press to indicate the centre. Arrange appliqué pieces on border, using the centre crease line as a guide. Add a contrasting corner or use a mirror to design your corner; *see below, centre.*

Contrasting corner Some border designs are difficult to resolve by simple mitring. If this is the case, add a contrasting square at each corner, picking up a design element from the quilt or from the border itself.

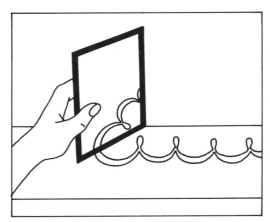

Designing a corner An ill-conceived border can ruin an otherwise beautiful quilt. Use a mirror to see what your border design will look like as it turns a corner. Rearrange pieces until the corner is to your liking, then work out the rest of the border to fit.

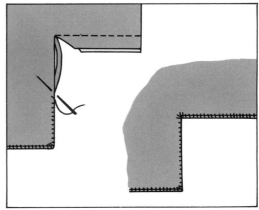

T-Quilt A T-quilt is used on a 4-poster bed; *see page 158.* The simplest way to finish the edge of the border is by fold finishing. Fold raw edges of quilt 6mm/¼in inside and slipstitch together. Clip fabric at corners and work extra stitches there for security.

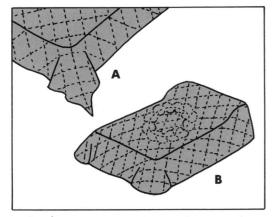

1 **Round corner** If you are making a quilt to cover the whole bed, squared corners will tend to drag on the floor (A). Make a round corner on your quilt for a more professional appearance (B).

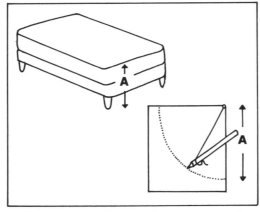

2 To make pattern for a round corner, measure from top of mattress to floor (A). Cut length of string to measurement A. Tie one end around pencil; pin other end to a sheet of paper. Swing pencil around to inscribe an arc. Cut out along curved line for pattern.

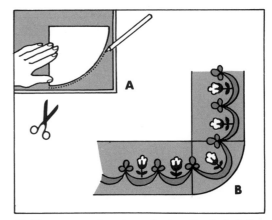

3 Use corner pattern to mark edge of a wholecloth quilt; trim away excess fabric (A). Or if adding a border to a quilt, use pattern to cut corner piece (B). Try to design border so it curves continuously around corner.

BINDING

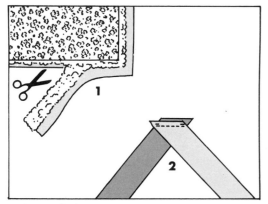

1 **Separate binding: square corner** Trim top, padding and back so edges are even (1). Cut four binding strips on straight grain of fabric, each 3.8–5cm/1½–2in wide, and length of each side of quilt plus 2.5cm/1in extra. For length, join on the diagonal (2).

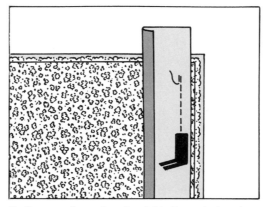

2 Press one long edge of each binding strip 6mm/¼in to WS. Position binding on quilt top with RS facing and 13mm/½in extension at top edge. Beginning 6mm/¼in from corner, sew binding to quilt. Stitch from corner to corner; backstitch at ends.

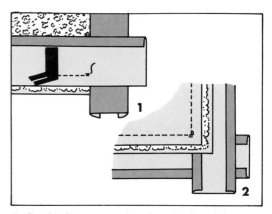

3 Sew binding to opposite edge of quilt and then to the remaining two edges in same manner, again allowing 13mm/½in to extend beyond corners (1). Open both bindings and turn quilt so back is facing up (2).

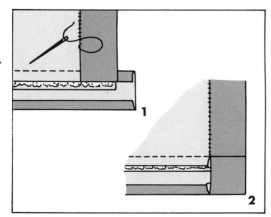

4 Fold pressed edge of first binding onto quilt back; pin so pressed edge covers line of stitching. Slipstitch binding to quilt back invisibly; trim fabric at top and bottom (1). Fold over edge of adjacent binding, covering edge of first binding (2).

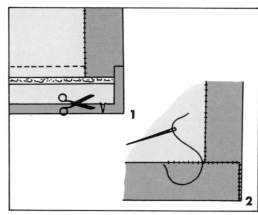

5 Trim excess binding from fold, leaving a 6mm/¼in extra to form an "L" shape as shown (1). Fold binding up to meet line of stitching, hiding all raw edges inside. Slipstitch binding invisibly in place starting in corner and then working across quilt (2).

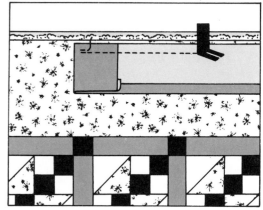

1 **Separate binding: mitred corner** Cut binding strip 3.8–5cm/1½–2in wide and length of perimeter of quilt plus 10cm/4in. Press one long edge 6mm/¼in to WS. Begin in centre of one side of quilt. Fold binding end 13mm/½in to WS. Stitch RS binding to quilt top.

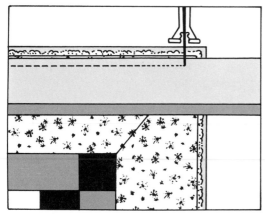

2 Stitch to first corner, making smaller stitches as you approach. When needle is 6mm/¼in from edge of quilt, stop stitching, leaving needle in corner point. Raise presser foot. Pivot quilt on needle to get ready to sew next edge.

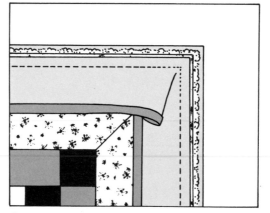

3 Adjust binding so raw edge is parallel to next edge of quilt. A tuck will form in binding; do not catch tuck in stitching. Lower presser foot and continue stitching with small stitches for 6mm/¼in. Adjust stitch length and continue stitching to next corner.

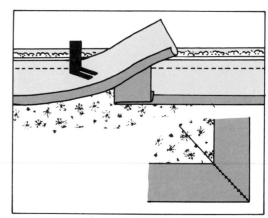

4 Stitch binding to quilt, sewing each corner in same way. Trim binding at end, leaving 13mm/½in which will overlap beginning of binding. Wrap binding over to quilt back, covering stitching line and folding tucks diagonally at corners. Slipstitch in place.

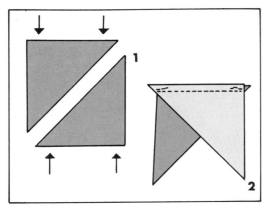

1 **Bias binding** Cut a square of fabric on straight grain; cut in half diagonally (1). With RS facing, stitch short straight edges (marked with arrows) together, making a 6mm/¼in seam; backstitch at ends to secure (2).

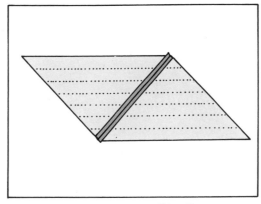

2 Press seam allowance open. Trim allowances to 3mm/⅛in. Mark parallel lines on WS of seamed fabric, each 3.8–5cm/1½–2in apart. Be careful not to stretch fabric as you mark it.

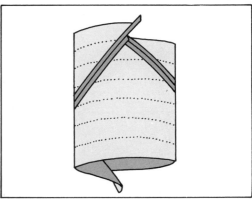

3 With RS facing, pin diagonal edges of marked fabric together, offsetting edges so that the top edge of fabric aligns with first line. Match marked lines as you pin. Stitch together making 6mm/¼in seam. Press seam allowance open and trim to 3mm/⅛in.

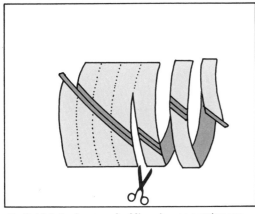

4 Cut fabric along marked lines in one continuous spiral as shown. Apply bias binding to a quilt or project by one of the methods described on the facing page. Bias binding is particularly useful when finishing quilts or projects with curved edges.

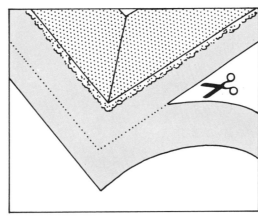

1 **Self binding** For self binding, quilt back must be at least 2.5cm/1in wider at each edge than quilt top. Trim quilt top and padding evenly. On WS of quilt back, mark a line 2.5cm/1in away from trimmed quilt top all around; cut along line.

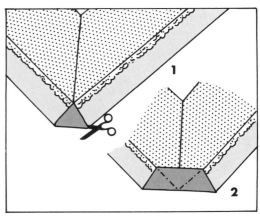

2 At each corner, fold quilt back so corner point of back touches corner point of quilt top and padding. Cut off corner as shown (1). Fold trimmed corner onto quilt top diagonally as shown (2).

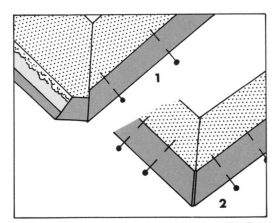

3 Fold raw edges of quilt back 6mm/¼in to WS. Fold quilt back onto quilt top along one side; pin to secure (1). Then fold the adjacent edge onto quilt top, forming a diagonal mitre at the corner (2).

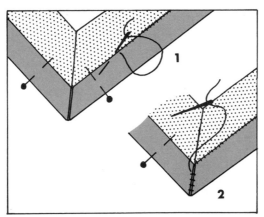

4 Slipstitch folded edge of binding invisibly to quilt top using thread to match binding (1). Remove pins as you go along. Slipstitch mitred edges together at corners (2). Continue until quilt is bound.

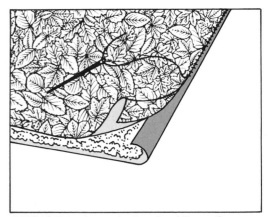

Fold finish Trim the top, back and padding so they are even. Fold the back 6mm/¼in over the padding. Fold the top 6mm/¼in to WS. Slipstitch folded edges of top and back together invisibly.

Unusual Finishes

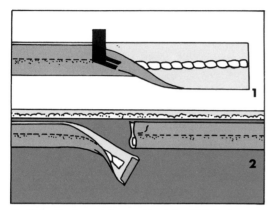

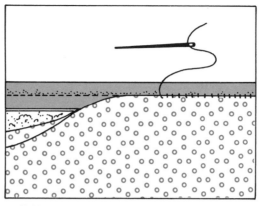

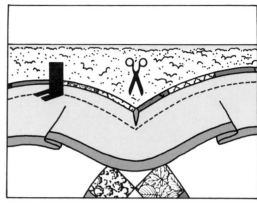

1 **Piping** Enclose piping cord in strip of fabric the perimeter of quilt (plus 5cm/2in) using a zipper foot. Stitch piping to quilt back with raw edges even. Overlap beginning by 13mm/½in. Cut excess piping; lap end of strip over beginning; cover raw edges.

2 Fold raw edges of quilt back and piping inside quilt, then fold raw edge of quilt top 6mm/¼in to WS. Pin so folded edge of quilt top just covers stitching line attaching piping to quilt back. Slipstitch folded edge of quilt top to piping.

1 **Angled edge** Do not trim padding or back until binding is sewn in place. With RS facing and raw edges even, stitch bias binding to quilt top. At each dip, clip seam allowance of binding; keeping needle in fabric, pivot and realign edges to sew next curve.

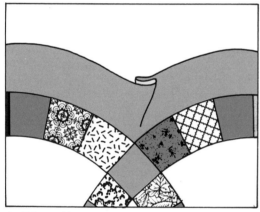

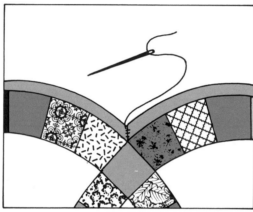

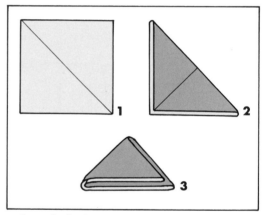

2 Trim padding and back even with quilt top. Wrap binding over to back of quilt; a tuck will form at each dip. Fold raw edges of binding 6mm/¼in to WS. Slipstitch folded edge of binding to quilt back, covering line of stitching.

3 Smooth the tucks evenly at each dip. Slipstitch the folded edges of the tucks together.

1 **Sawtooth edge** Cut squares of fabric and fold in half on the diagonal (1). Fold triangle thus formed in half (2) to make each sawtooth triangle (3).

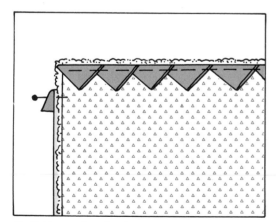

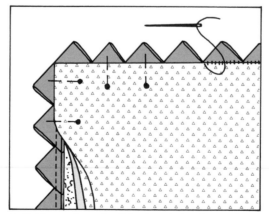

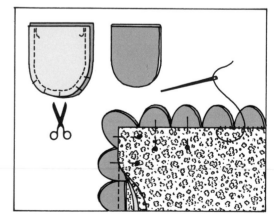

2 Fold raw edge of quilt top down and out of the way; pin to secure. Arrange triangles along raw edge of quilt back and padding, overlapping triangles as necessary so that they fit evenly across the edge. Baste, then stitch raw edges of triangles in place.

3 Fold raw edges of quilt back and triangles inside quilt so triangles extend beyond quilt back. Fold raw edge of quilt top 6mm/¼in to WS. Pin so folded edge of quilt top just covers stitching line attaching triangles to quilt back. Slipstitch top in place.

Clamshell Cut two U-shaped pieces of fabric for each Clamshell; stitch together with RS facing. Clip curves, turn to RS and press. Attach Clamshells to edge of quilt following directions for Sawtooth edge. For a rounded corner, turn one Clamshell at an angle.

SIGNING AND HANGING

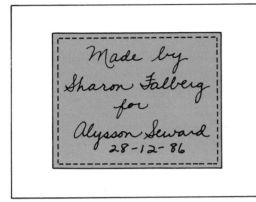

1 Signing Always sign and date your quilted projects. On a small piece of fabric, embroider your name and the date in cross stitch or outline stitch or write your name with indelible ink. You can even type the label. Hem all edges.

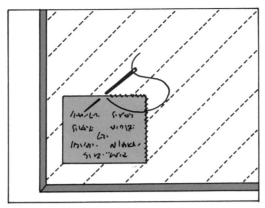

2 Slipstitch label to back of quilt using matching thread.

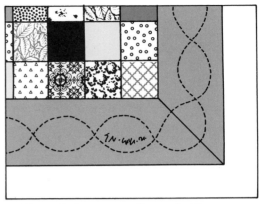

3 Alternatively, you can quilt or embroider your name on the front of the project, making your signature and the date part of the design.

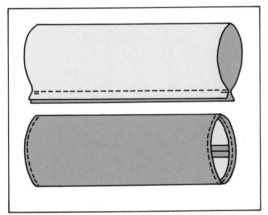

1 Hanging sleeves Cut fabric 2.5cm/1in wider than project and about 19cm/7½in deep. Fold in half lengthwise; stitch long edges together. Turn RS out and press with seam centred on one side. Fold raw edges at end 6mm/¼in inside and stitch in place.

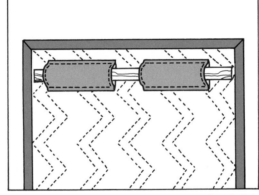

2 Pin sleeve to back just below top edge. Slipstitch in place so stitches penetrate padding, but not top. Do not stitch so sleeve is taut against project; allow some "give". Use one sleeve for small projects; divide into two or three sections for large ones.

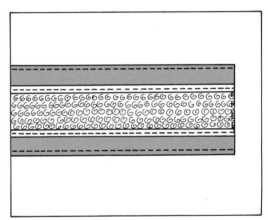

1 Velcro method Cut 5cm/2in-wide Velcro, slightly shorter than width of project. Cut two fabric strips to same length as Velcro and 7.6cm/3in wide; hem all edges. Separate strips of Velcro and machine-stitch each half to RS of one fabric strip.

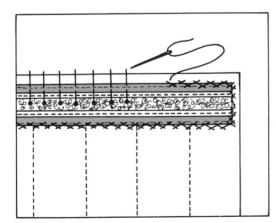

2 Pin fabric strip with smooth Velcro to back of project just below top edge. Secure all edges of strip to project with herringbone stitches; work stitches so they penetrate padding but not top.

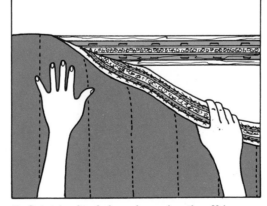

3 Cut strip of sealed wood same length as Velcro; glue or staple fabric with gripper side of Velcro to wood. Nail or screw wood to wall. Press top of project against strip of wood so Velcro strips grip together. Use this method to hang antique quilts.

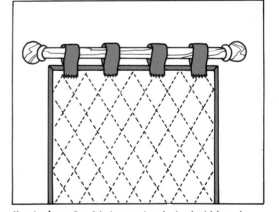

Hanging loops Cut fabric to twice desired width and about 15–18cm/6–7in long. Fold in half lengthwise; stitch long edges together. Turn RS out; press with seam centred on one side. Fold raw edges inside; slipstitch ends to quilt back, along top edge.

CARE OF QUILTS

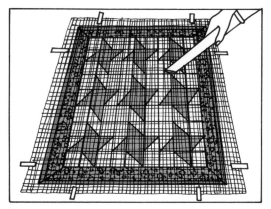

Cleaning To clean a fragile quilt, lay quilt on a flat surface; cover securely with net or muslin/cheesecloth. With vacuum cleaner at lowest setting, vacuum away loose dirt, holding hose above the surface so quilt is not drawn up by the suction.

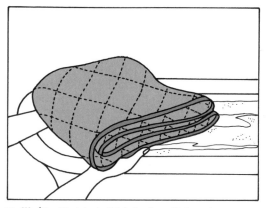

1 Washing First test all fabrics in quilt for colour fastness. Dampen white blotting paper and gently pat each fabric. If dye runs onto paper, do not wash. Fill bathtub with warm water; add mild detergent. Fold quilt loosely and gently place it in the water.

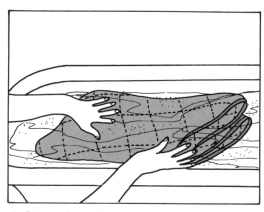

2 Press quilt into the water with your hands so that all parts are wet. Knead the quilt gently with your hands and soak for a short time. Drain and add fresh water to rinse. Continue rinsing and draining quilt until water runs clear.

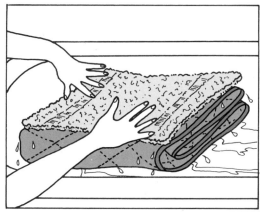

3 Drain water for the final time. Press quilt gently with your hands to remove excess water. Place thick towels on quilt and press again to remove as much of the water as possible.

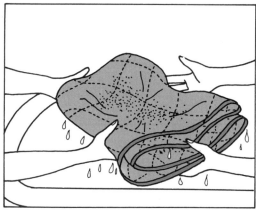

4 Because of the water it has absorbed, quilt will be quite heavy, placing stress on fabric and stitching. With another person, carefully lift the semi-dry quilt out of the bathtub, using both hands so as to put the least amount of strain on the quilt.

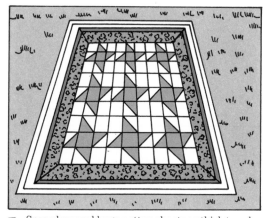

5 Spread several large cotton sheets or thick towels in a shady spot on the grass or in a warm, dry location indoors. Unfold quilt gently and place it on the sheets or towels. Allow quilt to dry thoroughly. Do not expose quilt to direct sunlight or heat.

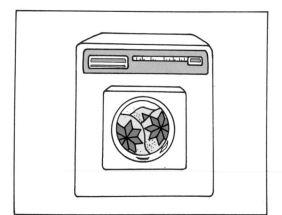

6 You can machine wash and dry a small quilt filled with synthetic padding. Pre-test fabrics for colour fastness as described above. Machine wash in warm water with mild detergent; tumble dry on a cool setting. Quilt must fit comfortably in machine.

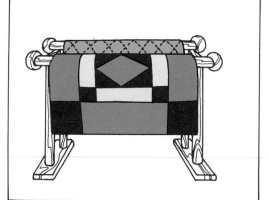

1 Storage To store a quilt, lie it flat in a cool, dry and dimly lit location. An excellent place to store a quilt is on an unused bed. Or hang it from a quilt rack as shown. Keep quilts out of direct sunlight and flourescent light.

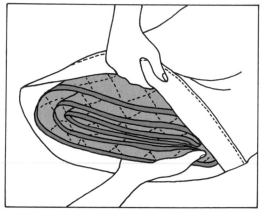

2 To store quilts out of sight, fold and place in a clean, white, 100% cotton pillowcase or an acid-free box in a dry place. Do not store quilts in plastic which encourages mildew. Crumple acid-free paper in folds of old quilts.

Small Projects

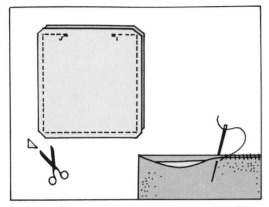

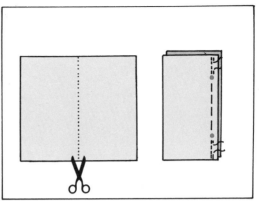

Cushion Cut 2 pieces of fabric to size, adding 6mm/¼in for seams, to each edge. Stitch together with RS facing, leaving an opening along one edge for turning. Clip corners, turn to RS and stuff. Fold raw edges 6mm/¼in inside; slipstitch together.

1 **Cushion cover** Make front of cover in one of the techniques described in this book. For back, cut piece of matching fabric to same height as front (allow extra for seams) and 2.5cm/1in wider. Buy a zipper about 5cm/2in shorter than height of cushion.

2 Cut back in half widthwise. Mark position of zipper, centred between top and bottom edges. With RS facing, stitch cut edges together making 13mm/½in seam. Make small stitches above and below position of zipper; baste edges where zipper will be inserted.

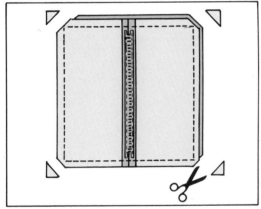

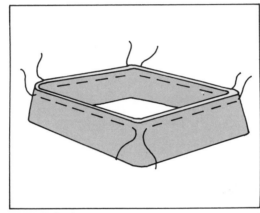

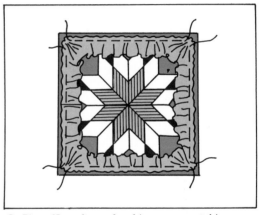

3 Press seam open. Baste zipper centred RS down over seam allowance. Stitch in place using matching thread and a zipper foot. Remove basting. With RS facing, stitch front and back together. Clip corners, turn to RS through zipper and insert cushion.

1 **Ruffled cushion cover** Cut ruffle to twice desired width and at least double cushion's circumference; add 6mm/¼in seam allowances. Sew short edges together. Fold in half with WS facing; press. Baste raw edges together, dividing ruffle into quarters.

2 Pin ruffle to front of cushion cover, matching quarter marks with each corner. Pull basting, gathering ruffle to fit perimeter of front. Adjust gathers with extra fullness at each corner. Baste, then stitch ruffle all around, making 6mm/¼in seam.

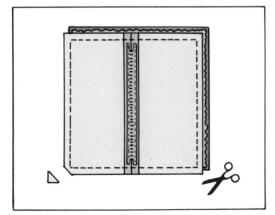

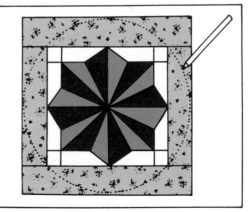

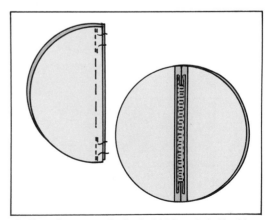

3 Assemble back as described for *Cushion cover*. Pin front to back with RS facing, raw edges even and ruffle in between. Baste and stitch together all around. Clip corners. Turn to RS through zipper opening. Insert cushion.

1 **Round cushion cover** Use a round design such as Double Wedding Ring or Folded Star. To make a square block round, add fabric border strips to each edge. Draw circle on RS of bordered square as shown. Cut off excess; leaving 6mm/¼in seam allowance.

2 To make pattern for back, fold front in half; add 13mm/½in seam allowance to straight edge. Cut out two fabric pieces using pattern. Insert zipper as for *Cushion cover*. Stitch back to front with RS facing. Turn to RS through zipper opening. Insert cushion.

SMALL PROJECTS

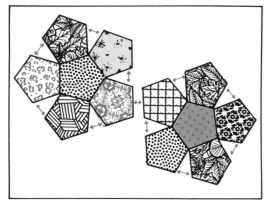

1 **Pentagon ball** Cut 12 pentagons from fabric; *see page 93 for pattern*. Prepare patches over papers; *see pages 52-53*. Whipstitch together in 2 groups with 6 patches in each group, joining 5 pentagons to a central patch as shown. Join arrowed side edges.

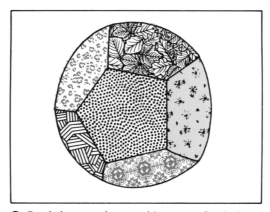

2 Sew halves together, matching seams. Just before sewing last seam, fill ball with stuffing to make a child's toy. For a pretty drawer or room freshener, fill ball with rose petals or lavender. Tie a ribbon into a bow and slipstitch to the top.

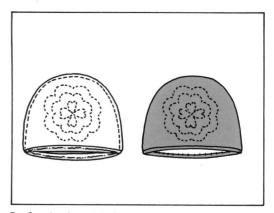

Tea Cosy Cut 2 semicircles of fabric to fit over handle and spout of teapot. Use as pattern to cut 2 padding and 2 lining pieces. Assemble and quilt layers together to form a design. Stitch quilted layers together with RS facing. Turn to RS. Bind lower edge.

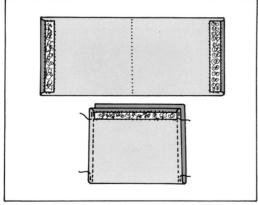

1 **Secret pouch for valuables** Cut strip of fabric about 23 × 43cm/9 × 17in to match quilt back. Fold short edges 6mm/¼in to WS and press. Cut Velcro shorter than edge and stitch over each raw edge. Fold fabric in half crosswise and stitch side edges together.

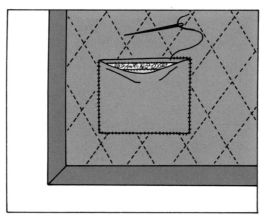

2 Turn to RS and press. Position pouch on back of quilt near one corner and slipstitch in place using matching thread. To close pouch, press Velcro edges tightly together. Store small valuables, money or important papers in pouch.

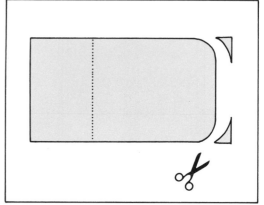

1 **Change purse** Cut backing fabric about 30.5 × 15cm/12 × 6in. Trim one short edge to round off corners as shown. Draw line on RS of backing 10cm/4in from straight edge. Use fabric as pattern to cut a layer of padding. Baste padding to WS of back.

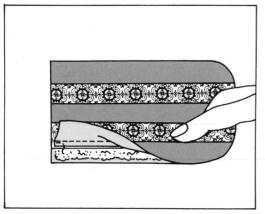

2 Cut strips of fabric and stitch to padding and backing following directions for *Quilt-and-sew* on *page 145*. Finger-press each strip to RS as you stitch it in place; *see page 43*. Trim edges of strips even with rounded edge of base fabric.

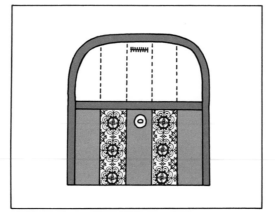

3 Bind straight edge of quilted fabric. Fold quilted fabric along marked line with backing inside. Baste side edges together. Bind all raw edges with bias binding. Make a buttonhole at centre of rounded edge. Sew a button to straight edge to match.

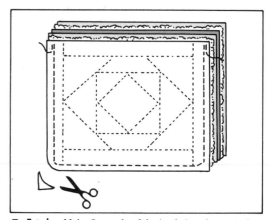

1 **Tote bag** Make 2 panels of desired size, decorated with patchwork or appliqué, and quilted if desired. With RS facing and raw edges even, stitch together at sides and bottom edge. Clip off lower corners. Fold raw top edges 6mm/¼in to WS and baste in place.

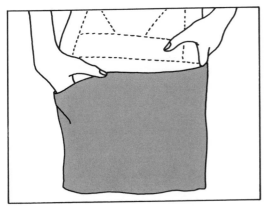

2 Cut 2 panels of lining fabric same size as outer panels. Stitch together at sides and bottom and clip off lower corners. Press raw top edges 6mm/¼in to WS and baste in place. Insert bag inside lining with WS facing.

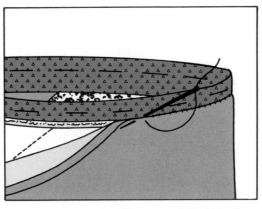

3 Pin folded top edge of lining over folded top edge of bag. Slipstitch together using matching thread. Tack lining invisibly to bottom of bag, matching corners. Turn bag RS out.

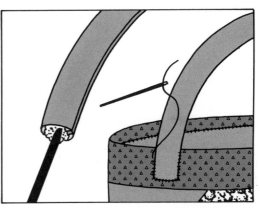

4 For straps, cut 2 strips of fabric 7.6cm/3in wide and desired length plus 13mm/½in. Stitch long edges together; turn to RS using a tube turner. Stuff each tube. Fold raw edges at ends inside; stitch closed. Stitch handles to front and back of bag on inside.

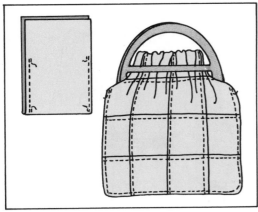

5 If you are using purchased handles, allow an extra 3.8cm/1½in at top edge of bag. Do not stitch sides together along this excess allowance. Insert each top edge through a handle, gathering fabric as necessary to fit.

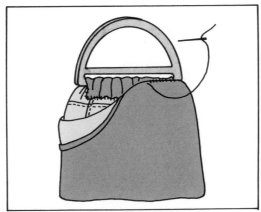

6 Fold raw edge down and slipstitch invisibly to WS of bag. Cut and stitch lining as described in step 2 above. Insert bag inside lining with WS facing. Slipstitch top edges of lining to bag close to handle, covering all raw edges.

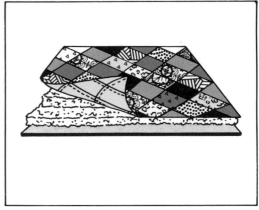

1 **Decorative lid** Cut sturdy cardboard to fit lid of purchased box. Cut padding same size as cardboard; glue to cardboard. Cut another layer of padding slightly smaller all around than the first; centre and glue to first layer. Place fabric on top.

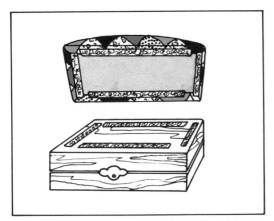

2 Fold raw edges of fabric smoothly to WS of cardboard and glue in place. Glue Velcro strips over each raw edge of fabric. Glue matching Velcro strips to box lid. Press decorative lid onto box lid so the Velcro strips match.

1 **Framed patchwork** Show off an intricate patchwork or appliqué block by framing it. If desired, add a wide border in matching or contrasting fabric, mitring corners; *see pages 164–165*. Press carefully. Insert into a standard wooden frame.

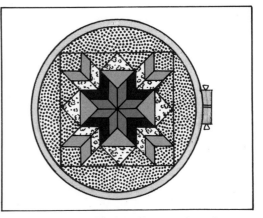

2 You can frame a block inside a round wooden quilting hoop for a more informal effect. Cut border strips wide enough to fit inside hoop. Centre block in hoop. On back, secure raw edges with sturdy thread; cover with fabric to hide raw edges.

CLOTHING

Quilted clothing looks best when the patterns are simple and based on straight lines. Select a suitable pattern and make a rough sketch of it on paper, then embellish the pattern with lines representing patchwork, quilting or appliqué. Use coloured pencils to indicate fabrics. Then study your design to see if it works. It is easier to make adjustments to your design in the planning stage rather than after the garment is completed. Try to visualize the way the finished garment will look when it is on you. A garment should always enhance your appearance, so do not place a bold design over a part of your body best left unnoticed. If you have wide hips, for example, do not make a patchwork skirt or you will end up looking like a walking quilt. Rather, draw attention away from your hips by making a patchwork blouse, or a dramatic quilted jacket.

Next, make up your garment in lightweight fabric and try it on; adjust for size, then use the fabric as your pattern. You will be putting more effort into making quilted clothing than regular clothing, so take a bit of time to ensure that your project fits just right. If you are planning to quilt the garment, do not buy a pattern that is larger than your normal size. This is never successful because the finished garment will always look as if it is one size too big. There are two methods that you can choose from to ensure that your quilted garment will fit beautifully. The first method is to make up patchwork or quilted yardage first, then cut your pattern from it. The second method is for those who prefer designing on a foundation. Cut the foundation slightly larger all around. Secure the pieces to it or quilt the foundation, then replace the pattern and cut the piece to the correct size.

Some types of clothing will not be enhanced by patchwork, even if worn by the slimmest model. Trousers and gathered skirts or dresses made entirely in patchwork or quilting are the worst offenders. If making these garments, add only a subtle accent in patchwork or appliqué.

If you are adding padding to your garment, use a thinner one than you would use to make a quilt. If you are using cotton, wool or silk padding, you must quilt closely or risk lumps when the piece is washed. Use a glazed polyester padding for garments that will be washed often.

If you are making a garment entirely out of quilting, use a solid rather than printed fabric to show off your stitches to their best advantage. Use unusual fabrics in your work that you may not consider using in a quilt. Shiny satin or sleek velvet will make a very special evening outfit. Add ribbons and lace to personalize the garment.

Appliqué is mentioned only briefly here because it should be added after a garment is made up; it wouldn't make sense to create a beautiful appliqué fabric and then cut it apart. Appliqués can do much to enhance a garment, but study your composition critically before sewing to make sure the design is balanced.

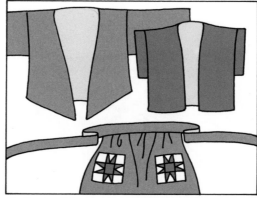

1 Planning Select patterns with straight lines, few seams and no darts. Simplicity is the key to a successful quilted garment. Also, you needn't make an entire garment in patchwork or quilting; you can add simple accents such as pockets on an apron.

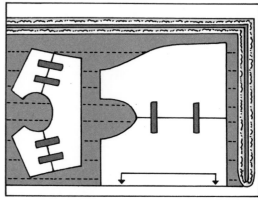

2 The fewer the seams in a quilted garment the better. Eliminate extra seams by taping pattern pieces together before using them to cut out your fabric.

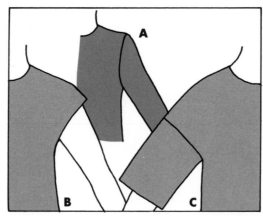

3 Do not use patterns with gathered or puffy sleeves. Rather, choose a simple set-in sleeve (A), a cap sleeve (B), or a pattern with a dropped shoulder (C).

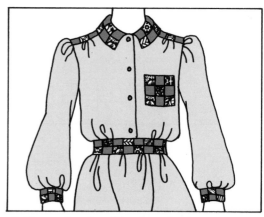

4 Use patchwork, quilting or appliqué to trim collars, cuffs, pockets, belts, and yokes. Often, just a simple accent will be more effective than making an entire garment in patchwork or quilting.

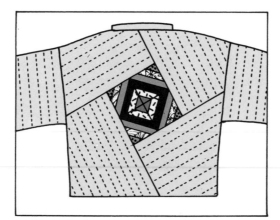

5 The back of a garment is an excellent place to add a bold design in patchwork, quilting or appliqué. The space is big enough for a large block or circular pattern. Your garment will then look just as interesting from the back as from the front.

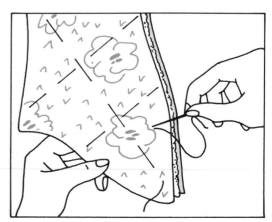

6 For a very simple yet effective quilted garment, select a lovely patterned fabric and outline-quilt around the printed design. Assemble the garment following the manufacturer's instructions, then finish the garment as shown on the facing page.

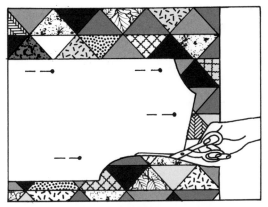

1 Cutting yardage Make the required amount of patchwork or quilted yardage for your garment. Use a commercial pattern to cut out the garment pieces from the yardage. The pattern directions will tell you how many pieces to cut.

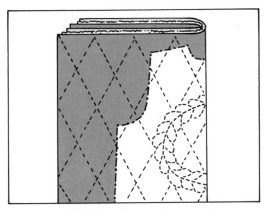

2 If you wish to add a design to the centre front opening of a garment, fold patchwork or quilted fabric in half at design area. Place front edge of pattern on fold, centre design and add allowance for seams. Cut out pattern; cut front edges apart.

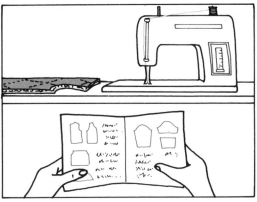

3 Assemble garment following the pattern instructions. If you are working with quilted material, finger-press the seam allowances. To reduce bulk, grade all your seams and remove as much padding as possible from the seam allowances.

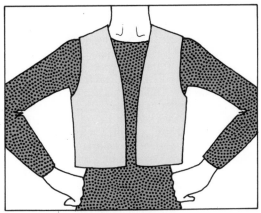

1 Working on a foundation Select a lightweight, plain fabric for the foundation. Use a commercial pattern to cut out the garment in the foundation fabric. Baste the garment together and try it on for fit; adjust as necessary, remove basting.

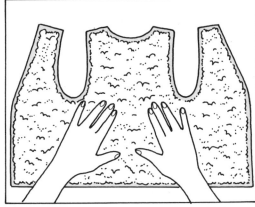

2 If you wish the garment to be quilted, add a layer of padding to WS of the foundation, smoothing the padding gently so that there are no lumps or thin spots. Baste the padding in place.

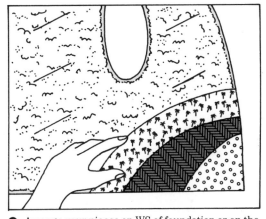

3 Arrange your pieces on WS of foundation or on the padding. When you are satisfied with your design, stitch the pieces in place by the *Press-Piecing* method; *see pages 75-76*. Or you can fold the raw edges under and slipstitch them in place by hand.

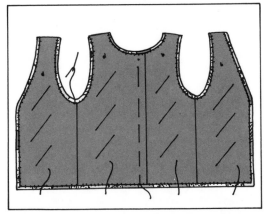

1 Finishing Unquilted patchwork garments must be lined. Fold raw edges of garment and lining to WS; press and slipstitch together. Sew shoulder seams without catching lining in seam, then slipstitch edges of lining together over the seam.

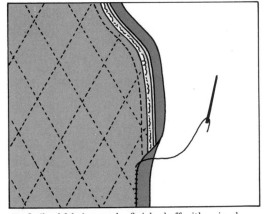

2 Quilted fabrics can be finished off with a simple binding; *see pages 166–167*. Use bias binding on curved edges. Machine-stitch binding to RS of garment, then wrap binding over to WS and slipstitch securely in place.

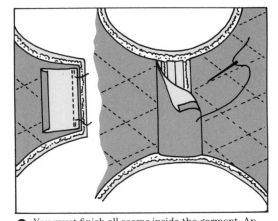

3 You must finish all seams inside the garment. An easy way is to add a narrow strip of fabric while you are sewing the seam. Fold raw edge of fabric strip 6mm/¼in to WS, then smooth over seam allowances and slipstitch in place, covering all raw edges.

A-Z OF QUILTING TERMS

A

Acid-free paper: Used for storing antique quilts; available in most art supply shops.

Adhesive/fusible web: Material composed of fibres that melt when an iron is applied to them; used for fusing 2 layers of fabric together.

Album quilt: Friendship quilt popular in the 19th century in America where each block, usually elaborate in design and workmanship, was made by a different person. The finished quilt was presented as a gift to a bride, a young man celebrating his 21st birthday, a church minister or an outstanding member of the community.

Amish patchwork: A style of patchwork made by the Amish or "plain people", that is characterized by bright bold colours, simple geometric forms and elaborate quilting.

Appliqué: From the French word, *appliquer* which means to put on or lay on. n. A piece of fabric that is secured (or "applied") onto a background fabric with hand or machine stitches. v. The process of sewing an appliqué to a background fabric; this can be done by hand with slipstitch, running stitch or a variety of embroidery stitches, or by machine with a close zigzag satin stitch.

B

Back: The bottom layer of a quilt sandwich. The back (also called the backing) is constructed of fabric pieced to the size of the quilt top plus about 5cm/2in excess to allow for take up.

Basting: Holding two fabrics or the layers of a quilt sandwich together temporarily with large hand or machine stitches, or with pins.

Batting: The American term for wadding, as it is known in Great Britain. See *Padding* for definition.

Bearding: A fuzzy coating on the surface of a quilt caused when loose fibres of padding migrate through the fabrics.

Beeswax: Used to strengthen thread and keep it from kinking and tangling.

Best quilt: Also known as a masterpiece quilt, this was the quilt that the maker considered her very best work. A best quilt could be a complex patchwork design or an elaborate appliqué work. Best quilts were put on the beds of favoured guests or used for special occasions such as a wedding night.

Betweens: Short needles used for quilting. The higher the number, the shorter the needle.

Bias: The diagonal grain of a fabric. This is the direction that has the most give or stretch, which is why it is used for sewing curves and binding curved edges.

Bias appliqué: See *Stained-glass appliqué.*

Binding: n. Narrow fabric strip used to finish off the edges of a quilt or a project; it can be cut on the straight grain of fabric or on the bias. v. To finish off the edges of a quilt in one of three ways: by attaching a separate binding, by folding the back over the top (or the top over the back) and stitching it in place, or by folding the raw edges of the top and back inside and sewing the folded edges together.

Bleeding: Bleeding occurs when dye has not been firmly bonded to a fabric, resulting in a loss of colour when the fabric is washed. Running dyes will usually discolour surrounding fabrics which is highly undesirable. Always prewash fabrics and test questionable fabrics before using.

Block: A single design unit comprising a patchwork or appliqué quilt. A block can be square, hexagonal or rectangular. Blocks can be sewn together or joined with sashing to create a quilt top.

Blocking: To straighten a crooked quilt block by using steam, heat and pressure.

Block style quilt: A quilt composed of separate blocks of patchwork, appliqué or quilting sewn together in rows to create a quilt top.

Bonded wadding/batting: Wadding/batting that is coated with chemicals to prevent it from fraying or coming apart when washed. Bonding is also meant to prevent bearding. The chemicals add a slight stiffness which may give body to a finished project but which will make it less easy to quilt through.

Border: A frame of fabric that edges a quilt. Borders are used to unify a design, to make a quilt larger, or to showcase fancy quilting. Borders can be narrow or wide, pieced, plain or appliquéd. Not all quilts have borders.

Broderie perse: An appliqué technique whereby fabrics with printed designs are cut apart and sewn to a background fabric. Chintz fabrics are normally used for this purpose.

C

Calico/muslin: In Great Britain, this term refers to a cotton plain-weave fabric in a natural cream colour; calico is known as muslin in America. Calico/muslin is strong and hardwearing, and is an excellent fabric to use for a quilt back. In America, the word calico refers to a patterned cotton fabric, usually a tiny floral print.

Candlewicking: A series of knots embroidered in a design on plain-woven cloth using candlewick threads.

Cathedral window: A form of patchwork whereby folded and refolded squares of fabric are sewn together to form a frame. A square of contrasting fabric is secured over the stitched seam. The resulting design resembles a stained-glass window.

Charm quilt: A patchwork quilt composed of many different fabrics collected over a period of time; no two pieces in the quilt are cut from the same fabric.

Cheesecloth: A loosely-woven pure cotton fabric that would be an excellent material to use for the back of Trapunto and Corded Quilting.

Comfort: An old-fashioned name for a very warm bedcovering consisting of several layers of padding secured between two layers of fabric by tying.

Comforter: A thick wholecloth quilt.

Compass: A tool required for drawing accurate circles and curves.

Corded quilting: A quilting technique whereby two layers of fabric are sewn together with parallel lines of running stitches to form a design. A length of cord is inserted between the fabrics and threaded between the lines of running stitches to throw the design into relief. It is also known as Italian Quilting.

Corduroy: A ribbed cotton fabric with a pile running the length of the material. Because the pile has a nap, all pieces must be cut the same way unless you are trying to create special effects. Press corduroy fabrics lightly on WS.

Cotton: Fabric woven from the natural fibre by the same name. Cotton fabric is very strong yet easy to work with. It is hard wearing and can be washed frequently with excellent results.

Counterpane: A summer-weight pieced or appliquéd quilt top that has no filling.

Crazy patchwork: The random arrangement of a variety of irregularly-shaped fabric pieces on a foundation; fabrics usually differ widely in fibre content, texture and colour. The edges of the patches are disguised by elaborate embroidery.

Crêpeline: A fine, transparent French fabric made especially for textile conservation work. It is used for cleaning and repairing antique quilts.

Crewelwork quilt: A quilt top composed of a sturdy fabric such as linen that has been embroidered with yarn or wool in a variety of colours.

Cushion quilting: A method of making a novelty quilt whereby small cushions or pillows are stuffed individually, then sewn together by machine.

D

Découpé: A form of Reverse Appliqué that is worked on the sewing machine.

Ditch quilting: Also known as "quilting in the ditch". The quilting stitches are worked very close to or actually in the seamlines to add texture to a pieced project. This technique is often used on thick fabrics that would be difficult to quilt through, or in cases where it is not desirable for the quilting stitches to show.

Double wedding ring: A style of patchwork whereby curved pieces are sewn together, creating a design of interlocked rings.

Dressmaker's carbon paper: Paper with a special waxy finish on one side, available in a variety of colours, that is used for marking placement or cutting lines on fabric. Before using, test to make sure that the marks will wash or iron out. Use a colour that matches closely to the fabric so markings will be less noticeable.

E

Echo quilting: A style of quilting whereby the stitches run parallel to the edges of a patchwork or appliqué piece, so the lines of the quilting seem to "echo" the shape. When more than one line of stitching is used, it is also known as contour or wave quilting, and is associated with Hawaiian Appliqué.

Embroidery: The embellishment of fabric with surface stitchery.

F

Fabric gluestick: An adhesive in a solid form used for joining fabrics. Although manufacturers state that it will not stain fabrics, it is a good idea to test a gluestick on a fabric scrap before using.

Feed dogs: The part of a sewing machine located within the needle plate which rhythmically moves up and down to help pull the fabric along while sewing.

Felt: A non-woven fabric, usually wool, that is made by pressing the fibres together with heat and moisture. Felt has no grain and will not fray. It is not a strong fabric nor is it washable.

Filling: The cotton, wool, silk or synthetic wadding/batting that is used between the two layers of a quilt sandwich. In this book it is mostly referred to as the "padding", although it can also be called the fill or stuffing.

Finger-press: A technique of pressing without an iron whereby the fabrics are flattened between the thumb and forefinger, or creased with a fingernail into the desired position.

Folded star: A patchwork technique whereby rectangles or circles of fabric are folded into triangular shapes and arranged on a base in a pattern which resembles a star. It is also known as Somerset Patchwork or Mitred Patchwork.

Foundation: A base upon which patchwork or appliqué pieces are sewn. The foundation can be a lightweight fabric, interfacing or soft paper.

Four block quilt: A quilt consisting of four large patchwork or appliqué blocks, usually surrounded by a border; *see page 159*. According to Ruth Finley, in *Old Patchwork Quilts and the Women Who Made Them*, page 125, four-block quilts went out of fashion before 1850. Since they took less time to make than other quilt styles, they were used as everyday quilts; thus few antique quilts of this type have survived.

Frame: See *Quilting frame*.

Freedom quilt: An album quilt popular in America during the 19th century that was made for a young man reaching his 21st birthday. Usually his female relatives and friends would design the quilt for him, with each person making a different block which they would sign.

The young man would bring this quilt with him into marriage.

Friendship quilt: A quilt popular in America during the 19th century made for a woman or family that was moving away. Each patchwork or appliqué block would be made by a different person, often with a relevant saying, or the name of the town and date. The blocks were assembled into a quilt which was presented to the person who was leaving.

Fusible interfacing: A web of fibres that will stick to a fabric upon the application of heat and pressure, as from an iron, and will provide a certain amount of stiffness and body to the fabric.

G

Gathered patchwork: A style of patchwork whereby the techniques of piecing and quilting are incorporated into one operation. The top fabric, larger than the base, is pleated over a mound of padding. The three layers are held together with running and stab stitches.

Godey's Lady's Book: A women's publication of the mid-19th century which gave patterns for many forms of needlework, including patchwork, quilting and appliqué.

Grain: The direction in which the threads run in a woven fabric. In a vertical direction it is called lengthwise grain and in a horizontal direction, crosswise grain. Diagonally, the grain is called the bias. For a professional result, the grain of fabric should always run in the same direction on a quilt block, or on the sashing and borders.

H

Hawaiian appliqué: A style of quiltmaking practised by the women living on the Hawaiian Islands, characterized by a bold intricate motif centred on a foundation.

Hem: To finish the edge of a project by folding the fabric to the wrong side and slipstitching it in place. The stitches should be invisible on the right side.

Honeycomb: A form of patchwork consisting of many hexagons sewn together randomly or to create a variety of geometric patterns. Honeycomb patchwork is usually worked by hand over paper templates for accuracy. The most common Honeycomb quilt design is called Grandmother's Flower Garden.

I

Inlay appliqué: Variations of basic appliqué. Simple Inlay is done by fitting two pieces together and sewing them to a foundation. Machine Inlay or Découpé is a simple method of Reverse Appliqué done on a sewing machine. In Applied Inlay, additional pieces are sewn on top of appliqués. In Reverse Inlay, two appliqué

pieces are cut out at the same time, switched and sewn in the other's frame.

Isometric paper: A grid of equilateral triangles produced in sheets or pads and sold in art supply stores. Will aid in drafting patchwork patterns that are not easily drafted on squared graph paper, such as diamonds, hexagons and octagons.

Italian quilting: See *Corded quilting*.

L

Lace: Delicate openwork fabric made from cotton, or synthetic fibres. It is an excellent material to use for adding dimension to a patchwork or appliqué design.

Ladies' Art Company: An American company that specialized in producing quilt patterns commercially. Their catalogues of patterns were published in the 1890s and into the 20th century and are now valuable sources of design to quilt historians.

Lamé: A fabric with metallic fibres woven into it which creates a shiny effect. It is non-washable.

Lap throw: A small quilt or coverlet made to cover the lap and knees. These were extremely popular during the late 19th century when they were often made in Crazy Patchwork.

Lattice: Also known as sashing, a lattice is a narrow strip of fabric used to separate the blocks of a patchwork or appliqué quilt.

Linen: A fabric made from the natural fibre of the flax plant. The plain-weave fabric usually has a slightly uneven texture; it is very strong and highly absorbent.

Linsey-woolsey: A coarse fabric with a linen warp and a woollen weft. Linsey-woolsey quilts were usually richly-coloured wholecloth quilts embellished with intricate quilting stitches and used primarily in the winter months. This term is often used to describe all early woollen quilts.

Log cabin: A style of patchwork whereby strips of fabric are sewn around a central shape, usually a square.

Loose stuffing: Fibres of cotton, wool, kapok or a synthetic such as polyester used to fill projects such as cushions and toys. The most readily available loose stuffing is called polyfil in Great Britain and polyester fiberfill stuffing in America.

M

Marking: Transferring a design to fabric.

Marriage quilt: Also known as a Bride's Quilt, this was the 13th quilt that a girl would take with her into marriage; it was used as the spread on her marriage bed. Marriage quilts were very elaborate, and were usually decorated with hearts, flowers and doves. It was considered bad luck for a girl to work on her marriage quilt before she became engaged.

Medallion quilt: A quilt style whereby a large central motif is surrounded by several different

A-Z OF QUILTING TERMS

borders. This is the earliest style of patchwork quilt. The central panel is usually a very elaborate and eye-catching patchwork or appliqué design, although early medallion quilts often had a printed fabric such as chintz or a commemorative handkerchief as the centre panel.

Milliner's needle: A long needle used in the millinery trade, but useful for basting the layers of a quilt together.

Mitre: To finish a corner by sewing fabrics together at a 45° angle.

Moiré taffeta: A sturdy fabric that has a wavy, watermarked appearance due to the application of heat and heavy pressure after weaving. It is usually made of acetate and is often used in evening wear.

Mola: A short-sleeved blouse worn by the Kuna Indian women of the San Blas Islands in Panama; it is decorated with their traditional form of intricate Reverse Appliqué work.

Mordant: Used to produce a fixed colour in a textile fibre during the dyeing process.

Mosaic quilt: A quilt style composed of many pieces of fabric sewn together to create an all-over design. An example of a Mosaic quilt can be seen on the front cover of this book: the Thousand Pyramids quilt.

Muslin: In Great Britain, muslin is an inexpensive, open-weave cotton fabric such as cheesecloth. In America, muslin is a strong, plain-weave cotton fabric in a natural cream colour.

N

Needlemarking: A method of quilting that is done after the quilt sandwich is basted together. Templates are placed on the quilt top and a thick, blunt yarn needle is used to mark around the edges, creating indentations or crease marks which are then quilted. This type of marking is favoured by advanced quilters who do not need to mark the entire quilt before beginning.

Notch: A triangular-shaped piece cut out from the edge of a patchwork template. Notches are marked on fabric pieces to aid in matching when the pieces are sewn together.

O

Organdy: A fine, transparent cotton fabric that has been permanently stiffened.

Organza: A fine, transparent silk or synthetic fabric that has a slight sheen.

P

Padding: The term used in this book to mean wadding as it is known in Great Britain, or batting as it is known in the United States. It is the middle layer of a quilt sandwich. Padding can be made of cotton, wool, silk or synthetic fibres and can be bought in sheets or as loose stuffing.

Pandau (pronounced pond ouw): The name literally means "flower cloth", but it has come to mean the embroidered or appliquéd needlework of the Hmong (pronounced mung) people who originated in Indochina, but who now live in Laos, Thailand, Vietnam and in communities scattered throughout the United States.

Patch: n. A small piece of fabric used to cover a worn area, or a piece used to make a patchwork pattern. v. The act of piecing together sections of fabric to make a patchwork design.

Patchwork: The technique of sewing small pieces of fabric together to create a larger piece of fabric, usually forming a design.

Pearl cotton: A cotton embroidery thread that is silky in appearance because of the way it is twisted in manufacturing. Available in a variety of colours, pearl cotton comes in three diameters: fine—no. 8; medium—no. 5; coarse—no. 3. This is an excellent thread to use when embroidering Crazy Patchwork. It can also be used for tying quilts.

Pieced quilt: A quilt composed of patches.

Pin baste: Securing layers of fabric together with straight pins instead of stitching. Pin basting is used for holding small patches together, or when the job is very simple and will be completed quickly. The term also means to secure the three layers of a quilt together using safety pins.

Polyester: A synthetic fabric that can be woven or knitted into a number of different weights of cloth. It is also used to make strong thread.

Polyfil: A British trade name for loose stuffing that is used for filling cushions and toys; the American equivalent is polyester fiberfill stuffing.

Presentation quilt: An album quilt made for a special person in a community, such as a local politician or a minister and his wife, and given in commemoration of good works.

Press: To flatten a fabric using heat, steam and pressure.

Presser foot: The part of a sewing machine that holds the fabric firmly onto the needle plate so that the needle can pass through the fabric.

Puff patchwork: Two layers of fabric are sewn together and stuffed to create small "puffs" which are then joined to make a patchwork top.

Putting in: The process of inserting the three layers of a quilt into a quilting frame.

Q

Quilt: A bedcovering composed of a top, padding and back held together with quilting stitches or ties.

Quilt-as-you-go: A type of quilting that is done in sections; the pre-quilted sections are later joined to create a quilt or other project.

Quilting frame: A four-sided structure designed to hold the three layers of a quilt taut to facilitate even stitching. A full frame will hold an entire quilt at one time. A roller frame takes up less room than a full frame; the quilt is wrapped around rollers and the quilt is unrolled, one section at a time for quilting.

Quilting hoop: A portable round or oval frame used to hold small portions of a quilt taut to facilitate even stitching.

Quilting stitch: A running stitch that is sewn through the quilt top, padding and back to hold the three layers together. Quilting stitches are usually worked in some form of design, although they can be random.

R

Reducing glass: The opposite of a magnifying glass, it is used when viewing patchwork before it has been sewn together to determine how the finished design will look. A reducing glass will diminish the size of a project so that it looks as if it has already been sewn together. It is available in art supply stores.

Remnant: A small piece of fabric that has been left on the bolt. Remnants are often excellent buys because they are reduced in price for a quick sale. Check to ensure that remnants do not have seconds or irregularities before buying them.

Reverse appliqué: The opposite of basic appliqué. A layer or layers of fabric are removed to reveal the design.

Rickrack: A type of trimming where a fabric strip is woven so that the edges form a zigzag pattern.

Rolling: Winding a quilt around the bars of a roller frame so as to expose a portion for stitching. When that portion has been quilted, the quilt is rolled again to expose a fresh part.

Rotary cutter: A device that is used to cut up to six layers of fabric at one time. A sharp circular blade is drawn along the edge of a thick plastic ruler to cut through fabric that has been placed on a special cutting mat.

Rotary ruler: A thick clear plastic ruler printed with lines that are exactly 6mm/¼in apart. It is used in conjunction with a rotary cutter. Diagonal lines indicating 45° and 60° are sometimes marked on the ruler.

S

Sampler quilt: A block-style quilt in which all of the blocks are different from one another. Making a sampler quilt is a good way to learn how to do different techniques

Sashiko: A form of Japanese embroidery that is worked on indigo-coloured fabric with white thread. This form of geometric embroidery lends itself beautifully to quilting.

Sashing: The strips of fabric used to join blocks when making a quilt top; it is also known as a lattice. Sashing is used to frame blocks, to unify a quilt design, to enlarge a quilt, or to showcase fancy quilting stitches.

Satin: A shiny silk, cotton or synthetic fabric. Because of the way it is woven, satin is a slippery and supple fabric that is difficult to handle.

Sawtooth edging: A method of finishing the edge of a quilt by inserting squares of fabric folded into triangles. A variation is called Prairie Points.

Scrap quilt: A quilt made entirely out of leftover pieces of fabric (scraps). Scrap quilts are usually very bright and colourful because of all the different fabrics used to create them.

Second: An irregularity or mistake in a length of fabric such as a skipped thread, knot or slub, or dirt such as oil or grease. Seconds can be used for patchwork and appliqué if you carefully cut around the irregularities; be sure to mark these areas before you begin cutting.

Selvages: The finished edges of fabric yardage. Do not be tempted to use selvages in your work (except for special decorative reasons) because the threads are much more firmly woven than the rest of the fabric, and are thus apt to shrink more when the fabric is washed. Also, selvages are difficult to quilt through because of the firm weave.

Seminole patchwork: A patchwork technique practised by the Seminole Indians in Florida whereby strips of fabric are sewn together, then cut into segments and resewn, creating intricate looking geometric designs.

Set: n. The way that the parts of a quilt top are arranged. v. The act of joining the parts of a quilt to complete the top.

Setting-in: A patchwork technique whereby one shape is sewn into an angle formed by the joining of two other shapes.

Shell patchwork: A form of Mosaic Patchwork consisting of patches that resemble shells or fishscales, by which name the technique is also known.

Shadow appliqué: A form of appliqué whereby brightly coloured fabric shapes are secured to a foundation; a layer of transparent fabric is placed on top, and then sewn to the foundation around the edges of the appliqués. When the project is finished, the appliqués are seen as shadows through the top fabric.

Shadow quilting: When Shadow Appliqué is done over a padded foundation, so that you are quilting and sewing at the same time.

Silk: A natural fibre produced by the silkworm. Silk is quite strong and lustrous and can be woven into a wide variety of fabrics of different weights and textures.

Sleeve: A fabric casing sewn to the back of a quilt so that it can be hung.

Squared paper: Graph paper.

Stained-glass appliqué: A style of appliqué whereby the raw edges of the appliqué are covered with narrow folded bias strips of fabric, usually in a dark colour, such as black. The result resembles a stained-glass window.

Stay-stitching: A line of machine stitches sewn just inside a seam allowance to stabilize the edge of the fabric; these stitches are not meant to be seen.

String or strip: A long narrow piece of fabric left over from cutting out a garment or some other project.

String patchwork: When strings of fabric are sewn together to make material which is then cut into various shapes. Or, when fabric strings are sewn to a foundation to create a design. The appearance is usually random, although String Patchwork can also be planned.

Strip piecing: In this book it means sewing strips of fabric together to create an abstract or pictorial design. It can also mean the technique of sewing strips together, creating a pieced cloth from which patchwork or appliqué shapes can be cut.

T

Tacking: Securing fabric layers together by means of invisible stitches worked on top of one another. It is also another word for basting.

Taking out: Removing a completed quilt from a frame.

Templates: A pattern piece used as a guide for marking fabrics for patchwork, appliqué and quilting. Usually made of sturdy material, templates can be reused many times.

Throw: A small patchwork or appliqué coverlet, simply lined without a layer of padding.

Tied quilting: A quick and easy way to hold the three layers of the quilt sandwich together without using the traditional running stitches. Thread or yarn is inserted through the quilt at regular intervals and tied in a square knot or bow, or secured using buttons.

Top: The upper layer of a quilt sandwich. A quilt top can be patchwork, appliqué or a whole piece of fabric. Quilting stitches are marked and worked on the top.

T-quilt: A quilt designed for a four-poster bed. The two bottom corners of the quilt are cut out so that the quilt can fit smoothly between the posters; the finished quilt resembles the letter T.

Tubular quilting: A method of making a quilt whereby strips of fabric are sewn to a foundation and then stuffed to form tubes.

Turkey red: A type of fabric dye known for its extreme colour-fastness. The process was developed in Turkey before the late 18th century. From that time, turkey-red fabrics were used extensively for making clothing and quilts. Many antique quilts can be dated by the inclusion of turkey-red dyed fabrics.

Trapunto: A style of quilting whereby two layers of fabric are joined together with stitches that form a design. Certain areas are stuffed from the wrong side so that the design stands out in high relief.

Tube turner: A long metal implement with an eye or a hook and catch at one end that is used for turning a tube of fabric inside out, or for drawing cord through a fabric tube. It is also known as a rouleau tubing needle.

Twilling: A continuous series of elaborate knots which form a flowing embroidered design on a fabric. Also known as Double Knot, Palestrina Stitch and Smyrna Stitch. It can be used to embellish a quilt border or appliqué pieces.

U

Unpicker/seam ripper: An implement with a sharp, curved and pointed tip that is used to undo stitches.

V

Velvet: A pile fabric woven from cotton, silk or synthetic fibres. The pile is formed by extra warp threads; the loops are sheared off to create a rich-looking brushed surface.

Voile: A transparent plain-weave cotton or synthetic fabric.

W

Wadding: The British term for batting. *See Padding.*

Warp: The vertical threads running the length of a woven fabric.

Weft: The horizontal threads of a woven fabric; it is also known as the woof.

Weighting: Adding metallic salts to silk to give weight and firmness to the fabric for proper draping. The metallic salts are corrosive which is why weighted silks in some antique quilts are in tatters.

Wholecloth quilt: A quilt made from two large pieces of fabric, either plain or printed, with padding in between. Fabrics comprising wholecloth quilts can be seamed together to achieve the proper size. Wholecloth quilts are usually elaborately quilted, often with Corded quilting or Trapunto work.

Window template: A template that is simply the outline of the patchwork or appliqué shape plus a 6mm/¼in seam allowance; the template thus appears to be a window through which the fabric can be seen. This is useful when fabric designs need to be centred on a piece.

Wool: A natural fibre woven from the fleece of sheep. Woollen fabrics are warm, resilient and absorbent. Many early utilitarian quilts were made of woollen fabrics.

Wrinkle quilting: A type of novelty quilting where the quilt top is larger than the back; the quilting stitches holding the layers together cause the quilt top to wrinkle.

Y

Yo yo: A style of patchwork whereby fabric circles are gathered, flattened and sewn together to create a lightweight coverlet or shawl.

BIBLIOGRAPHY

REFERENCE

Betterton, Sheila. *Quilts and Coverlets.* The American Museum in Britain. Bath. 1978.

Binney, Edwin 3rd & Gail Binney-Winslow. *Homage to Amanda: Two Hundred Years of American Quilts.* R K Press. San Francisco. 1984.

Bishop, Robert and Patricia Colbentz. *New Discoveries in American Quilts.* E P Dutton & Company, Inc. New York. 1975.

Bishop, Robert and Carter Houck. *All Flags Flying: American Patriotic Quilts as Expressions of Liberty.* E P Dutton & Company, Inc. New York. 1986.

Bishop, Robert and Elizabeth Safanda. *A Gallery of Amish Quilts.* E P Dutton & Company, Inc. New York. 1976.

Bresenhan, Karoline Patterson and Nancy O'Bryant Puentes. *Lone Stars: A Legacy of Texas Quilts, 1836–1936.* University of Texas Press. Houston, Texas. 1986.

Bullard, Lacy Folmar and Betty Jo Shiell. *Chintz Quilts: Unfading Glory.* Serendipity Publishers. Florida. 1983.

Carlisle, Lilian Baker. *Pieced Work and Appliqué Quilts at Shelburne Museum.* The Shelburne Museum Pamphlet Series, No. 2. Shelburne, Vermont. 1957.

Cavigga, Margaret. *Quilts.* Shufunotomo Company, Ltd. Japan. 1981.

Clabburn, Pamela. *Patchwork.* Shire Publications. Aylesbury, England. 1983.

Colby, Averil. *Patchwork.* B T Batsford. London. 1958.

Colby, Averil. *Quilting.* Charles Scribner's Sons. New York. 1971.

Conroy, Mary. *Three Hundred Years of Canada's Quilts.* Griffen House. Toronto. 1976.

Curtis, Phillip H. *American Quilts in the Newark Museum Collection.* The Newark Museum Association. Newark, New Jersey. 1974.

Denver Art Museum Textile Department. *American Patchwork Quilts.* Denver, Colorado.1986.

De Pauw, Linda Grant and Conover Hunt. *Remember the Ladies: Women in America 1750–1815.* The Viking Press. New York. 1976.

Dillmont, Th de. *The Complete Encyclopedia of Needlework.* Running Press Inc. Philadelphia. 1972.

Dunton, William R, Jr. *Old Quilts.* Self-published. Catonsville, Maryland. 1946.

Dyer, Margie. *Pennsylvania German Quilts.* Goethe House. New York. 1983.

Finley, Ruth. *Old Patchwork Quilts and the Women Who Made Them.* J B Lippincott Company. Philadelphia. 1929.

Fitzrandolph, Mavis. *Traditional Quilting.* B T Batsford Ltd. London. 1954.

Fox, Sandi. *Small Endearments: 19th-Century Quilts for Children.* Charles Scribner's Sons. New York. 1985.

Good Housekeeping. *Patchwork and Appliqué.* Ebury Press. London. 1981.

Good Housekeeping. *Quilting and Patchwork.* Ebury Press. London. 1983.

Haders, Phyllis. *Sunshine and Shadow: The Amish and Their Quilts.* Universe Books. New York. 1976.

Haders, Phyllis. *The Main Street Pocket Guide to Quilts.* The Main Street Press. Pittstown, New Jersey. 1981.

Hake, Elizabeth. *English Quilting Old and New.* B T Batsford Ltd. London 1937.

Hall, Carrie A and Rose G Kretsinger. *The Romance of the Patchwork Quilt in America.* Bonanza Books. New York. 1935.

Hechtlinger, Adelaide. *American Quilts, Quilting, and Patchwork.* Stackpole Books. Harrisburg, Pennsylvania. 1974.

Hinson, Dolores A. *Quilting Manual.* Dover Publications, Inc. New York. 1966, 1970.

Holstein, Jonathan. *Abstract Design in American Quilts.* Whitney Museum of Art. New York. 1971.

Holstein, Jonathan. *The Pieced Quilt.* New York Graphic Society, Ltd. Connecticut. 1973.

Holstein, Jonathan. *Kentucky Quilts 1800–1900: The Kentucky Quilt Project.* Pantheon Books. New York. 1982. Distributed by Dicmar Publishing Company, P O Box 35333, Washington, DC 20007.

Horton, Laurel and Lynn Robertson Myers. *Social Fabric: South Carolina's Traditional Quilts.* Quilt Project, McKissick Museum, University of South Carolina. Columbia. 1985.

Ickis, Marguerite. *The Standard Book of Quiltmaking & Collecting.* Dover Publications, Inc. New York. 1949.

Irwin, John Rice. *A People and Their Quilts.* Schiffer Publishing Company. Exton, Pennsylvania. 1983.

Johnson, Mary Elizabeth. *A Garden of Quilts.* Oxmoor House.

Birmingham, Alabama. 1984.

Katzenberg, Dena S. *Baltimore Album Quilts.* The Baltimore Museum of Art. Baltimore, Maryland. 1981.

Kihn, Yvonne M. *The Collector's Dictionary of Quilt Names & Patterns.* Acropolis Books Ltd. Washington, DC. 1980.

Kolter, Jane Bentley. *Forget Me Not: A Gallery of Friendship and Album Quilts.* The Main Street Press. Pittstown, New Jersey. 1985.

Lasansky, Jeannette. *In the Heart of Pennsylvania: 19th & 20th Century Quiltmaking Traditions.* Oral Traditions Project. Lewisburg, Pennsylvania. 1985.

Lipsett, Linda Otto. *Remember Me: Women & Their Friendship Quilts.* The Quilt Digest Press. San Francisco. 1985.

Martin, Nancy J. *Pieces of the Past.* That Patchwork Place, Inc. Bothell, Washington. 1986.

McMorris, Penny. *Crazy Quilts.* E P Dutton & Company, Inc. New York. 1984.

McMorris, Penny and Michael Kile. *The Art Quilt.* The Quilt Digest Press. San Francisco. 1986.

Michigan Hmong Arts: Textiles in Transition, The Museum, Michigan State University. Michigan. 1984.

Montgomery, Florence M. *Printed Textiles: English and American Cottons and Linens 1700–1850.* The Viking Press, Inc. New York. 1970.

Nelson, Cyril I. and Carter Houck. *The Quilt Engagement Calendar Treasury.* E P Dutton & Company, Inc. New York. 1982.

New Jersey Quilters: A Timeless Tradition. Morristown Museum of Arts and Sciences. Morristown, New Jersey. 1982.

Orlofsky, Patsy and Myron. *Quilts in America.* McGraw-Hill Book Company. New York. 1974.

Pellman, Rachel and Kenneth. *The World of Amish Quilts.* Good Books. Intercourse, Pennsylvania. 1984.

Pellman, Rachel and Kenneth. *Amish Crib Quilts.* Good Books. Intercourse, Pennsylvania. 1985.

Pellman, Rachel and Kenneth. *Amish Doll Quilts, Dolls and Other Playthings.* Good Books. Intercourse, Pennsylvania. 1986.

Peto, Florence. *Historic Quilts.* The American Historical Company, Inc. New York. 1939.

Peto, Florence. *American Quilts and Coverlets.* Chanticleer Press. New York. 1949.

Plews, Edith Rice. *Hawaiian Quilting on Kauai.* Kauai Museum Publication. Kauai, Hawaii. 1976.

Pottinger, David. *Quilts from the Indiana Amish.* E P Dutton & Company, Inc. New York. 1983.

The Quilt Digest 1. Kiracofe and Kile. San Francisco. 1983.

The Quilt Digest 2. Kiracofe and Kile. San Francisco. 1984.

The Quilt Digest 3. The Quilt Digest Press. San Francisco. 1985.

The Quilt Digest 4. The Quilt Digest Press, San Francisco. 1986.

Quilting in the Northeast. Tyne and Wear County Council Museum. Shipley Art Museum. Shipley Art Gallery, Gateshead. n.d.

Quilts: The State of an Art. Schiffer Publishing Ltd. Exton, Pennsylvania. 1985.

Ramsey, Bets and Merikay Waldvogel. *Quilts of Tennessee: Images of Domestic Life Prior to 1930.* Rutledge Hill Press. Nashville, Tennessee. 1986.

Safford, Carleton L and Robert Bishop. *America's Quilts and Coverlets.* E P Dutton & Company, Inc. New York. 1980.

Sienkiewicz, Elly. *Spoken Without a Word.* Turtle Hill Press. Washington, DC. 1983.

Smith, Wilene. *Quilt Patterns: An Index to the Kansas City Star Patterns 1928–1961.* Self-published. Wichita, Kansas. 1985.

Swann, Susan Burrows. *Plain & Fancy: American Women and Their Needlework, 1700–1850.* Holt, Rinehart and Winston. New York. 1977.

Symonds, Mary and Louisa Preece, *Needlework Through the Ages.* Hodder & Stoughton, Ltd. London. 1928.

Tomlonson, Judy Schroeder. *Mennonite Quilts and Pieces.* Good Books. Intercourse, Pennsylvania. 1985.

Webster, Marie D. *Quilts: Their Story and How to Make Them.* Tudor Publishing Company. New York. 1915.

White, Margaret E. *Quilts and Counterpanes in the Newark Museum.* The Newark Museum. Newark, New Jersey. 1948.

Woodard, Thomas K and Blanche Greenstein. *Crib Quilts and Other Small Wonders.* E P Dutton & Company, Inc. New York. 1981.

Woodard, Thomas K and Blanche Greenstein. *The Poster Book of Quilts.* E P Dutton & Company, Inc. New York. 1984.

Yabsley, Suzanne. *Texas Quilts, Texas Women.* Texas A &M University Press. College Station, Texas. 1984.

Yakima Valley Museum & Historical Association. *Quilt Masterpieces in Full Color.* Dover Publications, Inc. 1986.

TECHNIQUE

Amico, Yvonne L. *Shadow Appliqué.* Gick Publishing. Irvine, California. 1983.

Avery, Virginia. *Quilts to Wear.* Charles Scribner's Sons. New York. 1982.

Bass, Charlotte Christiansen. *Appliqué Quiltmaking.* B T Batsford Ltd. London. 1984.

Benjamin, Bonnie. *Sashiko: The Quilting of Japan from Traditional to Today.* Needlearts International. Glendale, California. 1986.

Beyer, Jinny. *The Scrap Look: Designs, Fabrics, Colors and Piecing Techniques for Creating Multi-Fabric Quilts.* EPM Books. McLean, Virginia. 1985.

Bonesteel, Georgia. *Lap Quilting with Georgia Bonesteel.* Oxmoor House. Birmingham, Alabama. 1982.

Bonesteel, Georgia. *More Lap Quilting with Georgia Bonesteel.* Southern Living Books. Birmingham, Alabama. 1985.

Bradkin, Cheryl Greider. *The Seminole Patchwork Book.* A Yours Truly Publication. Atlanta, Georgia. 1980.

Burbridge, Pauline. *Making Patchwork for Pleasure and Profit.* John Gifford Ltd. London. 1981.

Conroy, Mary. *The Complete Book of Crazy Patchwork.* Sterling Publishing Company, Inc. New York. 1985.

Culver, Ruth. *How to Hold a Quilt Show: A Practical Guide.* Culver Publications. Kingston, New York. 1985.

Dubois, Jean. *Patchwork Quilting with Wool.* Dover Publications, Inc. New York. 1978.

Elwin, Janet B. *Hexagon Magic.* EPM Publications, Inc. McLean, Virginia. 1986.

Florence, Judy. *Award-Winning Quilts and How to Make Them.* Wallace-Homestead Book Company. Lombard, Illinois. 1986.

Fournier, Frances. *Quilt It and Wear It.* Prints and Patches Press. Vancouver, British Columbia. 1981

Gutcheon, Beth. *The Perfect Patchwork Primer.* Penguin Books Ltd. Harmondsworth, England. 1973.

Gutcheon, Jeffrey. *Diamond Patchwork.* Alchemy Press. New York. 1982.

Hassel, Carla J. *Creating PA NDAU Appliqué.* Wallace-Homestead Book Company. Illinois. 1984.

Haywood, Dixie. *Crazy Patchwork.* Dover Publications, Inc. New York. 1986.

Higgins, Muriel. *New Designs for Machine Patchwork.* Charles Scribner's Sons. New York. 1980.

Hopkins, Mary Ellen. *The It's Okay if You Sit on My Quilt Book.* A Yours Truly Publication. Atlanta, Georgia. 1982.

Horton, Roberta. *Stained Glass Quilting Technique.* Self-published. Berkeley, California. 1978.

Horton, Roberta. *Calico and Beyond: The Use of Patterned Fabric in Quilts.* C & T Publishing. Lafayette, California. 1986.

Hughes, Trudie. *Template-Free Quiltmaking.* That Patchwork Place. Bothell, Washington. 1986.

James, Michael. *The Quiltmaker's Handbook.* Prentice-Hall, Inc. New Jersey. 1978.

James, Michael. *The Second Quiltmaker's Handbook.* Prentice-Hall, Inc. New Jersey. 1981.

Johannah, Barbara. *The Quick Quilt Making Handbook.* Pride of the Forest Press. Menlo Park, California. 1979.

Kline, Mary Ryder. *Cathedral Window: A New View.* That Patchwork Place, Inc. Bothell, Washington. 1983.

LaBranche, Carol. *A Constellation for Quilters: Star Patterns for Piecing.* The Main Street Press, Inc. Pittstown, New Jersey. 1986.

Laury, Jean Ray. *Quilts and Coverlets.* Van Nostrand Reinhold. New York. 1970.

Laury, Jean Ray. *Quilted Clothing.* Harper & Row, Inc. New York. 1982.

Leman, Bonnie. *Quick and Easy Quilting.* Hearthside Press Inc. New York. 1972.

Leman, Bonnie and Judy Martin. *Log Cabin Quilts.* Moon Over the Mountain Publishing Company. Wheatridge, Colorado. 1980.

Leman, Bonnie and Judy Martin. *Taking the Math Out of Making Patchwork Quilts.* Moon over the Mountain Publishing Company. Wheatridge, Colorado. 1981.

Leone, Diana. *The Sampler Quilt.* Leone Publishing Company. Santa Clara, California. 1980.

Leone, Diana. *Investments.* Leone Publications. Santa Clara, California. 1982.

Leone, Diana. *Fine Hand Quilting.* Leone Publications. Los Altos,

Calfornia. 1986.

Mahler, Celine Blanchard. *Once Upon a Quilt*. Van Nostrand Reinhold Company. New York. 1973.

Martin, Judy. *Patchworkbook: Easy Lessons for Quilt Design and Construction*. Charles Scribner's Sons. New York. 1983.

Martin, Judy. *Scrap Quilts*. Moon Over the Mountain Publishing Company. Wheatridge, Colorado. 1986.

Martin, Nancy J. *Sew Easy Strip Quilting*. That Patchwork Place. Bothell, Washington. 1980.

Martin, Nancy J. *The Basics of Quilted Clothing*. That Patchwork Place. Bothell, Washington. 1982.

McKelvey, Susan Richardson. *Color for Quilters*. Yours Truly Publication. Atlanta, Georgia. 1984.

McMorris, Penny. *Quilting: An Introduction to American Patchwork Design*. British Broadcasting Corporation. London. 1984.

Millard, Debra. *A Quilter's Guide to Fabric Dyeing*. Self-published. Englewood, Colorado. 1984.

Millett, Sandra. *Quilt-As-You-Go*. Chilton Book Company. Radnor, Pennsylvania. 1982.

Morgan, Mary and Dee Mosteller. *Trapunto and Other Forms of Raised Quilting*. Charles Scribner's Sons. New York. 1977.

Newman, Thelma R. *Quilting, Patchwork, Appliqué, and Trapunto*. Crown Publishers, Inc. New York. 1974.

O'Bryant, Nancy. *First Aid for Family Quilts*. Moon Over the Mountain Publishing Company. Wheatridge, Colorado. 1986.

Ota, Kimi. *Sashiko Quilting*. Self-published. Washington. 1981.

Pasquini, Katie. *Mandala*. Sudz Publishing. Eureka, California. 1983.

Patera, Charlotte. *Cutwork Appliqué*. New Century Publishers, Inc. New Jersey. 1983.

Patera, Charlotte. *Mola Making*. New Century Publishers, Inc. Piscataway, New Jersey. 1984.

Porcella, Yvonne. *Pieced Clothing*. Porcella Studios. Modesto, California. 1980.

Porcella, Yvonne. *Pieced Clothing Variations*. Porcella Studios. Modesto, California. 1981.

Puckett, Marjorie. *String Quilts 'n Things*. Orange Patchwork Publishers. California. 1979.

Puckett, Marjorie. *Patchwork Possibilities*. Orange Patchwork Publishers. California. 1981.

Puckett, Marjorie. *Lighter Shades of Pale: Shadow Quilting*. Orange Patchwork Publishers. California. 1983.

Puckett, Marjorie and Gail Giberson. *Primarily Patchwork*. Cabin Craft. Redlands, California. 1975.

Risinger, Hettie. *Innovative Machine Quilting*. Sterling Publishing Company, Inc. New York. 1980.

Risinger, Hettie. *Innovative Machine Patchwork Piecing*. Sterling Publishing Company, Inc. New York. 1983.

Robbins, Judy and Gretchen Thomas. *Hands All Around: Making Cooperative Quilts*. Van Nostrand Reinhold. New York. 1984.

Rose, Helen. *Quilting With Strips and Strings*. Dover Publications, Inc. New York. 1983.

Rush, Beverly with Lassie Wittman. *The Complete Book of Seminole Patchwork*. Madrona Publishers. Seattle. 1982.

Schaefer, Becky. *Working in Miniature: A Machine Piecing Approach to Miniature Quilts*. C & T Publishing. Lafayette, California. 1987.

Shedletsky, Andrea. *Making an Old-Fashioned Patchwork Sampler Quilt on the Sewing Machine*. Dover Publications, Inc. New York, 1984.

Stewart, Charlyne Jaffe. *Snowflakes in the Sun*. Wallace-Homestead. Lombard, Illinois. 1986.

Swim, Laurie. *The Joy of Quilting*. Penguin Books Canada Ltd. Toronto. 1984.

Vogue Patterns. *The Vogue Sewing Book*. New York. 1973.

Walker, Michele. *Quiltmaking in Patchwork and Appliqué*. Ebury Press. London. 1985.

Wiechec, Philomena. *Celtic Quilt Designs*. Celtic Design Company. California. 1980.

Wien, Carol Anne. *The Log Cabin Quilt Book*. E P Dutton & Company, Inc. New York.1984.

Wooster, Ann Sargent. *Quiltmaking: The Modern Approach to a Traditional Craft*. Drake Publishers, Inc. New York. 1977.

Young, Blanche and Helen Young. *The Lone Star Quilt Handbook*. Young Publications. Oak View, California. 1979.

Young, Blanche and Helen Young. *Trip Around the World Quilts*. Young Publications. Oak View, California. 1980.

Young, Blanche and Helen Young. *The Boston Commons Quilt*. Young Publications. Oak View, California. 1983.

Young, Blanche and Helen Young. *The Flying Geese Quilt*. Young Publications. Oak View, California. 1983.

Young, Blanche and Helen Young. *The Irish Chain Quilt*. Young Publications. Oak View, California. 1986.

PATTERNS

Anthony, Catherine H. *Sampler Supreme*. Leone Publishing Company. Santa Clara, California. 1983.

Baker, Jane. *Country Quilt Design Cut & Use Stencils*. Dover Publications, Inc. New York. 1984.

Beyer, Jinny. *Patchwork Patterns*. EPM Publications, Inc. McLean, Virginia. 1979.

Beyer, Jinny. *The Quilter's Album of Blocks & Borders*. EPM Publications, Inc. McLean, Virginia. 1980.

Bond, Dorothy. *Embroidery Stitches from Old American Quilts*. Self-published. Cottage Grove, Oregon. 1977.

Bryant, Claire. *Candlewicking*. Dover Publications, Inc. New York. 1983.

Cory, Pepper. *Quilting Designs from the Amish*. C & T Publishing. California. 1985.

Fairfield, Helen. *Patchwork from Mosaics*. B T Batsford Ltd. London. 1985.

Grafton, Carol Belanger. *Traditional Patchwork Patterns*. Dover Publications, Inc. New York. 1974.

Grafton, Carol Belanger. *Geometric Patchwork Patterns*. Dover Publications, Inc. New York. 1975.

Grafton, Carol Belanger. *Early American Patchwork Patterns*. Dover Publications, Inc. New York. 1980.

Gutcheon, Beth & Jeffrey. *The Quilt Design Workbook*. Pawson Associates Publishers, Inc. New York. 1976.

Houck, Carter. *Nova Scotia Patchwork Patterns*. Dover Publications, Inc. New York. 1981.

Macho, Linda. *Quilting Patterns*. Dover Publications, Inc. New York. 1984.

Malone, Maggie. *1001 Patchwork Designs*. Sterling Publishing Company, Inc. New York. 1982.

Malone, Maggie. *120 Patterns for Traditional Patchwork Quilts*. Sterling Publishing Company, Inc. New York. 1983.

Malone, Maggie. *115 Classic American Patchwork Quilt Patterns*. Sterling Publishing Company, Inc. New York. 1984.

Malone, Maggie. *Heirloom Quilts You Can Make*. Sterling Publishing Company, Inc. New York. 1984.

Malone, Maggie. *Quilting: Techniques & Patterns for Machine Stitching*. Sterling Publishing Company, Inc. New York. 1984.

McCloskey, Marsha. *Wall Quilts*. That Patchwork Place, Inc. Bothell, Washington. 1983.

McIntyre, Ione Benck. *American History in Patchwork Patterns: The Charter Oak*. The Patchwork Press. Bemidji, Minnesota. 1981.

McKim, Ruby Short. *101 Patchwork Patterns*. Dover Publications, Inc. 1962.

Mills, Susan Winter. *Illustrated Index to Traditional American Quilt Patterns*. Arco Publishing, Inc. New York. 1980.

Murwin, Susan Aylsworth and Suzzy Chalfant Payne. *Quick and Easy Patchwork on the Sewing Machine*. Dover Publications, Inc. New York. 1979.

Murwin, Susan Aylsworth and Suzzy Chalfant Payne. *The Quick and Easy Giant Dahlia Quilt on the Sewing Machine*. Dover Publications, Inc. New York. 1983.

O'Dowd, Karen. *Quick-and-Easy Heart-Motif Quilts*. Dover Publications, Inc. New York. 1986.

Ondori. *Patchwork & Quilting Book*. Ondorisha Publishers, Ltd. Tokyo, Japan. 1981.

Ondori. *Fine Patchwork & Quilting*. Ondorisha Publishers, Ltd. Tokyo, Japan 1983.

Ondori. *Patchwork for Your Home*. Ondorisha Publishers, Ltd. Tokyo, Japan. 1984.

Payne, Suzzy Chalfant and Susan Aylsworth Murwin. *Creative American Quilting Inspired by the Bible*. Fleming H. Revell Company. Old Tappan, New Jersey. 1983.

Pelletier, Henry Louis. *Favorite Patchwork Patterns*. Dover Publications, Inc. New York. 1984.

Porter, Elizabeth and Marianne Fons. *Classic Basket Patterns*. Ginger Snap Station. Atlanta, Georgia. 1984.

Rolfe, Margaret. *Australian Patchwork Designs*. Sterling Publishing Company, Inc. New York. 1985.

Seward, Linda. *Patchwork Quilts for Kids You Love*. Sterling Publishing Company, Inc. New York. 1985.

Seward, Linda. *Christmas Patchwork Projects*. Sterling Publishing Company, Inc. New York. 1986.

Seward, Linda. *Small Quilting Projects*. Sterling Publishing Company, Inc. New York. 1987.

Shirer, Marie and Barbara Brackman. *Creature Comforts: A Quilter's Animal Alphabet Book*. Wallace-Homestead Book Company. Chicago, Illinois. 1986.

Wilson, Erica. *Erica Wilson's Quilts of America*. Oxmoor House, Inc. Birmingham, Alabama. 1979.

Wiss, Audrey & Douglas. *Folk Quilts and How to Recreate Them*. The Main Street Press. Pittstown, New Jersey. 1983.

DESIGN IDEAS

Chapman, Suzanne E. *Historic Floral and Animal Designs for Embroiderers and Craftsmen*. Dover Publications, Inc. New York. 1977.

Eaton, Connie. *Oval Stained Glass Pattern Book*. Dover Publications, Inc. New York. 1983.

Menten, Ted. *Folk Art Cut & Use Stencils*. Dover Publications, Inc. New York. 1985.

Mirow, Gregory. *A Treasury of Design for Artists and Craftsmen*. Dover Publications, Inc. New York. 1969.

Sibbett, Ed Jr. *Stained Glass Pattern Book*. Dover Publications, Inc. New York. 1976.

Sibbett, Ed Jr. *Art Nouveau Stained Glass Pattern Book*. Dover Publications, Inc. New York. 1978.

Sibbett, Ed Jr. *Christmas Cut & Use Stencils*. Dover Publications, Inc. New York. 1978.

Sibbett, Ed Jr. *Easy-to-Make Stained Glass Lightcatchers*. Dover Publications, Inc. New York. 1981.

Sibbett, Ed Jr. *Floral Stained Glass Pattern Book*. Dover Publications, Inc. New York. 1982.

Sibbett, Ed Jr. *Snowflake Cut & Use Stencils*. Dover Publications, Inc. New York. 1984.

PERIODICALS

American Quilter. The American Quilter's Society, Division of Schroeder Publishing Co., Inc., 5801 Kentucky Dam Road, Paducah, Kentucky 42003.

The Independent Patchworker. National Patchwork Association, P.O. Box 300, Hethersett, Norwich, Norfolk NR9 3DB, England.

Lady's Circle Patchwork Quilts. Lopez Publications, Inc. 111 East 35th Street, New York, New York 10016. USA.

Patchwork & Quilting. Traplet House, Severn Drive, Upton-upon-Severn, Worcestershire WR8 0JL, England.

Popular Patchwork. Argus Specialist Publications, Argus House, Boundary Way, Hemel Hempstead, Hertfordshire HP2 7ST.

The Quilter. The Quilters' Guild, OP66 Dean Clough, Halifax HX3 5AX, England.

Quilter's Newsletter Magazine. Leman Publications, Inc., 741 Corporate Circle Suite A, Golden, CO 80401-5622. USA.

Quiltmaker. Leman Publications, Inc., 741 Corporate Circle Suite A, Golden, CO 80401-5622. USA.

INDEX

ACKNOWLEDGMENTS

On the Mitchell Beazley staff, thank you to Sue Egerton-Jones and Jack Tresidder, who encouraged me to write this book. Much appreciation to Jill Raphaeline for her superb book design and moral support and to Bob Saxton, an excellent and understanding editor. And an enormous thank you to Jill Shipley who turned my rough sketches into clear illustrations. She always had a smile, even when I asked her to correct a piece of art for the sixth time.

Writing a book is never easy, but writing one with a brand new baby is not an experience I would recommend. I could never have finished this without the help of the people who looked after Alysson so I could get on with the work: Alice Androkites, Pat Lake, Annlee Landman, my mother—Evelyn Macho—and my husband Robert.

A very special thank you to Sharon Falberg, who gave advice, encouragement, constructive criticism and suggestions in addition to allowing me to rifle through and borrow from her library. And many thanks to the new team of talented people who worked on the revision of this book: Judith More, Julia North, Janis Utton and Glen Wilkins. Thanks also to Brian John Wilkins who drew the new artwork for the expanded rotary cutting section.

COLOUR PHOTOGRAPHY

Thanks to those who supplied transparencies of their quilts: Jeanne Lyons Butler, Jane Burch Cochran, Lynne Edwards, Nancy Herman, Inge Hueber, Irene MacWilliam, Sara Ann McLennand, Ann Stamm Merrell, Paula Nadelstern, Linda Negandhi, Diana Robinson and Ursula Stürzinger. And to Amelia Adams, Monica Millner and Judith Hammersla for loaning their quilts for photography and Myron Miller and Carter Houck who supplied photographs of the antique quilts. I'd also like to thank Rosemary E Allan of the Beamish North of England Open Air Museum, Pauline T Laffitte of the South Carolina State Museum, Linda Skolarus of the Henry Ford Museum & Greenfield Village, Mrs Amy Emms MBE, Judy Greenwood, Jan Jefferson and Beryl J White at the Quilters' Guild.

PHOTO CREDITS

Lada Bartos: page 11 (Cold-Warm with Perturbations); Karen Bell: pages 16, 17 (By Moonlight); Roland Hueber: page 10 (Network); Jacqui Hurst: page 10 (Movement); Monique Le Luhandre: Jacket photography and pages 14 (Keith's Quilt), 18, 22 (African Magic), 23; Sara Ann McLennand: page 14 (Eating Disorder); James Merrell: page 13; Myron Miller: page 9 (Young Man's Fancy), 12, 19, 20, 21; Pam Monfort: page 22 (Southern Devotion); David Montgomery: pages 24, 25, 26; Ajit Negandhi: page 11 (Arachnida); Joseph Painter: page 15; Tom Yarish: page 17 (Fissures).

ARTWORK

The following Dover books proved invaluable as sources of inspiration for some of the designs: Suzanne E Chapman. *Historical Floral and Animal Designs for Embroiderers and Craftsmen*. 1977; Ted Menten. *Folk Art Cut & Use Stencils*. 1985; Gregory Mirow. *A Treasury of Design for Artists and Craftsmen*. 1969; Ed Sibbett, Jr. *Stained Glass Pattern Book*. 1976; Ed Sibbett, Jr. *Snowflake Cut & Use Stencils*.1984. The animal patterns featured in Emily's Quilt on page 18 can be found in Margaret Rolfe's book *Go Wild With Quilts. That Patchwork Place*. 1993.

FOOTNOTES

[1] Ruth E Finley, *Old Patchwork Quilts and the Women Who Made Them*, J.B. Lippincott Company, Philadelphia, 1929, page 168. The planned use of fabrics in many old quilts illustrates that despite primarily using scraps, women were not adverse to buying new fabrics for a quilt: "The scrapbag necessarily was a jumble of old and new; and always, with the exception of certain appliqué patterns for which new cloth was purchased to carry out a colour scheme or meet the requirements of large patches, quilt materials are older than the quilts themselves."

[2] Averil Colby, *Patchwork*, B T Batsford Ltd, London, 1958, page 22.

[3] Ruth E Finley, *Old Patchwork Quilts and the Women Who Made Them*, page 22.

[4] Averil Colby, *Patchwork*, page 30.

[5] Dolores Hinson, *Quilting Manual*, Dover Publications, Inc., New York, 1970, page 21.

[6] Mavis Fitzrandolph, *Traditional Quilting*, B T Batsford Ltd, London, 1954, Figures 41 and 43.

[7] Averil Colby, *Patchwork*, page 42.

[8] Jean Dubois, *Patchwork Quilting with Wool*, Dover Publications, Inc., New York, 1978, page 139.

[9] Jonathan Holstein, *The Pieced Quilt: An American Design Tradition*, New York Graphic Society, New York, 1973, plate 28.

[10] Averil Colby, *Patchwork*, page 20.

[11] Marie D Webster, *Quilts: Their Story and How to Make Them*, Tudor Publishing Co., New York, 1973, page 38.

[12] Ruth E Finley, *Old Patchwork Quilts and the Women Who Made Them*, page 118.

[13] Dolores Hinson, *Quilting Manual*, page 33.

[14] Ruth E Finley, *Old Patchwork Quilts and the Women Who Made Them*, page 127. The author states that "the appliquéd quilt was considered more worthy than any but the masterpieces of pieces patchwork and was cherished accordingly. For this reason the collector now finds in good condition many more appliquéd than pieced antiques."

[15] Robert Bishop and Carter Houck, *All Flags Flying: American Patriotic Quilts as Expressions of Liberty*, E P Dutton, New York, 1986, page 8.

[16] Ruth E Finley, *Old Patchwork Quilts and the Women Who Made Them*, page 122. The author points out that "Appliqué is unlike piecing in that it offers more possibilities of diversification and embellishment. It has little or none of the mathematical rigidity of the geometrical design."

[17] Jonathan Holstein, *The Pieced Quilt: An American Design Tradition*, page 18.

[18] Ruth E Finley, *Old Patchwork Quilts and the Women Who Made Them*, page 163. "So determined were the sheep and flax farmers and the woolen and linen manufacturers to save their time-honoured monopoly from being encroached upon by cotton that in 1721 George 1 deemed it politic to prohibit by law the use or wear of 'any printed, painted, stained or dyed callico', imported or otherwise."

[19] Jonathan Holstein, *The Pieced Quilt: An American Design Tradition*, page 21.

[20] Sheila Betterton, *Quilts and Coverlets*, The American Museum in Britain, Bath, 1978, page 59.

[21] Edith Rice Plews, *Hawaiian Quilting on Kauai*, a Kauai Musum Publication, 1976, page 2.

[22] Ibid, page 3.

[23] Eric Crystal, "Hmong Traditions in the Crucible of Social Change," *Michigan Hmong Arts: Textiles in Transition*, The Museum, Michigan State University, Michigan, 1984. page 12. The author states, "The tribal Lao textile tradition is part and parcel of an integral culture, often pregnant with symbolic meaning, intimately linked to ethnic identity, reflective of ancient mythological and contemporary historical traditions of the Hmong people."

[24] Carla J. Hassel, *Creating Pandau Appliqué*, Wallace-Homestead Book Company, 580 Water's Edge Road, Lombard, Illinois 60148, USA, 1984.

[25] Mary Symonds and Louise Preece, *Needlework Through the Ages*, Hodder & Stoughton, Ltd., London, 1928, page 82.

[26] Mavis Fitzrandolph, *Traditional Quilting*, page 39. The author notes that the terms "stamper" and "stamped quilt" were used in the belief that the designs were marked on the fabric by using a transfer, when in reality they were drawn in exact detail on a the material with a blue pencil.

[27] Ibid, page 33.

[28] Marie D Webster, *Quilts: Their Story and How to Make Them*, page 150. The author quoted the following passage from the "Annals of Tennessee", published by Dr J G M Ramsey in 1853: "A failure to ask a neighbour to a raising, a clearing, a chopping frolic, or his family to a quilting, was considered a high indignity .... Each settler was not only willing but desirous to contribute his share to the general comfort and public improvement, and felt aggrieved and insulted if the opportunity to do so were witheld."

[29] Eric Wilson, *Quilts of America*, Oxmoor House, Inc., Birmingham, Alabama, 1979, page 21.

[30] Carrie A. Hall and Rose G. Kretsinger, *The Romance of the Patchwork Quilt in America*, Bonanza Books, New York, 1935, page 33.

[31] Marie D Webster, *Quilts: Their Story and How to Make Them*, page 101.

[32] Averil Colby, *Quilting*, Charles Scribner's Sons, New York, 1971, page 75.

[33] Kimi Ota, *Sashiko Quilting*, self-published, Seattle, Washington, 1981, page 7.

[34] Averil Colby, *Quilting*, page 14.

[35] Marie D Webster, *Quilts: Their Story and How to Make Them*, page 155.

[36] Ruth E Finley, *Old Patchwork Quilts and the Women Who Made Them*, plate 64.